DELEUZE ANI

An increasing number of scholars, students and practitioners of psychology are becoming intrigued by the ideas of Gilles Deleuze and Félix Guattari. This book is a critical introduction to these ideas, which have so much to offer psychology in terms of new directions as well as critique.

Deleuze was one of the most prominent philosophers of the twentieth century and a figure whose ideas are increasingly influential throughout the humanities and social sciences. His work, particularly his collaborations with psychoanalyst Guattari, focused on the articulation of a philosophy of difference. Rejecting mainstream continental philosophy just as much as the orthodox analytical metaphysics of the English-speaking world, Deleuze proposed a positive and passionate alternative, bursting at the seams with new concepts and new transformations.

This book overviews the philosophical contribution of Deleuze, including the project he developed with Guattari. It goes on to explore the application of these ideas in three major dimensions of psychology: its unit of analysis, its method and its applications to the clinic.

Deleuze and Psychology will be of interest to students and scholars of psychology and those interested in continental philosophy, as well as psychological practitioners and therapists.

Maria Nichterlein, PhD, is a Psychologist working both in private practice and as a Senior Clinician at the Youth Brief Intervention Service at Austin CAMHS in Melbourne, Australia.

John R. Morss, PhD, is a Senior Lecturer at Deakin University Law School, and a member of the Alfred Deakin Institute for Citizenship and Globalisation, Melbourne, Australia.

Concepts for critical psychology: disciplinary boundaries re-thought
Series editor: Ian Parker

Developments inside psychology that question the history of the discipline and the way it functions in society have led many psychologists to look outside the discipline for new ideas. This series draws on cutting edge critiques from just outside psychology in order to complement and question critical arguments emerging inside. The authors provide new perspectives on subjectivity from disciplinary debates and cultural phenomena adjacent to traditional studies of the individual.

The books in the series are useful for advanced level undergraduate and postgraduate students, researchers and lecturers in psychology and other related disciplines such as cultural studies, geography, literary theory, philosophy, psychotherapy, social work and sociology.

Most recently published titles:

Race, Gender, and the Activism of Black Feminist Theory
Working with Audre Lorde
Suryia Nayak

Perverse Psychology
The pathologization of sexual violence and transgenderism
Jemma Tosh

Radical Inclusive Education
Disability, teaching and struggles for liberation
Anat Greenstein

Religion and Psychoanalysis in India
Critical clinical practice
Sabah Siddiqui

Ethics and Psychology
Beyond codes of practice
Calum Neill

The Psychopolitics of Food
Culinary rites of passage in the neoliberal age
Mihalis Mentinis

Deleuze and Psychology
Philosophical provocations to psychological practices
Maria Nichterlein and John R. Morss

Rethinking Education through Critical Psychology
Cooperative schools, social justice and voice
Gail Davidge

DELEUZE AND PSYCHOLOGY

Philosophical provocations to psychological practices

Maria Nichterlein and John R. Morss

Routledge
Taylor & Francis Group

LONDON AND NEW YORK

First published 2017
by Routledge
2 Park Square, Milton Park, Abingdon, Oxon OX14 4RN

and by Routledge
711 Third Avenue, New York, NY 10017

Routledge is an imprint of the Taylor & Francis Group, an informa business

British Library Cataloguing in Publication Data
A catalogue record for this book is available from the British Library

Library of Congress Cataloging in Publication Data
Names: Nichterlein, Maria, author. | Morss, John R., author.
Title: Deleuze and psychology : philosophical provocations to
psychological practices / Maria Nichterlein and John R Morss.
Description: 1 Edition. | New York, NY : Routledge, 2017. |
Series: Concepts for critical psychology | Includes bibliographical
references and index.
Identifiers: LCCN 2016002769 (print) | LCCN 2016005275
(ebook) | ISBN 9781138823679 (hardback) |
ISBN 9781138823686 (pbk.) | ISBN 9781315741949 (ebook)
Subjects: LCSH: Deleuze, Gilles, 1925–1995. | Psychology and
philosophy. | Psychology–Research–Methodology. | Philosophy,
French–20th century.
Classification: LCC BF41 .N53 2017 (print) | LCC BF41 (ebook)
| DDC 194–dc23
LC record available at http://lccn.loc.gov/2016002769

ISBN: 978-1-138-82367-9 (hbk)
ISBN: 978-1-138-82368-6 (pbk)
ISBN: 978-1-315-74194-9 (ebk)

Typeset in Bembo
by Wearset Ltd, Boldon, Tyne and Wear

In loving memory of
Natassja A. Jorkowski
One of a kind

CONTENTS

Foreword   viii
Preface   x

PART I
Reading Deleuze psychologically   **1**

1   A walk in the park   3

2   A question of failed identity: psychology's unit of
     analysis   27

3   Empirical becomings: the problematic position of
     psychology's method   53

PART II
Putting the assemblage to work   **89**

4   The actuality of multitudes   91

5   A practical approach: Deleuze and the clinic   142

Afterword   168
Index   170

FOREWORD

Michel Foucault, whose work has provided coordinates for thinking about the discipline of psychology as a component of the 'psy-complex', once commented that the twentieth century will one day be thought of as being 'Deleuzian'. This compliment by Foucault to his friend Gilles Deleuze is one indication that critical psychologists must take seriously the work of this theorist if they are to take forward a 'Foucauldian' perspective on psychology, on the disciplining of populations and individuals. But more than that, it indicates that there is something of the nature of our contemporary reality that is at stake in the claim that the last century was 'Deleuzian', and for how we try to disentangle ourselves from the past as we move on in this twenty-first century. This means that we must not only grasp different arguments about the forms of societal control and regulation that Foucault himself described so well, but also grasp how the system of concepts that we use to make sense of those forms of control and regulation are themselves part of the problem. Not only does radical theory and politics shift from a concern with 'vertical' tree-like systems of control to 'horizontal' rhizomatic networks of regulation, from hierarchical forms of power to sets of relationships between people, but society itself is mutating so that at the very moment that we try to escape old bad power we find ourselves tangled up in new, dense networks of obligations and responsibilities to each other. If the world itself is indeed becoming 'Deleuzian', then we desperately need Deleuze to describe it and open up 'lines of flight' to new forms of description and action.

This book takes up the challenge, providing a historical and conceptual overview of the context for the development of Deleuze's work, and then also enabling us to see what might happen to our psychology if we took his arguments on board. The deep challenge that he poses to psychologists is precisely to step aside from the endeavour to plunge 'deep' into the human subject, to step aside from the attempt to discover things under the surface that will allow the psychologists to better present themselves as experts who will tell us how we should think and how we should behave. This challenge, as Maria Nichterlein and John Morss explain so clearly and patiently, requires that we question dominant notions of ontology – what we think the things in the world are really like – and epistemology, which is how we elaborate a knowledge about those things.

We can then move on from finding 'things' much-beloved of traditional ontology and rethink what it means to build knowledge about them, tracing instead the surface of things, how they connect with each other and with who we think we are. We can move on from digging out static things from below the surface, from inside the mind, to 'process'. Once we do step aside, we are able to look sideways at the way that our 'psychology' operates as a series of language games, and we better appreciate how the discipline of psychology operates as a series of 'assemblages' which expand and insinuate themselves in our everyday lives. *Deleuze and Psychology* is a book about 'critical' psychology at the very same moment that it unravels almost every assumption about what psychology should be, and it is about 'clinical' psychology. It connects with the activities of systemic therapists, accumulating an argument for a new kind of practice in the clinic, putting together a different space for 'becoming' which might even make a claim to become a different kind of psychology altogether. In this way, Deleuze becomes a guide who is with us inside psychology but arguing against us from outside it, 'outwith' psychology all the better to be able to creatively transform ourselves.

Ian Parker
University of Leicester

PREFACE

What on earth is 'Deleuze'? I am a busy clinician and I do not have time for fancy theory! Why should I bother about the ideas of a continental philosopher who was on the 'radical' end of the spectrum? My work is not about ideas but about *actual* people and *real* suffering!

These words are echoes of many conversations that one of us – Maria – has engaged in through the years of clinical work. These are true and relevant considerations and should not be dismissed out of hand. Let's face it – psychology's contemporary practice, in particular the dominance of evidence-based practice, is highly contested. But this is the 'official' story and psychologists need to establish their professional identity by reckoning with these forces. This is already hard enough. The current orientation that characterises psychology leaves little space for considerations of the kind that Deleuze invites us to.

There are many ways of introducing Deleuze to a psychological audience. In this book we have been guided by Deleuze's own reflections:

> My ideal, when I write about an author, would be to write nothing that could cause him sadness, or if he is dead, that might make him weep in his grave. Think of the author you are writing about. Think of him so hard that he can no longer be an object, and equally so that you cannot identify with him. Avoid the double shame of the scholar and the familiar. Give back to an author a little of the joy, the energy, the life of love and politics that he knew how to give and invent.
>
> *Deleuze and Parnet, 2006, p. 88*

Even then, we have a range of options. We could make reference to his unique personal style and, for example, observe that many, including Deleuze himself, remarked on his unusually long fingernails and his rather dishevelled, non-bourgeois presentation. We could interpret this presentation in the context of his long-standing academic career as one of the professors of the experimental University of Vincennes, a true son of the students' revolution of May'68. We could focus on defining a psychological profile of the struggles he had with health and comment on the fact that he endured the effects of having one of his lungs removed due to tuberculosis when 44 years old, and even comment that he did not give up smoking as a result. We could perhaps focus on a more tender aspect of his persona and comment on the admiration shown to Deleuze by French society, as well as by friends and family. One of his friends – Yves – recalled how his wife, 'in one of the most beautiful gestures of love I have ever seen, stretched out her arms, took Gilles' hands in her long, slender fingers, and said to him, "Yves is right. I also think you're a saint"' (Dosse, 2010, p. 500). Our preference instead is to employ the description offered by the director of what was to become the film of the Deleuze *Abecedaire*:

> He was a great actor of his texts. He had this wonderful knowledge of how to use his body and silhouette. And a strong self-deprecating streak.... It is a rare occurrence to shoot someone who's so at ease in his body, in his voice, who's completely present in what he's doing, yet at the same time maintaining a distance from which he can look upon himself, and chuckle at being filmed. He's in the aquarium, he has chosen the water of his aquarium, and he does what he wants.
>
> *Boutang, 2004*

We are aware that these are rather unorthodox presentations of Deleuze and we are aware that this book is intended to introduce the value of his work to the profession of psychology. Here our automatic, instinctive response is to say that Deleuze is *the* philosopher of Difference and that some in psychology have been reading Deleuze and thinking about his contributions for some time. Particular mention should be made of Steve Brown, Johanna Motzkau and Hans and Kathleen Skott-Myhre in the English-speaking world, and to Pietro Barbetta in Italy. Brown (2012) identifies four areas of Deleuze's thought that are of relevance to psychology. First, Deleuze's works propose a 'flat ontology' wherein plurality is explained not in transcendental terms but in immanent terms. Second,

Deleuze presents a robust critique of common sense as the basis for thought and proposes instead that 'thinking only really begins when its faculty is confronted by a "sign" that throws it into "discord" or a "violence which brings it face to face with its own element"' forcing thought to 'make sense' (p. 106). Third, Deleuze 'demolishes' the subject; and, last, in his work with Guattari, Deleuze offers an account of power that connects power with desire as an alternative to subjugation by external forces.

These are important points, ones we think will become clear as you read the book and become more familiar with Deleuze's project. To add to what is said by Brown, something we think is perhaps the most powerful effect of Deleuze's ideas for the clinic is Deleuze's relentless affirmation of critical and creative functions in human endeavour. Here, the connections that Deleuze establishes between literature and the clinic are central to understanding how a philosophy of Difference articulates itself in grounded practices. We need to be clear that literature is not understood in the familiar sense of narrative approaches in therapy, but as a way of being in language.

We hope our attempts to translate and explicate Deleuze for a psychology audience proves of interest to you as a reader. It has been a challenge to do so in the way that Deleuze prescribes in the quotation above. We would not have been able to tackle this without the support of each other and many friends. We would like to particularly thank Ian Parker and Erica Burman, and acknowledge their profound commitment to critical thinking in the discipline. We also want to thank Michael Strang and Routledge for their faith in this project and the belief that we could 'provide the goods'. Special thanks also to Paul Patton and James Williams for their generous support. Maria would like to particularly thank Carmel Flaskas and Michael Wearing, whose support in the writing of her PhD thesis at the University of New South Wales – where the early seeds of this project were sown – was invaluable. Equal thanks need to be given to the examiners of the thesis – Britt Krause and Steven Brown – whose generous feedback was the source of further productive thought. Maria would also like to thank her team – the AIMS and YBIS team within CAMHS – at the Austin Hospital in Melbourne, in particular Catherine Coffey and Barbara Woods, who supported her in finding time for writing. Hayden Jones also requires particular mention, for it was he who had to cover for Maria's distractedness. John would like to acknowledge the support of colleagues in the Alfred Deakin Institute for Citizenship and Globalisation at Deakin University, especially Fethi Mansouri, Sean Bowden, Jack Reynolds, Matt Sharpe and Patrick Stokes. Last, we would also like to give big thanks to all friends who were around during the hours of writing, in particular Zoe, Felix and Claire.

References

Boutang, P.-A. 2004. Everything about Gilles Deleuze and nothing about Gilles Deleuze. *RevueVertigo*, 25.

Brown, S. 2012. Between the planes: Deleuze and social science. *In:* Jensen, C.B. and Rodje, K. (eds), *Deleuzian intersections: science, technology, anthropology*. New York: Berghahn Books.

Deleuze, G. and Parnet, C. 2006. *Dialogues II*. London: Continuum.

Dosse, F. 2010. *Gilles Deleuze & Félix Guattari: intersecting lives*. New York: Columbia University Press.

PART I

Reading Deleuze psychologically

1

A WALK IN THE PARK

In 1972, Gilles Deleuze and his friend Félix Guattari published *Anti-Oedipus: Capitalism and Schizophrenia*. This is how the book starts:

> It is at work everywhere, functioning smoothly at times, at other times in fits and starts. It breathes, it heats, it eats. It shits and fucks. What a mistake to have ever said *the* id.

A beginning like this is designed to shock and, getting on for fifty years later, it still does. Those five-letter words grab our attention. But what does it mean? As it turns out, that question indicates the answer. '*What does "it" mean?*' For, as the title of the book states it, one of the main targets of *Anti-Oedipus* is Freud's account of human mental life, with its representation of subconscious forces as 'the it': literally thus in the original German (das Es). This term was turned into the even more impressive-looking Latin form 'Id' – still capitalised – by Freud's English translators.

Like in the 1950s science fiction movie *Forbidden Planet*, Deleuze and his henchman Guattari are taking on 'Monsters from the Id'. There are no monsters, they say; there is no id. There is no such 'thing'. Instead of a thing or things, there are flows and connections: connections of production, of consumption, of desire and of ecology. Not 'it' but 'machines'. For Deleuze and Guattari, 'Everywhere *it* is machines.' The syntax is a little unconventional but we can figure out what they are driving at if we just keep reading:

> Everywhere *it* is machines – real ones, not figurative ones: machines driving other machines, machines being driven by other machines, with all the necessary couplings and connections.... Hence we are all handymen: each with his little machines.... A schizophrenic out for a walk is a better model than a neurotic lying on the analyst's couch. A breath of fresh air, a relationship with the outside world.... There is no such thing as either man or nature now, only a process that produces the one within the other and couples the machines together. Producing-machines, desiring-machines everywhere, schizophrenic machines, all of species life: the self and the non-self, outside and inside, no longer have any meaning whatsoever.
>
> *Deleuze and Guattari, 1983, pp. 1–2*

They started their years of collaboration in 1969, the year after the shock of student-led protests and strikes in Paris. Perhaps, then, it is not surprising that their style is direct and provocative. *Anti-Oedipus* became an instant best-seller in France, where it was acclaimed as the book that best articulated the new sensibilities emerging out of May'68 (Colebrook, 2002b, p. xvii).

Turbulent times

The events of May'68 had a significant impact on Deleuze. As he himself recalled, he was one of the first students to defend his thesis after the revolt, a situation that gave rise to some comic relief, for his professors were more concerned about possible attacks by gangs than in evaluating his work (Boutang, 2012). On a more serious note, however, May'68 marked a significant rupture in French social and political life. Together with similar events elsewhere in Europe, especially West Germany as it then was, it affected the Western world in general. It shaped the spirit of the thinkers of that generation in what came to be known as 'French thought' (Roudinesco, 2008). As Colebrook points out (2002b, p. xxxiii), these were examples of human events that escaped the rationalities and definitions ascribed from all directions, expressing unexpected and uncontrollable forces. What made May'68 such a critical event for Deleuze was its 'unexpected *puissance*', its force in cutting through the established order, a disruption that afforded the creation of a space of possibility; a space that escaped descriptions and expectations. The student demonstrations began as protests against the Vietnam War, in solidarity with protest movements in the USA and elsewhere. But May'68 was neither planned nor controlled ... it happened; and its happening left all ideological mindsets speechless (Deleuze and Guattari, 1984). For Deleuze, May'68 was an example of how reality cuts through the ideologies showing the limits of language and of the attempt to make sense of novel events in terms of established structures and institutions.

Deleuze saw in May'68 a unique moment of life, an event, a moment where a collective intensity engaged people politically and created an event of significance, a rupture with the status quo that gave birth to the genuine possibility of change and newness. For Deleuze this was people – as a collective – reaching their limits and engaging in active protest, in a clamour of having 'had enough'. It was people alive in their gesture of discontent.

The emergence of a critical manifesto

Anti-Oedipus put together a manifesto of protest against the conceptual evils of modern life. Deleuze and Guattari's was an ambitious critique that is best grasped by recalling its subtitle: *Capitalism and Schizophrenia*. *Anti-Oedipus* attempted to capture the force of the event of May'68 by articulating the salient elements of this protest and working out the critical implications to constructively inform not just French but Western sensibilities. The critique was carried out by means of an exploration of the strengths and limitations of the two prevalent analytical frameworks of that era – Marxism and psychoanalysis. Deleuze and Guattari juxtaposed an analysis of Marx's conceptualisations on the flow of capital and on the conditions of production together with Freud's proposal of the existence of an unconscious and of an economy of desire or libido. Appropriating Nietzsche's ideas on the will to power, Deleuze and Guattari affirmed a material reading of reality and of our human activity as, fundamentally, a social production. Reality is no longer a representation of a specific point within a historical process of liberation but the creative expression that results from or emerges out of processes of production. In turn, production is not a proletarian activity in the way that Marx had described, but the expression of unconscious desires. Reality for Deleuze and Guattari is a delirium, a creative articulation of what is better described as 'a schizophrenic out for a walk' rather than 'a neurotic lying on the couch'. Not a passive introspection, isolated from the world, but an active and constructive engagement with the world, a getting out among it. Importantly, this engagement constructs what Deleuze and Guattari would later call '*assemblages*', mobile structures that in turn co-produce one's sense of one's self – as a subject with consciousness – and the sense of a world, and that world itself.

In relation to the discipline of psychology, the major critique presented by Deleuze and Guattari is, as the title indicates, against psychoanalysis. Psychoanalysis, they suggest, is the only true force to be reckoned with in psychology, a kind of back-handed compliment to its power. In *Anti-Oedipus* they portray psychoanalysis as, ultimately, fulfilling a constraining role within the broader framework of capitalism. Capitalism restrains the flow of capital by alienating production, especially by means of the creation of (artificial) ownership. In a complementary way psychoanalysis, they claim, undermines the promises of its discovery of the unconscious by reducing its potential and denying its true nature. Deleuze and Guattari accuse psychoanalysis of a 'reduction of the factories of the unconscious to a piece of theater [*sic*]' (Deleuze, 1995, p. 17), Oedipus or Hamlet; the reduction of the social investments of libido to domestic investments, and the projection of desire back onto domestic coordinates (Deleuze *et al.*, 1972).

Deleuze and Guattari articulate an alternative proposal: rather than psychoanalysis, 'schizoanalysis'. Rather than a neurotic lying on the couch of the psychoanalyst revisiting – endlessly so – the past familial dynamics, a schizophrenic walking in the park encountering and making connections with the outside in an attempt to break free from the binds inherent to the human condition. Schizoanalysis attempts not to unveil the true dynamics of an unconscious searching for 'mummies and daddies' but to articulate the machinations and the trajectories of what Deleuze and Guattari call 'desiring machines' in their explorations of the circumstances of contemporary life. We will return to these issues throughout this book.

Anti-Oedipus marked the beginning of a new metaphysics, a metaphysics that would respond to the insights of science in the twentieth century as noted by Todd May (2005). This is particularly of relevance to psychology because, as Adkins clarifies in relation to *A Thousand Plateaus*, theirs is a metaphysics but not an ontology. 'It is an experimental, pragmatic metaphysics that replaces ontology's "to be" with a series generated by the conjunction "and ... and ... and..."' (2015, p. 24). Deleuze and Guattari's project is indeed a forceful critique of the established tenets of the West, tenets they saw embodied in a philosophy based on representation and identity. But it is much more than that. Their project was not merely negative but also an affirmative proposal that would become more fully articulated in the companion volume to *Anti-Oedipus*, written eight years later, *A Thousand Plateaus* (Deleuze and Guattari, 1987). This critically positive element in Deleuze and Guattari's ideas makes them particularly interesting for our discipline.

Developments that took place between these collaborative volumes also include the move from a vocabulary of 'desiring machines' to a vocabulary of 'assemblages' and what might cautiously be called a maturing of the style of presentation. But before we focus on the developments emerging in their project, there is value in noting the complexity of interplay between Deleuze's solo work and his collaborations with Guattari. There is little doubt that the collaborations between Deleuze and Guattari were unique and intensely creative and that, although Deleuze became more recognised, Guattari provided some significant contributions to their collaborative work (Lecercle, 2002, pp. 33–6). In many ways, their collaboration confirmed the coherence of their ideas of an actual relational knowledge in practice. Many have commented on the uniqueness of their friendship and how they complemented each other, to the extent that some see it as misleading to think of the work of the one without that of the other (Dosse, 2010). Deleuze himself commented on the complementary styles of himself and Guattari, a complementarity that would afford the creation of a third entity that was not simply an aggregate of the two but an emerging new persona (Deleuze and Parnet, 2006; Deleuze *et al.*, 1988). Not that the two writers lost their distinctiveness from each other. As Deleuze commented, they 'were never in the same rhythm, [they] were always out of step' (Deleuze and Parnet, 2006, p. 13). Guattari remarked that 'we're really not of the same dimension ... [Deleuze] always has the *oeuvre* in mind' (2006, p. 400). This difference can in part be accounted for by the fact that by the time Deleuze started his collaboration with Guattari, he was an experienced writer and teacher of academic philosophy. By the time he met Guattari, he had published ten books and numerous articles on the key thinkers and ideas that informed his philosophical investigations. Guattari, on the other hand, had established himself as a major psychoanalytic practitioner in the Lacanian tradition.

Understanding Deleuze's philosophical project

In a sense, and in some ways pre-empting the insights of *A Thousand Plateaus*, Deleuze's oeuvre can be best described as 'conceptualizations within a plateau'. Deleuze and Guattari borrowed the concept of plateau from Gregory Bateson to refer to a 'continuous, self-vibrating region of intensities whose development avoids any orientation toward a culmination point or external end' (1987, p. 22). Bateson's concept of a plateau (1958) helps us to focus on two central characteristics of Deleuze's work. In the first instance, and as Paul Patton has noted, Deleuze 'is an experimental thinker committed to a conception of movement in thought' (2010, p. 10). If anything is fixed in Deleuze's conceptual work, it is the centrality of difference and variation in all aspects of life, including conceptual work. Reading Deleuze requires the acceptance that all of his concepts carry with them a field of resonances and indeterminacy. It is hard to pin down his concepts to specific definitions not because he lacks precision but because, in line with his own insights, concepts suffer variations through time when they engage in material encounters with the outside. Like Deleuze and Guattari's central concept of assemblages, Deleuzian concepts are not static but in movement. Here lies a second fundamental commitment of Deleuze's work: to engage with philosophy in ways that are vitalist, that is to say directly informed by life. In the context of these 'constraints', it can be correctly stated that Deleuze's writing can be best understood as 'always on the move'.

Such movement needs to be understood as multidirectional. Perhaps it can be best thought of as a kind of landscape, an extension of sorts or, using an idea Deleuze and Guattari would often use, as 'establishing a territory'. Here lies a difference from the works of other great thinkers which can be reduced to lineal trajectories. Such trajectories may be chronological or might be thought of as representing a logical sequence with a straightforward structure. In contrast, Deleuze constantly calls us to engage with the whole – to see the landscape, in all its particulars. He invites us to see the forest while walking amidst the tall trees. There is something in the style of Deleuze's writing that always reminds us that there is a much larger picture at stake, a larger machine of which the particulars in question are but cogs. This is demanding and something that many have described as daunting. But such a territory – such a machine, such an assemblage – can be seen as demarcated by a number of defining coordinates. As May (2005) and others (e.g. Dosse, 2010) have commented, there are two main coordinates in Deleuze's work. The first is empiricism as a foundational methodology. The second is a trinitarian genealogy of philosophy through the work of Spinoza, Nietzsche and Bergson. These will be our bearings in this introductory exploration of Deleuze's work.

Empiricism: the opening of concepts to life

The term empiricism is familiar to those who have studied psychology in the English-speaking world. It connotes an openness to the world in all its sensory complexity and relatedly a respect for experimentation, for trying things out. Empiricism stands in opposition to dogmatic insistence on the validity of views imposed by those in positions of authority. All these characteristics are relevant to Deleuze's version of empiricism. But by comparison with Deleuze, the conventional understanding of empiricism in psychology is somewhat timid. We will come back to psychologist's timidity in the next chapters, focusing at this point instead on how Deleuze used the term.

Empiricism and Subjectivity (1991) was Deleuze's first book, the beginning of what was to become a life-long engagement with empiricism as methodology. As Deleuze states, empiricism constituted a continuous and central orientation in his work (1995, p. 89). What attracted him to empiricism was that, as a method, it 'sets out to present concepts directly' (Deleuze and Maggiori, 1986, pp. 88–9), thus engaging with raw concepts rather than 'approach[ing] things through structures, or linguistics or psychoanalysis, through science or even through history' (p. 89). It was Deleuze's way of grounding his philosophical investigations in what is concrete and material, an orientation that provided his work with the 'innocence' noted by Jacques Derrida (1998).

Deleuze followed the definition of empiricism given by the English philosopher Whitehead at the beginning of the twentieth century: 'the abstract does not explain, but must itself be explained; and the aim is not to rediscover the eternal or the universal, but to find the conditions under which something new is produced (*creativeness*)' (Deleuze and Parnet, 2006). There is a difference between this take on empiricism and the sense of 'empiricism' that is more familiar to professional psychologists. Perhaps a simple way to explain this difference is by looking at the role of concepts in the production of knowledge. In mainstream professional understandings of empiricism, great effort is put to ensure that concepts are based on facts. This orientation, if not problematised, can lead to a silencing of ideas in favour of concrete examples, a conservative tyranny of 'what is' instead of 'what is possible'. For Deleuze as for Whitehead before him, on the other hand, empiricism is not to be set against concepts per se. Empiricism for Deleuze is not a critique of thought or of theory in itself, but a critique of an idea of thought as static and distant from the ever-changing conditions constituting life. Empirical thought, for Deleuze, does not stand on a different level to, but operates in an open and creative relationship with, the outside: with the flow and variations present in everyday life. Instead of concepts serving a representational function – a crucial issue in his thesis *Difference and Repetition* (Deleuze, 1994) that we will discuss later – concepts are to be considered as powerful instruments in our engagement with the world. Concepts for Deleuze are not inert representations but productive forces: '[a]bstract ideas are not dead things, they are entities that inspire powerful spatial dynamism' (1997, p. 119). In this sense, empiricism affords and supports a philosophy of movement and of possibilities, allowing an engagement with concepts not as cut out – abstracted – from life but as recursively involved in the movements of life that they attempt to account for. We will return to discuss empiricism and the implications for psychology of this reading in more detail in Chapter 3.

Philosophy's history: Deleuze's particular genealogy of a material immanent trinity

In the curiously titled *Letter to a Harsh Critic*, Deleuze explained his work as manifesting a particular trajectory within philosophy. He saw this trajectory as his unique way of subverting what he perceived to be the repressive role played by the prevalent, canonical history of philosophy in the education of young philosophers. This involved Deleuze, in a move that is representative of his style of scholarship, focusing his attention on a small number of key thinkers of the past, thinkers for whom he felt a special affinity and whom he saw as 'compensating' for the power of prevalent dogmas.

Deleuze arrived at a unique combination of admired authors. Some were to be read in unfamiliar ways, partly accounting for the feeling of unfamiliarity that his work generates in traditionally oriented colleagues. In his introduction to Deleuze's work, May (2005) argues that although Deleuze writes about many thinkers, there are three who stand above the rest in providing the coordinates of Deleuze's work. They can each be linked to a key concept: 'Immanence, duration, affirmation: Spinoza, Bergson, Nietzsche. These are the parameters of an ontology of difference' (May, 2005, p. 26; see also Dosse, 2010, ch. 7). We will now briefly overview these important sources of influence on Deleuze.

Spinoza and immanence

Bento, Baruch or Benedictus Spinoza (1632–77) was, for Deleuze, 'the Christ of philosophers' compared to whom other great philosophers are mere apostles, approaching or seeking distance from this 'mystery' (Deleuze and Guattari, 1991, p. 60). For Deleuze, 'Spinoza rediscovered the concrete force of empiricism in applying it in support of a new rationalism, one of the most rigorous versions ever conceived' (1992, p. 149).

Spinoza's new rationalism focused on the articulation of an ontology based on *immanence*. Immanence is a monistic concept, in other words it rejects the split between appearance and reality so strongly proclaimed by Plato. Immanence is the doctrine in philosophy that affirms the existence of only one substance to explain reality. That is to say, everything that occurs arises from what is already in existence and is not informed by some mysterious 'outside'. This is not to say that the outside needs to be forgotten or not taken into account but, as we will discuss more extensively in Chapter 3, such outside is not external to the object but refers to chaotic singularities. Immanence thus stands in contrast to transcendence and to dualistic forms of philosophy. It points to an understanding that explains things 'from within' as compared to transcendental explanations that explain according to 'things in themselves'. 'Things in themselves' were to have a continuing career in the philosophical thought of Europe long after Spinoza's death. A hundred years after Spinoza's death, writing towards the end of the eighteenth century in the Enlightenment period, Immanuel Kant found the distinction between 'noumena' (things in themselves) and 'phenomena' (things as they appear) to be unavoidable. Indeed, twentieth-century 'phenomenology' owed much to this Kantian heritage. It is thus important to note that Spinoza 'failed' if by that is meant that Western philosophy failed to grasp his insights for some while. For Deleuze, however, Spinoza was the first philosopher to notice that the philosophical distinction between the two worlds of the material and the spiritual was an illusion.

Immanence 'is the first requirement of an ontology of difference' (May, 2005, p. 27). Deleuze saw in Spinoza's work on immanence an element foundational to the new metaphysics that he was developing. Spinoza's *Ethics* asserted that there is only one substance – which may be termed God or Nature. Everything that exists is merely a modulation of this substance. To put it another way, all that exists are 'attributes', not things, which is to say that everything is but different expressions of the wholeness. Deleuze uses this idea and conceives *events* in life (not people as such) as unique expressions of material articulation, expressions that differ from each other yet are all ultimately connected for they are all but manifestations of a unique substance. From this perspective, immanence as a core concept affords not only the idea of difference and of multitude, but also the idea of a fundamental union in the unfolding of life. This interplay between unity and diversity allows intimate relationships between apparently different events, including those that pertain to our felt experience. This in turn affords a central dynamic for Deleuze: that events have the capacity to affect and be affected by each other, making 'encounters' central. *Immanence*, then, is key in supporting a non-reductionist understanding of life.

For Spinoza, the infinite expressions of life are to be measured in terms of their effects. Deleuze explains this in his peculiar style by noting that Spinoza was 'too shrewd' to title his book 'Ontology', choosing instead 'Ethics' to remind readers that one can only judge claims in terms of the type of ethics that such claims brings forth (1980, para. 24). Deleuze refers to Spinoza's distinction of sad and joyful passions as the way such evaluation takes place, an evaluation that is not objective but highly singular.

Nietzsche and affirmation

Nietzsche and Philosophy (1986a) was Deleuze's second book. It was published in 1962, nine years after *Empiricism and Subjectivity* and, more than the latter, it was the book that positioned Deleuze as a philosopher of stature in academic circles (Boutang, 2012; Stivale, 2000). If Deleuze characterised Spinoza as 'the Christ of philosophy', it could be argued that he saw in Friedrich Nietzsche (1844–1900) an alternative figure to the 'Holy Spirit', for his concept of the 'eternal return' can ironically be positioned to refer to a sacred spirit, a spirit of holiness that is entirely abstract in its presence yet central to what we observe and, what is more important, what we live. According to Deleuze, Nietzsche's 'eternal return' is a powerful companion to the concept of immanence in Spinoza. Nietzsche's eternal return was a crucial contribution to Deleuze's subsequent development of the critique of identity and representation. This is because the Nietzschean eternal return is not the return of something identical. It does not refer to a predictable orbit by reference to which the next appearance of a planet or a moon can be confidently anticipated. The eternal return is about a *difference* that returns selectively to create the transient stability of images and things. The eternal return thus refers to a return that eliminates 'half-desires and hesitant yearnings' (Bogue, 1989, p. 31) and crystallises, at every moment, the full potential of differentiation and of the becoming of difference. In this shift, identity is possible by the returning of what is pure in difference. The eternal return is central to affirm what is ephemeral and in constant flux. It brings forth a subtle interplay between stability and change: of a certainty that something will return, and also of difference because what will return is a unique process of differentiation. The eternal return provided Deleuze, then, with a powerful alternative to the conventional idea of passive engagement with representations of 'something' already out there (Deleuze, 1967, p. 124). For Deleuze, the eternal return was central to Nietzsche's idea of life as tragedy (1886); a tragic throw of the dice (1954). Life, in this sense, articulates the ultimately undecidable throwing of the dice. We know life is constituted by imponderables and that our life as a human calls for an active engagement with the circumstances implied in the throws (throes?) that we are confronted with. Nietzsche talks about *good* and *bad* players, good players being those who engage with such a throw in constructive and affirmative ways while bad players get stuck in either guilt or resentment. What is unique in Nietzsche is that the evaluation of the quality of life one lives is not measured by external factors (such as systems of morality) but by factors that are immanent to the mode of living in question. This is what is of relevance to Deleuze and to a philosophy of difference. No longer are there stable and predictable values that work as judgements belonging to a transcendental (Christian) order, but particular evaluations that emerge out of the specific conditions of living which, 'in essence, are not values but ways of being, modes of existence of those who judge and evaluate' (Deleuze, 1986a, p. 1). As Deleuze explains elsewhere:

> Not that every interpretation therefore has the same value and occupies the same plan – on the contrary, they are stacked or layered in the new depth. But they no longer have the true and the false as criteria. The noble and the vile, the high and the low, become the immanent principles of interpretations and evaluations.
>
> *Deleuze, 1967, p. 118*

This conceptual twist helps understand another important point in Nietzsche: phenomena, more than simple signs, are 'symptoms' and the philosopher's work, rather than being analytical in a logical sense, is one of being a physician of sorts. The philosopher evaluates contemporary events as symptoms, that is to say, events are read in terms of what they say about themselves and about the society in which they emerge.

Bergson and duration

Nietzsche, like Spinoza, may be also said to have 'failed' if that is taken to refer to the immediate impact of their philosophical works. It was only many decades after his death in 1900 that Nietzsche's supreme importance as a philosopher was recognised across Europe, in France thanks to thinkers like Deleuze and Foucault. Henri Bergson (1859–1941), who completes Deleuze's trinity, was by contrast very successful through much of his academic working life although he sacrificed his status in protest against the Vichy government. Since Deleuze was born in 1925, their lifespans overlapped for some sixteen years.

Somewhat like Nietzsche, although more conventional in his career and in the mode of expression of his ideas, Bergson was sceptical of the capacity of rational human consciousness in the face of life's challenges. Or rather, he was sceptical about the ways that Western philosophy had understood and articulated the nature of human consciousness and its rational dimensions. Bergson was writing in an era when mainstream Western science seemed to be all-powerful not only in relation to industrial production both in peace and in war, but in relation to the ideology of knowledge. The laboratory sciences allied with mathematics seemed to be hegemonic in defining the scope and limits of human experience. Somewhat loosely this can be called a 'positivist' worldview that, as a package of ideas, coalesced around notions of human progress and the contribution that rational human thinking, focused on scientific advancement and industrial development, would make to that project.

Bergson was deeply sceptical about this *zeitgeist*. The scientific rationality on which it relied was, he felt, fragile. The risk was that the efforts of a scientific elite and of its allies in the establishment would be but petty tinkering in the face of the great crashing waves of historical movement and of organic diversity. Again like Nietzsche, Bergson seemed to Deleuze to have noticed the sheer scale of what we modern humans are up against and the feeble capacities with which we are supplied. Critically, however, Bergson, like Spinoza as well as Nietzsche in this respect, wrested a defiantly optimistic philosophy from these insights. Central to Bergson's philosophy was a rethinking of nothing less than the nature of organic life on Earth. In this re-thinking he appropriated elements of the so-called vitalism that had characterised Francophone zoology in previous centuries. This also was attractive to Deleuze. In the writings of Bergson, this vitalism occasionally verged on the spiritualist if by that is meant an idealism that loses contact with the materiality of this world. Certainly Deleuze felt that the value of vitalism, its capacity to energise and give urgency to the otherwise dry and dusty skeleton of evolutionary theory, was best ensured by maintaining contact with the writings of Bergson.

Consistent with the above attitudes, and like Spinoza in this respect, Bergson rejected the conventional division between a material and an intelligible world. In the words of Deleuze, 'Bergson replaced the differentiation between two worlds with the distinction between two movements' (Dosse, 2010, p. 138). *Movement* is a key trope for Deleuze, a theme or style of expression that captures something of his overall project. Bergson's sense of time as duration is closely linked to this.

With Spinoza as Son and Nietzsche as Holy Spirit, it seems convenient to use the image of the Father to refer to the influence that Bergson had on Deleuze. The convenience of this name is that Bergson can be said to have provided immanence with an articulation of time (May, 2005, p. 41). In particular, as Widder (2012, pp. 46–7) insightfully comments, Bergson provided Deleuze with an account of the past and the present as a springboard for the future. For Deleuze, Bergson's account of time provided a good complement to Nietzsche's eternal return. The time that Bergson calls forth is not a phenomenological time – the time of personal experience – but a foundational time that enables experience to make sense and to acquire meaning. As Eugene Holland (2011) observes, time for Deleuze and Guattari is like irreversible time in the understanding of modern physics. Deleuze and Guattari reject the more traditional scientific approach to time in which time is treated as a mathematical dimension along the lines of the three dimensions of space, turning time into – literally – a fourth dimension. That traditionally scientific view in effect treats time as reversible. Time is assimilated to the spatial dimensions in which we supposedly are free to move at will, backwards or forwards, up or down. Holland connects this orthodox or classical scientific approach with the philosophical position of Kant. In stark contrast to Kant, and in contrast to this somewhat domesticated view of time, Bergson thought of time as something terrible, awesome: like a wall of water moving forward and carrying all before it. This sense of the forward rush of time was very much a Bergsonian influence on Deleuze. At the same time, adding a twist to Bergson, Deleuze recognised that we are somehow like Alice's Red Queen, running to stand still.

With Bergson, we complete this initial exploration of the coordinates in Deleuze's thought. As already mentioned, these coordinates were already in action prior to the collaboration with Guattari on *Anti-Oedipus*.

Difference and repetition

Difference and Repetition was the published version of Deleuze's *aggregation* thesis and constituted a point of departure for his own project (Patton, 1994, p. xi). As Deleuze himself commented, it foreshadowed the ideas in *Anti-Oedipus* (1986b, p. 300). Published in 1968, *Difference and Repetition* is a sustained and comprehensive critique of the dominance of two related notions, central to Western philosophy since the time of Plato. These are the notions of 'identity' and of 'representation' as a fundamental activity of thought. Within the classical tradition based on identity and representation, *difference* is relegated to a secondary role. What is perhaps even more important for psychology, *change* is relegated in the same way. Thus in the Platonic tradition, difference is that which lies between two identities perceived at the same time. Change is difference occurring with time rather than at the same time. Difference, in this tradition, has a negative and reactive quality instead of having a presence in and of itself. Deleuze's thesis critiqued this arrangement by repositioning difference as an active and affirmative phenomenon central to our thinking and, ultimately, to life. This shift turned the 'order of things' upside down, relegating identity to a secondary role, as that which remains stable through repetitions across time.

One particularly important exploration takes place in *Difference and Repetition* when Deleuze addresses the way in which a focus on identity mystifies core activities in both philosophy and everyday life. He talks about a certain 'image of thought': a certain set of presuppositions that provide thought with a certain essence or identity, often under the name of 'common sense' or 'good sense'. For Deleuze common or good sense are not the friends of thought. Rather, they are 'fiends' that hinder the ability of thought to think anew. As Deleuze states, such presuppositions about thought 'crush thought under an image which is that of the Same and the Similar in representation, but profoundly betrays what it means to think and alienates the two powers of difference and repetition, of philosophical commencement and recommencement' (Deleuze, 1994, p. 167).

Deleuze offers further grounds for rejecting the identity-centred, stable image of thought. For Deleuze, it is a practical corollary of the identitarian position that it supports and is supported by morality (1994, p. 132). Deleuze distinguishes sharply between morality and ethics. He thought of morality as pertaining to static images of thought that provide correspondingly static and determinate expectations on how life ought to be lived. In contrast, Deleuze valued ethics, thought of in terms of an ongoing evaluative process of what is constructive and positive in life. Supporting the parameters mentioned above, this view of ethics had been indicated by Spinoza and further articulated by Nietzsche.

As an alternative to this static, identity-centred image of thought, Deleuze proposes a *nomadic* image of thought. Nomadic thought is a type of thought that is empirical. It is a thought that is best conceived as an 'encounter' with the outside: as 'something in the world [that] forces us to think' (p. 139) in an active and productive search for solutions to the dilemmas that life presents. It is in this sense that Deleuze's philosophy is sometimes considered to be 'constructivist', although many approaches go under that name.

Deleuze emphasises two points in relation to this shift from identity and representation to difference and repetition. First, he insisted that the change away from representation does not amount to a lack of foundations as such but, as noted above, an inversion in the explanation: no longer identity as central but difference. In such a world of difference, as we will expand through the book, what is central is not representation of a static and predictable world but the material emergence – the becoming – of the new. Second, Deleuze uses the concept of 'the virtual' in a formally equivalent position to 'the idea' in Plato's thought. For Plato, ideas correspond with and thereby represent a world of essence, of a true reality, obscure to any but the Gods or the properly trained philosopher. For Deleuze, the virtual is a concept that refers to a non-material dimension that informs the material world. This concept of the virtual creates interesting effects. In particular, its effects differ from those of the Platonic idea in that the relationship between the virtual and the material world is now not one of representation but one of *actualisation*. With this move from the Platonic idea to the Deleuzian virtual, the world as it is experienced is no longer a copy of an idea – of a transcendental and universal idea – but a concrete embodiment of a virtual possibility. Deleuze considers the virtual not as a world of ideas but as an undifferentiated mass – the cosmos, or the Spinozan monist nature – in which there is no empty or negative space. The actual is an emergent entity. That is, it emerges as a result of a process of actualisation in which the virtual acquires form through a transformation that takes place when a number of undifferentiated elements connect with or 'encounter' each other. In this process, an order is established out of disorder, a form emerges out of chaos. We will continue to discuss this idea throughout the book, in particular in Chapter 3, when we explore Deleuze's interest in empiricism and in *chaosmos*.

What is important to understand at this point, however, is that such a process is one of transformation and of embodiment. The actual is in no relationship with a supposed essence – which, in turn, has no relationship with the virtual – and it does not have a direct and predictable relationship with its origin. In this way, Deleuze honours the Nietzschean idea of the eternal return by asserting that 'difference must be shown *differing*' (Deleuze, 1994, p. 41, cited in Dosse, 2010, p. 152).

Bearing in mind this understanding of life as an infinite process of differentiation, it becomes clear that, for Deleuze, it is not possible to ascertain a 'right judgement of *what is*'. In a fluid world, where thought is not about representation and images but about engagement and finding ways forward, it is impossible to make accurate and reliable correlations between the world as one experiences it and the world as it is. This is so because there is no such 'thing' as 'the world as it is'. It is impossible to articulate the nature of 'things in themselves'. In some ways it was Kant's project to establish the cognitive infrastructure by which such correlations and articulations might be comprehended. In turn, for Kant, it would then be possible to establish a firmly based, objective ethics. As Nietzsche and Bergson had urged, this project cannot possibly work. This impossibility is not due to epistemological limitations – to the limits of the human capacity to appreciate knowledge of the true. To believe that this is the case would be to fall prey to the seductions of conscious activity either as guilt (what am I doing wrong or lacking that I cannot know) or as resentment (the world is a fiendish and deceptive world). There is no deficiency or evolutionary limitation either in our souls, our reason or our brain that lies at the base of it. The impossibility is a manifestation of something positive, something which constitutes a metaphysical condition that needs not only to be acknowledged, but also to be lived.

Trailblazing new conceptualisations of thought and knowledge

Difference and Repetition calls for a new understanding of the role of one's thought and knowledge. The position Deleuze was establishing stood in critical relation with the forms of philosophy dominant in 1960s France: phenomenology and structuralism. Phenomenology, in many ways the heir of Kant's work through Husserl, focused on subjective experience and perception and sought to establish reliable patterns of description for the everyday worlds of living and being in society. Structuralism studied the abstract codes by recourse to which, according to its adherents, sense is made of the many dimensions of cultural existence. Deleuze comprehended the aims, and greatly respected the rigour, of both phenomenology and structuralism (e.g. Deleuze, 1972, 1990). But he went beyond both. In relation to phenomenology, Deleuze called on the contribution of Heidegger to critique phenomenology for reducing the complexity of immanence to conscious awareness. Deleuze made reference to Heidegger's ontological intuition to indicate the necessity of what he called a differentiation of difference (Deleuze, 1994, p. 117). Immanence is an abstract principle and, as such, it always remains abstract/virtual, and its concrete/actual manifestations must be of a different kind. In other words, the relationship between the virtual and the actual must be one of differentiation and endless (viral) proliferation. As becomes clear in his later writings (e.g. Deleuze and Guattari, 1986), he named this foundational principle as 'the abstract machine'. For the purposes of psychology, perhaps the most 'concrete' articulation of such abstraction is the idea of desiring machines, of assemblages or of war machines as expressed later in the second volume of *Capitalism and Schizophrenia*.

For Deleuze, the concrete manifestations of life are understood as belonging to a different level than the abstract machine. Life in Deleuze's view needs to be considered as intimately connected with the virtual, yet working as material manifestations that are ever-differing expressions of the infinite possibilities of such an abstract principle. The collapsing or merging of immanence and consciousness that Deleuze sees taking place in phenomenology betrays this basic distinction and establishes an *Urdoxa* for experience (Lawlor, 1998, 2012), a type of foundational experience that frames all grounded phenomena and affords intersubjectivity (Rajchman, 2000, p. 10). *Urdoxa* is a portmanteau word, a combination of the German prefix *Ur*- and the Classic Greek word *doxa* – dogma – coined by Husserl to refer to a 'primary' or 'first' doctrine, a foundational experience common to all human beings. For Deleuze, Husserl's claim constituted a new type of dogmatism. Deleuze saw promise in the phenomenological concept of *sense* – in particular, of *making sense* – as a concept that marks a rather intuitive, at times a pre-conscious, type of knowledge as distinct from straightforward information or cognition. Yet he was wary of the totalising properties of *Urdoxa*. From a productive angle, the problem implied in an 'experiential' dogmatism is resolved in *Anti-Oedipus* where Deleuze and Guattari put forward the idea that desiring machines work through a series of unconscious syntheses, with conscious thinking emerging only as a product of the last synthesis. Consciousness is thus positioned as but an effect, the left-over residue of the workings of (unconscious) desiring machines.

As with phenomenology, Deleuze worked his way rapidly through structuralism and out the other end. Deleuze had already been acknowledged for his valuable contribution to structuralism through his article *How Do We Recognize Structuralism?* (1972) where he describes a number of criteria of recognition for structuralism, all intimately related to language. As he states, '[i]n fact, language is the only thing that can properly be said to have structure' (1972, p. 170). Consistent with his style, while defining structuralism he also pointed to the limitations of this approach. As Protevi explains, '*Difference and Repetition* conceptually works out a challenge to thinking of philosophy solely in terms of concepts as sets of signifiers. Rather, concepts are markers of problematic fields, and our encounter with those fields will affectively change us' (2010). The focus on the transcendence of symbolic structures was problematic for Deleuze. As Dosse explains, Deleuze was 'vigilant with regard to any reduction of the event to insignificance, as was practiced by structuralism' (Dosse, 2012, p. 129). Rather than thought being an abstract analytic tool supporting an 'ideal synthesis of recognition and representation adequate to the identical', thought for Deleuze is a core tool in the process of engaging with the articulation of a unique and distinctive life, a life that is constituted through finding unique solutions to the problematic complexities immanent to living. Although these solutions have to be found in the frame of concrete and material or actual structures, the solutions themselves have to be unique, singular. It is appropriate to stress repeatedly that what is central to Deleuze is difference, creativity and singularity.

It is in this context of asserting difference that Deleuze saw problems with language as instructive – as a neutral channel to exchange information – and representational. Instead of this transcendental and dualist understanding of language, Deleuze engages with language not as a stable system but as fluid and transformational, a medium for tools that are immanent to life and to the task of empirically dealing with and solving the problems that emerge in the process of living a life. Instead of language, then, Deleuze prefers the notion of signs and of expression such that, rather than representation, language involves a certain apprehension of the elements at hand and their consequent transformation so as to produce novel solutions to the (conceptual) problems. Instead of representation, Deleuze supports the idea of a transformative engagement with signs, a type of Baconian portraiture (2004) that expresses renewal, a commentary that acts as a veritable double. Deleuze explains this in relation to the history of philosophy with some humour: 'One imagines a *philosophically* bearded Hegel, a *philosophically* clean-shaven Marx, in the same way as a moustached Mona Lisa' (1994, p. xxi). We discuss Deleuze's critique of current understanding of language in more detail in Chapter 4.

The focus at this point is that it is precisely in Deleuze's attempts to develop a critical position toward these two traditions, phenomenology and structuralism, that we can best appreciate the point of departure for his work with Félix Guattari. Guattari, like many others, was impressed with Deleuze's *aggregation* thesis and made a presentation to his colleagues at the Freudian School (of psychoanalysis) in Paris in 1969, ahead of meeting Deleuze in person, on the differences between 'Machines' and 'Structure' (Guattari, 1984, pp. 111–19). Shaping what was to come in *Anti-Oedipus*, Guattari used the notion of machine 'to think what has been repressed by structuralism, namely, the joint processes of subjectification and the historical event' (Dosse, 2012, p. 127). Deleuze, in turn, was fascinated by Guattari's distinction between structure and machine, which seemed to him to be 'far more advanced in its critique of structuralism' (Dosse, 2012, p. 132) than his own investigations.

Machines in motion

In some ways, then, the concept of 'machine' marks the point of encounter between Deleuze and Guattari and becomes a central concept in their new, collaborative project, *Anti-Oedipus*. As May states, 'machine' is a versatile concept that 'can be situated at the level of the individual, the society, the state, the pre-individual, among groups and between people, and across these various realms' (2005, p. 122). Colebrook extends this analysis of the usefulness of the term for Deleuze and Guattari by noting that, unlike organisms or mechanisms, machines have 'no subjectivity or organising centre' and are 'nothing more than the connections and productions [they make]' (Colebrook, 2002a, pp. 55–6).

This reference to machines takes us back to the opening of this chapter and to Deleuze and Guattari's affirmation in *Anti-Oedipus* that what is central to life is its functioning as a machine. In terms of our human condition, the distinction is of relevance at many levels, starting with a questioning of the focus on consciousness and purposive action. Deleuze and Guattari talk instead of desiring machines and schizophrenic processes of synthesis, that is, processes that do not represent, but rather *produce*, experienced reality. Schizophrenic processes in this sense are not the same as in the clinical presentation of schizophrenia. Deleuze and Guattari are not romanticising the suffering of madness. In fact, they see the schizophrenic person as, in a sense, a 'failed' example of the schizophrenic process: an attempt at differentiation that, in whatever form and for whatever reason, has collapsed. What the schizophrenic person shares with the schizophrenic processes is the understanding of 'nature as a process of production' (Deleuze and Guattari, 1983, p. 3). Furthermore, the notion of schizophrenic calls forth the rupture and schisms inherent to these machines. The components of the desiring machines of Deleuze and Guattari are random and are boundless in the sense that they escape the confines that common sense and good sense gives to things in the world. These components are like the experiences of those who lived through May'68, traversing and being traversed by all sorts of expected and unexpected forces and establishing all sorts of connections with the outside. Desiring machines, then, put 'elements in play that are totally disparate and foreign to one another ... and yet they work' (Deleuze, 1975, p. 18). The idea of work will also need to be refined for, as indicated before, the workings of these machines lack purpose. These machines are instead just expressions of what is possible and what is important: endless experimentations of, and in, life.

From *Anti-Oedipus* to *A Thousand Plateaus*: a positive proposal to populate this earth

Anti-Oedipus has the subtitle of *Capitalism and Schizophrenia*. It aimed to be not only a critique of psychoanalysis, especially Lacanian psychoanalysis, but also a political critique – a critique of our place in society, in the *socius*. The critique is profound, intriguing and, as we hope to indicate in this book, of great significance for the discipline of psychology. Our book is an attempt to explain and enlarge on these implications, and those that emerge from the 'follow-up' to *Anti-Oedipus*, namely *A Thousand Plateaus* (1987). It might be said 'alleged' follow-up because, although similar in scope and ambition, the nature of the project undergoes significant transformation between these books. Instead of being predominantly a critique, a cry of protest, *A Thousand Plateaus* is a positive proposal explicating the metaphysics that Deleuze – both alone and with Guattari – had been exploring. The emphasis and the names given to the identified machines and structures, changes. As we will explain in the next chapter, in *A Thousand Plateaus* there is a radical departure from psychoanalysis and, with it, a transformation of desiring machines and processes of syntheses into the concept of assemblages – in particular, 'war machines' – actively engaged in the creation of 'territories', of existential planes. Assemblages roam not in the ordered world presupposed by both Descartes and Kant but in, borrowing a term from Joyce, a 'chaosmos' of multitudes.

Yet it is not just the geo-socio-political assemblages that populate this earth that are the target of Deleuze and Guattari. Holland (2011, 2013, pp. 30–1) identifies five different problems that they attempt to address in *A Thousand Plateaus*. First, there is an epistemological question that can be best stated as '[H]ow can thought operate in such a way that it thinks with the cosmos instead of about it?' The question of knowledge is posed by Deleuze and Guattari as a problem that needs to honour immanence, an immanence that reminds us that, given the multiplicity present in life, knowledge is useless if it attempts to describe what is outside of its sphere of functioning. Knowledge needs to be part of – must be embroiled in – the assemblage from which it speaks and within which it serves certain functions. Knowledge, then, like life, is not about static representations of a stable and ordered world. It is a strategic tool for active engagement with an untimely future, with what they would describe as the becoming of 'the people to come' (Deleuze and Guattari, 1991, p. 218).

A second problem addressed in *A Thousand Plateaus* falls into the domain of what Holland calls onto-aesthetics. Initially Holland discusses this as an ontological problem that could be posed in the following way: '[H]ow can the cosmos and Life within it exist in such a way that they are the result of constant change but also always susceptible to further change?' (Holland, 2011, p. 4). Holland adds the aesthetic dimension in his later book (2013, p. 53) to include the question of how to understand being as becoming in the context of open dynamic systems. The move that Deleuze and Guattari call for is one away from ontologies into onto-aesthetics, ultimately reminding us that life is an art in waiting.

A third problem addressed by *A Thousand Plateaus* is, as Holland describes it, anthro-ethological. Holland explains that this problem can be understood as referring only to 'the specifically human (or anthropological) portion of the universe of animal behaviour (ethology)' (p. 76). Yet it is only anthropological in 'the high-structuralist (and anti-humanist) sense involving the symbolic order' (Holland, 2011, p. 4). This problem refers to the ways humans socially self-organise themselves and the effects that such organisations recursively have on human life. There are three particular symbolic apparatuses that are explored: language and the notion of regimes of signs in human life; what Deleuze and Guattari call 'faciality'; and money, with its current manifestation as capital. We have already spoken of Deleuze and Guattari's critique of structuralism and these three topics are manifestations of struggles with rigid structures. It is at this level of struggle that the focus becomes directly relevant to our discipline. A Deleuzian understanding of knowledge is not only expressive of multiplicity – so that knowledge is decentralised – but also has to be constructive and actively engaging with the problems at hand.

Relatedly, the last two problems explored in *A Thousand Plateaus*, according to Holland, are politics and ethics. With politics, as Holland explains, the main question concerns the types of social self-organisations that we have access to, that is, in exploring the forms of government available to humankind, forms that range from 'repressive despotic tyrannies' to the 'expansive economic imperialism' of capital – both State-like forms of organisation – and the nomadic life they describe as 'the war machine'. Such an exploration is ultimately geared to face the ultimate problem: the question of ethics. That is to say, the end point is an engagement with the question of how we are to live our lives so as to maximise our chances of being both productive and joyful. Matters of ethics and politics permeate *A Thousand Plateaus* and Deleuze's work in general.

The present book will attempt to explain the impact of Deleuze in psychology and, in doing so, will not only provide a radical critique of traditional approaches in the discipline, but will also invite psychology to engage in a different way with its objects of study, that is to say, with life and with our human condition. It rests with you, as the reader of this book, to judge if we are successful in this project.

References

Adkins, B. 2015. *Deleuze and Guattari's A Thousand Plateaus: a critical introduction and guide*. Edinburgh: Edinburgh University Press.

Bateson, G. 1958. *Naven: a survey of the problems suggested by a composite picture of the culture of a New Guinea tribe drawn from three points of view*. Stanford, CA: Stanford University Press.

Bogue, R. 1989. *Deleuze and Guattari*. London: Routledge.

Boutang, P.-A. 2012. *Gilles Deleuze from A to Z*. Directed by Boutang, P.-A., MIT Press.

Colebrook, C. 2002a. *Gilles Deleuze*. London: Routledge.

Colebrook, C. 2002b. *Understanding Deleuze*. Crows Nest, NSW: Allen & Unwin.

Deleuze, G. 1967. Conclusions on the will to power and the eternal return. *In:* Lapoujade, D. (ed.), *Desert islands and other texts 1953–1974*. New York: Semiotext(e).

Deleuze, G. 1972. How do we recognize structuralism? *In:* Lapoujade, D. (ed.), *Desert islands and other texts 1953–1974*. New York: Semiotext(e).

Deleuze, G. 1975. Schizophrenia and society. *In:* Lapoujade, D. (ed.), *Two regimes of madness: texts and interviews 1975–1995*. New York: Semiotext(e).

Deleuze, G. 1980. *Deleuze/Spinoza: Cours Vincennes – 25/11/1980* [Online]. Available: www.webdeleuze.com/php/texte.php?cle=17&groupe=Spinoza&langue=2 [accessed 12 July 2013].

Deleuze, G. 1986a. *Nietzsche and philosophy*. London: Continuum.

Deleuze, G. 1986b. Preface to the American edition of *Difference and Repetition*. *In:* Lapoujade, D. (ed.), *Two regimes of madness: texts and interviews 1975–1995*. New York: Semiotext(e).

Deleuze, G. 1990. *The logic of sense*. London: Athlone Press.

Deleuze, G. 1991. *Empiricism and subjectivity*. New York: Columbia University Press.

Deleuze, G. 1992. *Expressionism in philosophy: Spinoza*. New York: Zone Books.

Deleuze, G. 1994. *Difference and repetition*. New York: Columbia University Press.

Deleuze, G. 1995. *Negotiations, 1972–1990*. New York: Columbia University Press.

Deleuze, G. 1997. *Essays critical and clinical*. Minneapolis, MN: University of Minnesota Press.

Deleuze, G. 2004. *Francis Bacon: the logic of sensation*. London: Continuum.

Deleuze, G. and Guattari, F. 1983. *Anti-Oedipus: capitalism and schizophrenia*. Minneapolis, MN: University of Minnesota Press.

Deleuze, G. and Guattari, F. 1984. May '68 did not take place. *In:* Lapoujade, D. (ed.), *Two regimes of madness: texts and interviews 1975–1995*. New York: Semiotext(e).

Deleuze, G. and Guattari, F. 1986. *Kafka: toward a minor literature*. Minneapolis, MN: University of Minnesota Press.

Deleuze, G. and Guattari, F. 1987. *A thousand plateaus: capitalism and schizophrenia*. Minneapolis, MN: University of Minnesota Press.

Deleuze, G. and Guattari, F. 1991. *What is philosophy?* London: Verso.

Deleuze, G. and Maggiori, R. 1986. Breaking things open, breaking words open. *In:* Deleuze, G. (ed.), *Negotiations, 1972–1990*. New York: Columbia University Press.

Deleuze, G. and Parnet, C. 2006. *Dialogues II*. London: Continuum.

Deleuze, G., Guattari, F. and Backes-Clement, C. 1972. Gilles Deleuze and Félix Guattari on *Anti-Oedipus*. *In:* Deleuze, G. (ed.), *Negotiations, 1972–1990*. New York: Columbia University Press.

Deleuze, G., Bellour, R. and Ewald, F. 1988. On philosophy. *In:* Deleuze, G. (ed.), *Negotiations, 1972–1990*. New York: Columbia University Press.

Derrida, J. 1998. I'm going to have to wander all alone. *Philosophy Today*, 42, 3–5.

Dosse, F. 2010. *Gilles Deleuze & Félix Guattari: intersecting lives*. New York: Columbia University Press.

Dosse, F. 2012. Deleuze and structuralism. *In:* Smith, D. and Somers-Hall, H. (eds), *The Cambridge companion to Deleuze*. New York: Cambridge University Press.

Guattari, F. 1984. *Molecular revolution: psychiatry and politics*. Harmondsworth: Penguin Books.

Guattari, F. 2006. *The Anti-Oedipus papers*. New York: Semiotext(e).

Holland, E.W. 2011. Deleuze & Guattari at 3,000 Plateaus an Hour. *Fourth International Deleuze Studies Conference*, Copenhagen, Denmark.

Holland, E.W. 2013. *Deleuze and Guattari: a thousand plateaus*. London: Bloomsbury Publishing.

Lawlor, L. 1998. The end of phenomenology: expressionism in Deleuze and Merleau-Ponty. *Continental Philosophy Review*, 31, 15–34.

Lawlor, L. 2012. Phenomenology and metaphysics, and chaos: on the fragility of the event in Deleuze. *In:* Smith, D. and Somers-Hall, H. (eds), *The Cambridge Companion to Deleuze*. New York: Cambridge University Press.

Lecercle, J.-J. 2002. *Deleuze and language*. Basingstoke. Palgrave.

May, T. 2005. *Gilles Deleuze: an introduction*. Cambridge: Cambridge University Press.

Nietzsche, F. 1886. The birth of tragedy: out of the spirit of music. *In:* Kaufmann, W. (ed.), *Basic writings of Nietzsche*. New York: Random House.

Nietzsche, F. 1954. *Thus spoke Zarathustra: a book for none and all*. New York: Penguin Books.

Patton, P. 1994. Translator's preface. *In:* Deleuze, G. (ed.), *Difference and repetition.* New York: Columbia University Press.

Patton, P. 2010. *Deleuzian concepts.* Stanford, CA: Stanford University Press.

Protevi, J. 2010. Preparing to learn from difference and repetition. *Journal of Philosophy: A Cross-Disciplinary Inquiry (Nepal),* 5, 35–45.

Rajchman, J. 2000. *The Deleuze connections.* Cambridge, MA: MIT Press.

Roudinesco, E. 2008. *Philosophy in turbulent times: Canguilhem, Sartre, Foucault, Althusser, Deleuze, Derrida.* New York: Columbia University Press.

Spinoza, B.D. n.d. *Ethics.* London: Heron Books.

Stivale, C.J. 2000. *P as in professor* [Online]. Available: www.langlab.wayne.edu/Romance/FreD_G/ABC3.html [accessed 26 February 2002].

Widder, N. 2012. *Political theory after Deleuze.* London: Continuum.

2

A QUESTION OF FAILED IDENTITY

Psychology's unit of analysis

What on earth is psychology?

We often wonder how an alien visiting this earth would comprehend the discipline and profession that we call 'psychology'. If this alien were to ask people in the street the question 'What is psychology?' the likely response it would get is that psychology is the study of we humans. As a species, what and how do we think? What do we feel, and why? What does it mean to us to live well? In Australia, the Psychological Society has adopted the logo 'Good Thinking'. The idea behind this logo, as well as behind the comments of our surprised pedestrians, is that psychology is a specific, expert kind of knowledge that, provided one upholds its assumptions and parameters, can help us to fulfil our opportunities in life because it helps us to make the right decisions.

Our naive alien might become curious as to how psychology can make such claims. We imagine that most of these pedestrian informants (if not as many as with the first question) would make some reference to the fact that psychology is a scientific study. By this they would probably mean that the information provided by psychology has some higher standing than other kinds of knowledge. To say that psychology is a science is to say that the knowledge it generates is objective, credible in its rigour and legitimate in relation to the reliability of its sources. In short, the alien may well be told that the knowledge that psychology has of the human condition stands closer to the truth than other claims. Should our alien continue its investigation, it would likely find itself going to a library or searching online through a multitude of disciplinary journals. The majority of these journals would share a similar research ideology: the application of specific methods of investigation to a defined sample from a defined population.

Should this intelligent alien have the resources and the technology to read all this information, it might feel reasonably confident that it could leave this planet with an understanding of what human beings are. After all, it will have listened to what people said, and read their objective knowledge. Such an understanding is what Deleuze would call 'an image of thought'. 'An image of thought' is a description that, notwithstanding its claim to 'represent' reality, ultimately not only fails in such a pursuit but also betrays both thought and life. Unless it stayed long enough on our planet and in its investigation to start noticing the inconsistencies and limitations of the kind of knowledge described as scientific psychology, our earnest alien would have left this earth with a distorted and, more importantly, a deficient image of our condition. Psychology as we understand it is just inadequate to its task. So what went wrong?

Attempting to engage with such a question requires something like arrogance. This is not entirely foreign to Deleuze's writing. There is a boldness in his writing that is reenergising, for it invites us always to consider an alternative organisation of what is known. What is known for Deleuze, in terms of forms of life, can always prove to be subject to change. This is the foundational point of a philosophy of difference. Representation, and the knowledge that emerges out of its practice, is limited and mostly generates *retrospective* definitions. These are definitions of the type that fall in the category of 'that is what it was', which is different from 'this is what it is'.

As we want to demonstrate through this book, there are a multitude of other ways in which psychology as a science could be conceptualised and could be practised. Above all we seek and celebrate *difference*. As Gregory Bateson puts it, the kind of difference we value is *a difference that makes a difference* (1973, p. 351). Thought of in this spirit, difference is not an ethereal concept but a material or concrete condition that is actualised through the creation of particular alternative forms of organisation that 'work'. The plurality is important. It is not one hegemonic 'critical' form of psychology that we seek or advocate. What we are proposing is not a takeover of traditional psychology or an arm-wrestle over legitimacy. We do not claim to speak on behalf of the oppressed. As for Deleuze, it is not a matter of who is right or who is wrong but of actively engaging in *thinking otherwise*.

For the purposes of this book, we have chosen to start this process by turning 'back to basics'. One way of doing this is (cautiously) to look at the ancients. The pre-Socratic Greek philosopher Heraclitus unfortunately left behind only fragments of his wisdom, but one interesting remark was this: 'If you do not expect the unexpected, you will not find it' (Kratochwil, 2014, p. ix). Psychology, we feel, is a discipline that refuses to expect the unexpected. It blocks out the unexpected, turning the study of our psyche and our condition into a subjugated and subdued discipline that is entirely distanced from its aspirations and from its possibilities.

Perhaps our hopes are too high. Perhaps we must just come to terms with the fact that the discipline of psychology is a timid and subservient discipline. To the extent this is so, this may well be a consequence of historical relationships with other disciplines, and the requirements of the various professions, as well as other cultural dimensions of psychology's past (Richards, 2002) and of its present. Dynamics between the institutionalised professions of psychology, psychiatry and medicine, for example, have given rise to a somewhat stable hierarchy or 'pecking order' among them. Generally speaking, medicine may peck at psychiatry and psychiatry may peck at psychology. Status, salaries and working conditions all reflect this reality. But whatever the reasons, the current situation is that psychology as a discipline prefers familiarity. It prefers to predict what it already knows and to have confirmed what it already has staked its resources upon. This approach is manifest in the training of psychologists in the universities where, at both undergraduate and postgraduate levels, extreme care is taken that the methods and forms of explanation currently valued by the academic leadership in the profession are transmitted to the next generation. This is not training that aims to engage more fully with, or become more insightfully aware of, our human condition, but one whose emphasis is on recruiting its students into a certain docility. The analogy with priesthood springs to mind. What many students of psychology find during the course of their training is their recruitment in a programme of studies that, in the name of a certain kind of reading of science, restrains and, at times, impoverishes both their senses and their imagination.

We are not denying that a certain education and training is required by the profession, and that such education requires a recruitment into a specific regime of signs, a certain way of observing, talking and acting. This happens in all disciplines and professions. Postgraduate training in the laboratory sciences is overwhelmingly a matter of training in specific investigative techniques, an apprenticeship in its more narrow sense. Analogous pedagogy holds for much of the humanities. But it seems especially worrying in our discipline of psychology because of its increasingly direct impact on everyday life, given its claims of subject expertise. It suffices to check out the magazines in the local newsagency to realise the privileged standing of psychology. Other social sciences or the humanities command nothing like the shelf-space of popular psychology. The alien that opens this chapter would not have been directed to scholars or experts in other disciplines for larger or more inclusive perspectives on psychology. And it is important to stress that popular psychology is an outgrowth of mainstream, respectable psychology – of psychology as a science – not a competitor. Indeed the official publications of the leading psychological organisations, such as *The Psychologist* – published monthly in the UK by the British Psychological Society (BPS) – strive to be popular.

In apparent contrast to its leading role in society, the study of psychology seems to demand a closing down of options, a deliberate imposition of blinkers. Required in the training, there is an acculturation into a prescribed way of looking at the world. It might be said with some hyperbole that psychology fears the unknown. It has frequently been suggested that psychology relies too much on its favoured methods and in so doing resembles a drunk searching for his keys near a lamp-post because that is where the light is.

It seems to us that psychology feels compelled to try to circumscribe the unexpected, to constrain the flood. Here something can be learned from psychology's approach to the topic of memory. Remember Marcel Proust? Even if his name were otherwise unfamiliar, students of psychology will probably have heard about the reclusive Parisian novelist, author of the multi-volume *In Search of Lost Time*. Proust, it seems, found as an adult that multisensory memories of his privileged childhood came flooding back when he tasted a 'madeleine' confection dipped in tea. English history has been fondly satirised as a jumble of half-remembered facts and a few dates (Sellar and Yeatman's *1066 And All That*) and the teaching of psychology typically includes a standard collection of anecdotal reference-points and illustrations. Proust's memory-drenched biscuit is one of these. Just before launching into an account of memory typically focused on the experimental investigation of information processing, a nod is frequently given to the French modernist in order to acknowledge the richness and complexity of human memory, perhaps even to hint at its unexpected and sometimes overwhelming power. The case of Proust dunking his madeleine, as appropriated by teachers of psychology, seems to capture the essence of psychology's double-bind style of presentation. 'This is something really important. And we are now going to investigate something else.' Or to put it in another way, it is typical of the teaching of psychology, and equally typical of published research in psychology, to make a preliminary gesture towards complexity and surprisingness before recoiling from the difficulties posed by this acknowledgement and pursuing instead a familiar methodology. Psychology does not so much ignore the complexity and open-endedness of human life as give up on it, throwing up its hands in despair. It turns a blind eye to the complexity so to speak – that is to say, it knowingly declines to engage with it.

At one level, this is what we are referring to as the failed identity of psychology, that is, we are referring to the struggles that the discipline has had with the task at hand. To be clear, we are not so much targeting particular contemporary practices as talking about persisting problems for psychology. We are not claiming that Western psychology of earlier times, either ancient or relatively modern, was in some sense more authentic and 'true to its name' than the psychology of our own time and place. We are not claiming that, since these times, psychology has lost its way, 'forgotten its roots' or 'lost its mojo'. We do not think that William James, who was writing about psychology in the late nineteenth century, had the answers – although he did have some of the questions (but perhaps no more than did his brother, the novelist Henry James). We are not in search of lost psychology. We are in search of a new psychology or better, new psychologies. Sketches and signposts are no doubt to be found in many places and in many times, past and present.

Psychology's attempts to engage with the task that it has set itself have failed to engage constructively with this task. As Deleuze might say, following Whitehead, psychology continues to reduce the power and the potential of the event into predictable forms of knowledge (Motzkau, 2011). In doing so, psychology continues to deny the complexity of its subject matter. It has failed because it persists in a desire to domesticate its subject instead of engaging with it constructively. In some ways Freud's treatment of the unconscious is, for Deleuze, an example of this. As discussed at the beginning of the previous chapter, Deleuze and Guattari vociferously rejected the Freudian account of mental life. In particular they attacked the form taken by psychoanalytic psychology in France in the decades after Freud's death. But the critique expressed by Deleuze and Guattari emerged out of their recognition of the important insights that Freud and others in the psychoanalytic movement had contributed. For the work of Freud and his followers was itself in important ways subversive of mainstream practices of the medical treatment of the clinical population. Some way must be found of articulating the role of the unconscious in human life, of that vast realm of psychological functioning that escapes conscious and intentional interrogation. Deleuze's critique of Freud was in many ways based on disappointment. Freud and his acolytes had betrayed their own earlier, critical insights and had focused instead on 'naming' and classifying what they came to think of as discoveries. Reification replaced critical research, with significant impact on clinical and other professional practice.

There is in psychology a pattern of domestication and of reification. This pattern – for it is not a specific 'thing' – is inextricably connected with the desire in psychology to 'shed light' onto, to create an image of, its subjects. Perhaps the major concern we have with psychology, then, is that it has turned into a type of King Midas, at whose touch everything turned to gold. Psychology is like a Midas who claims to be a chemical analyst who has 'discovered gold everywhere'. Midas might claim to have found gold but, in doing so, other dangerous mechanisms have been set in place that ensure that 'finding something else' is now impossible for him. That is his tragedy, and therefore it is ours.

Let's return to Proust and his unleashing of a lifetime's memories. This will both provide a more concrete example of these concerns, and assist us in starting to look at the contribution of Deleuze's project in helping psychology to find a way – or, as Deleuze would say, a line of flight – out of this 'domestic' condition and engage more fully with the dilemmas pertaining to the human condition. Proust's sense of memory was not of a phenomenon that can be reduced to neuronal activity, or reproduced in a mechanical manner as a result of good cognitive and behavioural conditioning. What is valuable is surely not fully captured by Jonah Lehrer's assertion that '[n]euroscience now knows that Proust was right' (2007, p. 80). Proust's life's work was the writing of an extended and highly singular narrative, what Deleuze calls 'the narrative of an apprenticeship' (2000, p. 3). It is composed in the form of an autobiography – of questionable factual accuracy if thought of as such. The narrative is all about relationships, small-talk, society. Despite its unique singularity, whatever is valuable to the reader in the books that make up *In Search of Lost Time*, it is not in its portrayal of an individual person. Marcel Proust's narrator is not a single unit of investigation. Nor is the value of the book to be found in the account of single incidents or of physical acts that Proust is said to have performed. As Deleuze observed, 'What is essential to the Search is not in the madeleine or the cobblestones' (2000, p. 3). In any case, it is a long way from the vision of psychology as we know it.

In this sense, a token reference to Proust in introducing the study of memory seems to be part of a larger pattern as to what psychology does with its research. Proust's literary elegance – including all the existential possibilities therein embedded whose aim is to move the reader to a deeper and more complex consideration of their lives – is reduced to a type of pre-credits sequence in which the audience is invited to notice that such-and-such is an interesting or challenging aspect of human life, after which the familiar plot gets into motion. Psychology's recognition of the surprising and the challenging is like a movie trailer (to adjust the analogy): the exciting bits that entice us to download the movie but which somehow we no longer notice in the disappointment of the full-length event.

Training effects

It is also important to pay attention to the effects that such disciplinary training has on those who practise psychology and who seek to apply it to benevolent ends. The systematic emphasis on 'objective knowledge' comes with a hidden requirement of students to limit their capacity to notice, let alone engage with, anything other than what is already familiar and has fulfilled the requirements of 'good science'.

It is a frequent response of psychology students that their years of study at university was not what they had expected. Instead of a serious engagement with the challenges and dilemmas inherent to the human condition, students often make sarcastic remarks about their studies being about nothing but 'rats and stats'. As Ben Bradley describes, recent graduates criticise the lack of preparedness consequential on the focus and style of a university education in psychology (2005, p. 186): '[I]n countries like Australia ... the bulk of psychology graduates go out into the workforce with no hands-on preparation for the kinds of job they get' (2005, p. 20). In the best of scenarios, candid and idealistic students, who have persevered in their training in mainstream psychology, realise that they will need to then negotiate a way of 'translating' such disciplinary knowledge into the complexities of 'real' life. But they are hampered by the style of professional engagement into which they have been systematically socialised. For, as Bradley again clarifies, 'In order to promote its case both within and beyond the university, psychology has availed itself of ... the justification of "technical-rationality"' (2005, p. 22). This phenomenon is well known to those supervising these budding practitioners in the nuances of the discipline as practised. For these hatchlings, the initiation into the actual practice of the profession is often experienced as confusing and overwhelming. It is often in these circumstances that the limitations of the disciplinary definitions become evident and the 'bubble' of 'real science' (as it is often presented) starts to burst. Psychology-trained clinicians report being overwhelmed by the complexity that they encounter, a complexity for which their 'scientific' form of training does not seem to have equipped them. In turn, professional bodies may well acknowledge the dilemmas experienced by students, yet plead necessity. Professional bodies and the training institutions whose programmes they regulate may well point to a curriculum under pressure of time and resources, and hence to a need to prioritise what is taught. This we understand. Our claim is rather that part of what is left behind is precisely the complex history behind the dominant ideas in the field. What is often left obscured is the multitude of calculations and decisions that resulted in the identification of some types of knowledge(s) as more desirable than others. Ironically, and in line with Foucault's insights on the intricate connections between knowledge, power and subjectivity, psychology students might be enabled to learn more if they were introduced to such nuances.

A positive alternative

So, for the sake of aliens and students alike, there is a pressing need for educators in psychology to widen their gaze, so as to notice and to honour more adequately what is going on in the natural and social worlds that we cohabit. This kind of 'liberation' of perception and of thought calls for the insights of philosophers more recent than Heraclitus and we feel that Deleuze has a great deal to offer in this regard. The writings of Deleuze (with or without Guattari) provide robust and provocative formulations, formulations that are bold and sometimes raucous. This attitude is in itself refreshing and energising. More importantly, as we indicated in the first chapter, if Deleuze stands out in his generation, it is because his work did not stop with the development of a critical attitude. It did not stop with pointing the finger at the limitations of prevalent knowledge. His critique served as a springboard for a different metaphysics from that which has informed Western thought since Plato (what one might call 'A Thousand Platos'). This new proposal calls forth an exploration and articulation of an alternative way of engaging with our professional knowledge and our professional practices. It generates a different epistemology that, as will become clear, puts ethics at the centre.

We would like to approach this new reading in psychology in a staged manner. As a first stage we will focus on two central structures of the discipline of psychology when it is defined as a science. The search for scientific knowledge can perhaps be best identified by the use of both a clear unit of analysis and a method to gain knowledge of such a unit. The remainder of this chapter will focus on the Deleuzian effects on the unit of analysis of the discipline – the individual through all its manifestations. This will provide the groundwork for a more detailed discussion of matters of method, in the chapter that follows. We will then proceed to the second part of the book, where we aim to engage in a positive and assertive proposal of what *a* (not *the*) Deleuzian psychology might look like.

Psychology's unit of analysis: the mysterious affair of the vanishing subject

What we mean by a unit of analysis is the conceptual basis of the vocabulary of mainstream psychology. In many ways, one might expect this to be a straightforward issue. 'As we all know', this is literally a matter of *units* – of atoms – which, in psychology, seems 'naturally' to refer to individuals: to individual 'subjects' as in the conventional research report. Common knowledge dictates that the psyche is an individual matter. But there are a number of significant tensions within the field of psychology on this point. These tensions are to be found within the mainstream of the discipline as it has developed, as well as between the mainstream and the critical commentaries. A historical review of the discipline would show that defining the unit and on this basis defining the scope of the discipline has been a source of significant debate. The psychologist's unit of analysis has varied in meaning through time and according to the instruments, both conceptual and technical, available to observe and measure such a unit. At different times the unit has been thought of as the individual soul, as the individual psyche, or as the individual mind. Importantly, a major school of psychology has focused on individual actions or 'behaviours' as the microscopic level of analysis, but it is the individual organism generating or being constituted by the stream of behaviours that remains, even in this approach, the basic unit. As a basic unit, however, this 'individual' is endowed with a significant number of unexamined characteristics. As Braidotti and Pisters comment, this is a subject that claims to be 'unmarked by political categories such as race and gender' (Braidotti and Pisters, 2012, p. 3) and as an image reflects 'the liberal model of an entity that coincides with self-reflexive individualism and is consequently capable of self-correcting agency, transcendental consciousness and moral universalism' (Braidotti and Pisters, 2012, p. 1).

A further alternative to the sub-structure of an individual organism being thought of as actions or behaviours can be found in the thought of this sub-structure in terms of functional anatomy. Thus, if we are to listen to the more recent neurophysiological descriptions, we are encouraged to look at fragmented and specialised or modularised mental functions (memory, speed of processing and so on). If only at first glance, this would seem to represent a revival of the phrenology of the nineteenth century according to which different mental capacities reside in different parts of the brain and may even be detected (as more or less highly developed) by a trained hand running over the subject's skull (Gould, 1981). And as with the phrenologist's model, the capacities and functions are all in some manner integrated into or at least contained within one single individual. They are parts of a whole. Even so, there has been a vigorous debate around the autonomy of such units. Can the integrity of the individual mind be thought of as sufficient to account for psychological dynamics? Is the core element in psychological investigations the individual conceptualised as a free agent? In some ways what seems to be happening in mainstream psychological explanation is that a leap is made between studying components or facets and celebrating the unifying holistic entity that encloses and integrates all those subsidiary factors. With what used to be called 'hand-waving' – patronisingly putting aside the difficulties of explanation – mainstream psychology jumps from its limited albeit rigorous experimental level of analysis to an intuitive appeal to what we all understand.

Another important point of tension is the role played by the environment, and in particular by the social environment, within psychological research. Even when psychology acknowledges the social domain, it mostly does so as secondary to the individual, as something that is background to it. For well over a century psychologists have written about crowds and groups as well as about relationships within the heteronormative Western family. Social psychology is a core unit in the psychology degree even if 'social behaviour' tends to be considered last, apparently as something of an afterthought, in the dominant introductory texts in psychology (Bradley, 2005, p. 196, referring to textbooks used in Australia). But as a series of critical accounts have shown, the basis of this research and of its consequences for practice is questionable.

Despite these tensions, it could be argued that irrespective of these differences in the micro- and the macro-analysis surrounding psychological knowledge and research, much still is centred on developing an understanding of the individual person *as* an individual person. Individuals are what counts, what is being counted, in research. Either numerically counted in statistical analysis, or counting as legitimate informants in qualitative research, the unit is the human 'subject'. Variation is recognised, yet, in line with Deleuze's critique, it has been subordinated to the supremacy of the individual.

If we are to take Deleuze seriously, however, this image of the unit, these cognate senses of a unit, are to be profoundly questioned. Critical movements in psychology have challenged the mainstream on these precise points, but – arguably – they lack the conceptual apparatus to move beyond critique and to reorientate our thinking. This is where we call on Deleuze. Deleuze proposes different ways of thinking about these matters in at least two senses. We can express this in the form of a slogan: *not the individual but an assemblage; not the subject but vitality*. We have already made brief reference to Deleuze and Guattari's concept of assemblage. Before returning to the assemblage, we will first discuss the concept of the vital. This is a foundational concept in the analysis and one that both explicates and contextualises the value of the concept of assemblage.

Chaosmos and (a problem of) vitality

The importance of *vitality* is succinctly explained by Brown and Stenner who write:

> The problem we face within psychology is not then, as is commonly assumed, the problem of 'the subject', but rather that of 'life'. Or more precisely, of understanding how particular lives are extracted from the modes of existence, relations, normativities and processes which comprise life-in-itself.
>
> *Brown and Stenner, 2009, p. 176*

Brown and Stenner here capture a concern central to Deleuze. The unit of analysis is not the individual subject but 'life', or rather as Deleuze puts it, 'a life' (2001): not 'the life of a subject' as mainstream psychology might put it but a moment of pure and unique material differentiation. Deleuzian differentiation must, however, be distinguished from the traditional usage that this concept has had in developmental psychology (e.g. Benjamin, 1987) or in family therapy (e.g. Bowen, 1978). Deleuze's differentiation can perhaps be best recognised through the notion of 'the event', of something that, although it affects and involves in meaningful ways the individual, is larger. Life is not just a matter of individual human organisms. Life also escapes the bounds of narrative and discourse. Instead, life is the frame in which both of these concepts emerge as meaningful, thus its centrality as a unit of analysis.

Deleuze is a philosopher who engages not with traditional understandings of thought, but with thought as a fundamental response to the complexity of life. Furthermore, Deleuze defined himself as a 'pure metaphysician' (Villani, 1999, p. 130). This is a particularly interesting and productive position to take for, as Stenner indicates, each of the influential philosophical ideas informing critical psychology during the late twentieth century 'defines itself against an idea of metaphysics' (2009, p. 203). These approaches – existential hermeneutics, post-structuralism and ordinary language philosophy – all, in their own way, attempt to 'deconstruct "truth"' making instead '"*discourse*" its central concern'. Martin Heidegger, whose career flourished during the Nazi era in Germany, was foundational to the continental European versions of these movements – existential hermeneutics and post-structuralism in particular.

Deleuze stood in stark contrast with Heidegger who, as Stenner explains, asserted 'the end of metaphysics in the philosophical context of a groundedness in being-in-the world' (Stenner, 2009, p. 203). Against this philosophical and critical tradition – still highly influential or even dominant in the French and German academy in the 1960s – Deleuze saw his project as a positive search for a metaphysics, but a metaphysics that responds to the insights of modern science (Smith and Protevi, 2013). In this context, Deleuze employed the term *chaosmos*. The word chaosmos itself was taken from James Joyce. Compressing 'chaos' and 'cosmos', Joyce had written in *Finnegans Wake* of 'every person, place and thing in the chaosmos of Alle'. Here 'Alle' is a Joycean-Germanic term for plurality. Given that modern science had taken the word 'quark' from the same source (*Finnegans Wake*) – in which it represents the sound of the seagull – the appropriation of Joyce seems appropriate. For Deleuze, this compression or jamming-up of concepts helps in grappling with the order of the cosmos, and with it the order of this world, as emerging out of a fundamental chaos. Deleuze had already connected up the Nietzschean notion of the eternal return with his own articulation of difference. The appropriation of chaosmos into his vocabulary helped him to provide a concrete background for these ideas. As he went on to explain, the eternal return 'is not an external order imposed upon the chaos of the world; on the contrary, the eternal return is the internal identity of the world and of chaos, the Chaosmos' (Deleuze, 1994, p. 299).

This is a very different vision of the world from the more familiar, Platonic one in which a sharp distinction is drawn between chaos and cosmos (Smith, 2012, p. 23). It is the Platonic account that has informed Western thinking for centuries. In that tradition, the cosmos emerges out of chaos and perhaps returns to it at the end of days; but the step from one to the other is in either case transcendental, it is a complete renewal. In contrast,

Deleuze sees the chaos as always present in the cosmos and the cosmos always present in the chaos. To put it another way, immanence instead of transcendence. In such a chaosmos, immanence is thus central to the understanding of life. Life is no longer a transcendental creation but, as for Spinoza, an exercise in immanent expression. What is central is not what is already 'visible' – what is already 'there' – but the active process of differentiation that is, precisely, life in itself. That is to say, Deleuze's metaphysics explains life not as static and structured but as packages of emerging epiphenomena that are, by definition, transient and dynamic in nature. Life for Deleuze needs to be understood in its capacity of self-organisation, in its ability to shape itself in the context of fluidity and of complex multiplicities.

This approach has much in common with the project of neurophysiologists Humberto Maturana and Francisco Varela (1980, 1998), whose work on 'autopoiesis' emphasises the recursivity implied in life. Autopoiesis is a word coined by Maturana and Varela to characterise the functioning of the living as a result of its own activity, as self-production. As they write, '[autopoiesis] was a word without a history, a word that could directly mean what takes place in the dynamics of the autonomy proper to living systems' (1980, p. xvii). The need for a new word was in the context of the desire of Maturana and Varela to find words that point to immanent processes of production, processes that are constitutive of emerging conditions. Static images of thought, images that focus on stable intrinsic essences like 'a subject with specific and determinate psychological qualities', miss a crucial element of life. A simple analogy would be the way that laboratory samples can only be understood as approximations to what takes place in 'real' conditions. Similarly, Bergson (1922) also addressed these issues when discussing a vital impetus, a certain force of life, inherent to evolution. His contribution was unfortunately poorly understood, and to some extent ridiculed in the Anglo-Saxon world after Bergson's death by translating his concept of '*élan vital*' as some mystical sort of spiritualism. This misguided translation missed the more complex understanding that Bergson, and later Deleuze, were striving for.

From individuals to assemblages

In such a vision of life – broadly shared by Bergson, Deleuze, Maturana and Varela – the human subject is fully conceptualised as an integral part of a larger ecology, a cog in a much more complex machine. With this point we move to the second sense in which Deleuze's reading of psychology challenges its unit of analysis: the assemblage. More than a phenomenon in itself, the human subject for Deleuze is an epiphenomenon, an emerging entity. The subject must be conceptualised as intimately connected to its circumstances, connected to the extent that any search for an internal essence is doomed to failure, for it relies upon forced and arbitrary distinctions. Further, thought is not exclusive to humans but to life in general, a situation that is evident when one understands evolution as an ongoing experimentation of what is possible in life.

This decentring of the human subject resonates strongly with Foucault's account of the historical emergence of the human and social sciences as separate areas of study. Since the nineteenth century, according to Foucault, these disciplines have arbitrarily endowed humans with a new status as 'an empirical entity' (2004, p. 375) and 'to include man ... among the *objects* of science' (2004, emphasis added, p. 376). This decentring of the human subject has a special meaning for those advocating a philosophy of difference. It certainly is not to endorse the reduction of psychology to biology (Morss, 1990). Rather, it is to call for a recognition that the study of our 'human' condition must start with an acknowledgement that this is a study not of static, essence-ridden identities, but of complex living processes. This is, of course, a direct challenge to the traditional emphasis on the individual as the core unit of analysis within psychology. As a specific critique, it runs parallel to the critique carried out within the systemic tradition, in particular by the work of Gregory Bateson (1958, 1973, 2002). The resonances between Deleuze's ideas and the systemic ones are such that, currently, some commentators in the social sciences are looking to the writings of Deleuze as providing perhaps the best model to understand the functioning of 'dynamic open systems' (Bell, 2006; Jensen and Rodje, 2012). Correspondingly, some of the advocates of Deleuze's work see in Bateson, and in particular Bateson's work in cybernetics, a paradigm of the type of science that Deleuze calls forth (Pickering, 2010, 2012).

Although the ramifications are complex, the contrast between an individualistic psychology and these newer ideas is simple to state: the focus should not be on individuals but on complex machines, machines that escape the individual skin. Resonating with Bateson (1970, 2002), Deleuze and Guattari's concept of the assemblage refers to a functioning whole that escapes not only a mind–body Cartesian dualism but also a multitude of other dualities informing common sense in the Western mind. For example, it avoids the false dualities of individual/context and of human/machine. As an interesting twist of fate, it could be argued that the Deleuzian concept of assemblage is more respectful of Bateson's insights than many of the concepts developed by psychologists out of Bateson's ideas. This contrast is especially clear in the case of family therapy (Nichterlein, 2013). As with the work of Bateson, Deleuze and Guattari's project advocates a relational type of constructive knowledge, a focus that is entirely different from the traditional focus on family dynamics. The latter treats 'the family', understood in a narrow manner, as the unit of analysis. Again the problem of inappropriate units of analysis emerges. Indeed it is not only the familiar but in many ways the familial on which psychology's gaze is fixed – on the world of parents and siblings. Freud's work is only one tradition within psychology according to which the nuclear family takes pride of place. Many approaches within psychology which entirely spurn psychoanalysis in all its varieties, such as experimental versions of developmental psychology, concur with this familial primacy (Burman, 2008, p. 105). Family therapy as we currently know it, with the significant influence of attachment theory, is another important example of the fetishising of the (hetero-normative) family. While attachment theory emerged from the psychoana-lytic work of Bowlby, with its concern for the origins of delinquency in early parenting, it has become more or less severed from those roots in the course of being operationalised and rendered into the form of empirical research technique. This brings us to a clarification of the ways in which Deleuze's project is to be distinguished from psychoanalysis.

Deleuze and Guattari's work has many significant relationships with psychoanalysis. Both projects demonstrate a recognition of extra-conscious forces. Yet the project of Deleuze and Guattari cannot be reduced to just another variety of psychoanalytic interpretation of unconscious forces. It is true that Deleuze makes some positive remarks on the insights of psycho-analysis in *The Logic of Sense* (1990) which was first published in 1969. But three years later he wrote with Guattari *Anti-Oedipus*, a book that cannot but be seen as a root-and-branch critique of psychoanalysis. Deleuze and Guattari are clear that they do not attack psychoanalysis because of its insights into the unconscious, but because, as they see it, psychoanalysis 'betrayed' these insights, forcing the study of the unconscious back to the familiar, back to family dynamics, rather than exploring further its ongoing revolutionary potential. *Anti-Oedipus* forcefully asserts the claim that psychoanalysis, rather than understanding the functioning of the uncon-scious in its productive potential, imposed on it an interpretative frame by which the unconscious activity is captured in familial dynamics. Deleuze and Guattari assert a very different image of the unconscious. The uncon-scious for them is not a theatre but a machine; not a repetitive representa-tion of a play – of a performance – but a productive encounter with the outside. It is in this sense that one can start to understand their famous claim that 'the unconscious isn't playing around all the time with mummy and daddy but with races, tribes, continents, history, and geography, always some social frame' (Deleuze *et al.*, 1988, p. 144).

What is powerful in the Deleuzian critique is that, in this collaboration with Guattari, Deleuze provides an alternative understanding of the unconscious as the source of our sense of self. He does this by building on his earlier critique of Kant (Deleuze, 1984). Deleuze had focused on Kant's *Critique of Practical Reason*, itself originally published in 1788. As Smith says, 'it was Kant who first defined the faculty of desire as a *productive* faculty' (2012, p. 318), thus establishing a connection between desire and autonomy and freedom. In doing so Kant was of course inspired by Hume, or at least 'woken' by Hume 'from his dogmatic slumbers'. It is the productive elements in desire that afford 'a free being [to] be the cause of something that is not reducible to the causal determinism of mechanism' (Smith, 2012, p. 318). This shift by Kant also implied another shift that was central to Deleuze's critique of (Lacanian) psychoanalysis. Kant's conceptualisation of desire was not 'in terms of *lack* (I desire something because I do not have it), but rather in terms of *production* (I produce the object because I desire it)' (Smith, 2012, p. 318). Deleuze uses Kant, then, not only to critique psychoanalysis but also uses his notions on synthesis to provide a substantial alternative to the conceptualisation of how experience is constituted within chaosmos.

What Deleuze does is to invert Kant's argument. Consciousness – and the subject's will – is no longer the locus of synthesis, but one of the products from the unconscious activities of the desiring machine. In this sense, consciousness is an epiphenomenon. In *Anti-Oedipus* Deleuze and Guattari describe in great detail their proposal of how the desiring machine functions through three syntheses. The result of these activities is the production of both, a certain subjectivity and a sense of the real – even if the latter is nothing but a delirium. The alternative to the prevalent psychoanalytic conceptualisations of the unconscious that is articulated by Deleuze and Guattari, including these syntheses, is well explained by Holland (1999, pp. 26–36).

The crossroads of a Wolf-Man

The move to *A Thousand Plateaus* constituted a decisive shift away from psychoanalysis as a key concern. This shift is difficult to fully grasp these days because some of Deleuze's current readers feel the need to reconcile

Deleuze with this orientation and bring him back into the fold of psycho-analysis (Baker, 2013; Dodds, 2011; Semetsky and Delpech-Ramey, 2012). It needs to be stated, however, that Deleuze and Guattari never backed down from their critique of psychoanalysis (Deleuze, 1973, 1977; Deleuze and Parnet, 2006). They continued to eschew references to psychoanalytical constructs, focusing instead on an appreciation of the radically constructive nature of knowledge and of life. And they continued to make critical points. The last focused reference to psychoanalysis is found in Plateau 2 of *A Thou-sand Plateaus*. This plateau is entitled '1914: One or Several Wolves?' It begins with the 'Wolf-Man', whose real name was Sergej Pankejeff, one of Freud's best-known cases. Indeed this case was to be the last to be reported in any detail by Freud (1977, p. 29). Pankejeff was a Russian aristocrat at the time of his treatment by Freud. He was referred to by Freud and his circle as the Wolf-Man because of the nature of one of his dreams – a winter's dream of wolves in a conifer tree – a dream which was seen as representing the underlying dynamics of the fears he reported having had as a child. Typically for Freud, the employment of the nickname or pseudonym served several functions. It served to confer anonymity on the patient with respect to the larger public, although a false but conventional name would of course have done the same; but it also, of course, labelled him. It classified him as an object of psychoanalytic scrutiny, as a 'case'. It identified Pankejeff as a neu-rotic individual, the bearer of a symptom. Here, then, is psychology's unit of analysis: Rat Man, Wolf-Man.

There are several ways in which the 'wolf' resonates in psychology's history. 'Wolf-children' – children defined as feral – had been identified in the early decades of the twentieth century (Candland, 1993, p. 53). Deleuze and Guattari find wolves interesting as social animals and they find Freud's baptising of Pankejeff as the Wolf-Man fascinating and illuminating. The Wolf-Man was well aware, write Deleuze and Guattari, that Freud 'knew nothing about wolves' (1987, p. 26). Moreover, '[Pankejeff] knew that this new and true proper name would be disfigured and misspelled, retran-scribed as a patronymic' (Deleuze and Guattari, 1987, p. 27). As with many claims made by Deleuze and Guattari, the references are at multiple levels, including the dating of the plateau. The year 1914 was both when World War I began, and when the four-year analysis of Pankejeff was terminated by Freud, who declared him officially cured. When writing about the Wolf-Man, Deleuze and Guattari might have been aware of a series of con-troversial interviews with a much older Sergej Pankejeff (Obholzer, 1982). In this series of interviews, carried out from 1973, Pankejeff provided some interesting reflections and raised significant concerns. Consistent with the comments of Deleuze and Guattari, the Wolf-Man admits his lack of engagement – to the extent of disbelief – with the interpretations provided by Freud and his circle at the time of his treatment. Perhaps more worryingly, in this interview Pankejeff also discloses that he had been financially supported by the Vienna Psychoanalytical Society in a manner that made it impossible for him to publicly question the psychoanalytical claims. He was provided free analysis for many years after having been declared 'cured'; and was provided with sums of money to help him through financially difficult times. The Wolf-Man's dependence on the psychoanalytic establishment was maintained for many years. As Paul Roazen, commented: 'Even now, as the Wolf-Man's life has grown less harmonious with old age, writing about his experiences with Freud has given a purpose to his life' (1971, p. 172). As Deleuze and Guattari clearly saw, he was betrayed by that establishment.

Apart from the issues regarding Sergej's financial dependence on psychoanalysis, Deleuze and Guattari critique Freud on conceptual matters. The relationship of Sergej Pankejeff to the wolf was, they say, completely misunderstood by Freud. They say that Freud failed to see what they call the 'becoming wolf' of the Wolf-Man. What was missed, write Deleuze and Guattari, was an awareness of the differences between the wolf and the dog. That is, the differences between a domesticated animal – an animal whose alliance is ultimately with a master – and a wild, unmastered animal that has a complex relationship within a certain social organisation, within a pack. A recognition of these distinctions calls for a novel rearrangement of what is central not just to the Wolf-Man but also to our discipline. Deleuze and Guattari move the discipline to a fully psychosocial orientation with a twist because 'the call of the wolf' is a type of social activity that pertains to a very different domain to the domains comprehended by contemporary psychology, even by versions of contemporary psychology that claim to be psychosocial.

Holland (2013) focuses on this distinction with the concept of Intra-Species Social Organization (ISSO), a concept he coined as a consequence of his reading of *A Thousand Plateaus*. The ISSO focuses attention on the social nature of the definition of species and, with this, reorganises the order of emergence of these different domains. As Holland explains, in the ongoing self-expanding organisation of the chaosmos, there is a moment when life emerges through becoming self-productive – the organic domain. Subsequently, a new 'critical threshold within the organic stratum is reached [and] some species start addressing the problem of survival by self-organizing socially' (Holland, 2013, p. 25). Holland makes the point here that ISSO is not a direct reference to a specific human quality but is an evolutionary step consistent with complexity, a step that can be applied to a multitude of different mechanisms. The crucial point here is that this is not a lineal or univocal step but that, consistent with a philosophy of difference, there are a multitude of responses or solutions to ISSO, including the social organisations of insects as well as (cattle) herds, (wolf) packs and (bird) flocks. For Deleuze and Guattari, wolves – and the social organisation of which they are part – are particularly interesting because they highlight 'a second threshold within the organic stratum, where species learning or problem-solving gives rise to individual learning' (Holland, 2013, p. 25). With individual learning we are then in the domain of a type of self-awareness, a phenomenon that affords in turn the emergence or construction of human subjectivity: a domain more familiar to psychology.

It is in this sense that, with Deleuze, the individual needs to be understood in terms of his or her individuation *within* a group and a circumstance *while still being part of such*. If psychology wants to study the individual, it needs to study it in its participation in a larger assemblage from which it emerges and from whence it acquires specific forms. Further, it needs to do so recognising that such individual configuration is *within* an equally unique configuration of the pack as a unique assemblage. This brings us to the second of the ways in which the study of Deleuze calls for changes in psychology's unit of analysis. When talking about assemblages, we go back to the opening of the previous chapter and the assertion of Deleuze and Guattari in *Anti-Oedipus* that we are fundamentally parts of functioning machines. As we have indicated in Chapter 1, their concept of machine has undergone transformations through time. Initially Deleuze and Guattari referred to these machines as desiring machines, marking its intimate connection with psychoanalysis. The concept of assemblages was first used in their second collaborative book, *Kafka: Toward a Minor Literature* (Deleuze and Guattari, 1986) and became central in *A Thousand Plateaus*, perhaps as another manifestation of their distancing from psychoanalytic terminology.

Some further clarification of this concept might prove helpful. MacGregor Wise comments that, as a concept, assemblage deals 'with the play of contingency and structure, organization and change' (2005, p. 77). Such a description helps perhaps to explain the occasional inclusion of the work of Deleuze under the rubric of post-structuralism, a gesture that at least has the merit of reminding us that post-structuralism is much more than a simple, negative critique of structuralism. For Deleuze, structures are structures in movement. It is here that we find the connections that Derrida saw between his project and that of Deleuze (1998; see also Morss and Nichterlein, 1999). Both

Derrida and Deleuze remind us, using the language of Spinoza, of the need to engage 'joyfully' (Spinoza, n.d.; see also Deleuze, 1988) – that is to say, to engage in a life-affirming way – in the play of meanings present in the complexity in which life occurs. For Deleuze in particular, this means that we must remember that any definition one uses has a limit defined by its utility to the machine in which it is embedded. This clarification demonstrates two important qualities of assemblages. First, assemblages are not unified nor stable entities, but work instead more like 'swarms of difference that actualize themselves into specific forms of identity' (May, 2005, p. 114). Rather than 'things' with some persistent essence, the assemblage takes the form of an emerging collective containing a number of different elements. Following from this, a second characteristic of assemblages is that they are not made *only* out of material elements, what Deleuze and Guattari refer to as 'content' including bodies, actions and passions – 'an intermingling of bodies reacting to one another' (Deleuze and Guattari, 1987, p. 88). They are also made out of 'expression', a concept that includes the 'incorporeal transformations attributed to bodies' (Deleuze and Guattari, 1987, p. 88) such as acts and statements, or what is more commonly known as a regime of signs (Zourabichvili, 2012, p. 145).

Assemblage, then, as a concept, refers to complex totalities in action. The movement of the assemblage brings forth another critical concept for Deleuze and Guattari: territory. In line with the ethological approach to humans (Buchanan, 2008), Deleuze was interested in how assemblages occupy space. This interest leads to significant connections with politics and the Deleuzian distinctions between State-like machines and nomad or war machines. Deleuze and Guattari saw significant importance in identifying the types of machine at work and their patterns of movement, a process they considered to be more akin to cartography than to traditional therapeutic analysis. Deleuze and Guattari introduced the term schizoanalysis in this context. We can return here to the Wolf-Man and the date of Plateau 2 to highlight the tensions they saw between their considerations and those of psychoanalysis. More than a forced return to familial themes, Deleuze and Guattari thought it was of far more relevance to understand Sergej Pankejeff's anxieties in terms of the changes in Sergej's life and culture. Such an analysis required a far more nuanced assessment of the types of assemblage in which Pankejeff could participate. The call of the wolf experienced by Pankejeff was a call to cross the line between a State-like lifestyle – a comfortable one, one must add – and the one within a pack, within a 'war machine' as Deleuze and Guattari would say, that would see his becoming in a very different world.

What is important to remember is that, in order to understand the individual as a unit of analysis, one has to keep in mind a twofold movement. At one level there is the movement of the assemblage – what Deleuze and Guattari refer as 'the position of the mass' (1987, p. 29) – and, at another, the unique style of the individual. As Deleuze and Guattari put it, style relates to 'the position of the subject itself in relation to the pack ... how the subject joins or does not join the pack, how far away it stays, how it does or does not hold to the multiplicity' (1987, p. 29). This brings us to a point central for Deleuze. The 'signs' of life can be best grasped in the individual through elements of style. That is to say, through an appreciation of the unique way in which this individual deals with the complexities of its existence so as to turn it into *a life*, a unique moment of differentiation within a collective. Such a life is, in itself, 'beyond good and evil' as Nietzsche would have put it: it is a life that stubbornly lives. This explains why Melville's *Bartleby, the Scrivener* (1853) is, for Deleuze (1997), the paradigm of such a life in modern times. What is important for Deleuze in this context is that the life of a person therefore cannot be measured, nor can it be defined, in relation to a norm. Life is instead that which escapes the norms. This is not to say that Deleuze denies the value of normative and definitional activities but that the human condition – in particular *a life* – cannot be reduced to the set of its predictable forces.

In this complex analysis, there is no requirement for a stable and integrated inner core for the subject. On the contrary, too much integration can easily turn into rigidity and death – rigor mortis comes to mind. Yet, too little integration can lead to disintegration. Individual style therefore resonates with the Deleuzian insight into life as chaosmos and with the Deleuzian understanding of assemblages in their endless process of creating an existential territory, a process Deleuze and Guattari refer as territorialisation–deterritorialisation–reterritorialisation. Deleuze and Guattari comment on this point with their usual directness: 'You have to keep small rations of subjectivity in sufficient quantity to enable you to respond to the dominant reality' (1987, p. 160).

What Deleuze and Guattari propose, then, is a reversal of the traditional causal order in which the social is explained by reference to the individual. Instead, the individual is seen as emerging out of the social, where the social is not 'context' but is rather considered a type of evolutionary response to the problem of life. In other words, it is not the individual, nor the social, but the ecological that matters; and the individual is explained through its intimate relation to its particular ecological niche, a niche that is better explained by Bateson (1973) than by mainstream biological ecology. Here there is a clear contrast with social constructionist formulations, influential in contemporary psychology both clinical and scholarly. It is true that social constructionist thinking rejects the more patent forms of individualism and biologism. But the Deleuzian formulation emphasises patterns of interaction and of ethical engagement, of flight and risk, of pulling apart and pulling together. Social constructionism explains subjectivity and experience as developing out of social discourse, as Bradley (2005, p. 129) has described, like the chicken from the egg. The explanation is causal and developmental. Deleuze jolts us out of such a comfortable frame.

On wolves and herds: an emerging political field within psychology

Now we can at last appreciate the full force of the cry in *Anti-Oedipus*: '[T]he unconscious isn't playing around all the time with mummy and daddy but with races, tribes, continents, history, and geography, always some social frame' (Deleuze *et al.*, 1988, p. 144).

It is in this particular conceptualisation of our human condition that the socio-political implications of Deleuze's project for the human and social sciences begin to make sense and to bring forth a number of questions that have yet to be considered by psychology. Holland – channelling Nietzsche – asks 'are we a herd animal or a pack animal?' (2013, p. 25) Despite appearances, questions like this are ultimately political in nature and they give rise to ethical dilemmas rather than definitive answers. These dilemmas inform and continually engage with a multiplicity of domains of psychological activity that need to be identified in the context of the social organisations they call forth. This is Deleuze's critique of static 'images of thought' as manifested in States. It is here that State organisations – mass or herd-like organisations – are starkly contrasted with nomad ones. As Deleuze and Guattari write:

> The classical image of thought, and the striating of mental space it effects, aspires to universality. It in effect operates with two 'universals', the Whole as the final ground of being or all-encompassing horizon, and the Subject as the principle that converts being into being-for-us. *Imperium* and republic.... It is now easy for us to characterize the nomad thought that rejects this image and does things differently. It does not ally itself with a universal thinking subject but, on the contrary, with a singular race; and it does not ground itself in an all-encompassing totality but is on the contrary deployed in a

horizonless milieu that is a smooth space, steppe, desert, or sea. An entirely different type of adequation is established here, between the race defined as 'tribe' and smooth space defined as 'milieu'.

Deleuze and Guattari, 1987, p. 379

This distinction between the State and the nomad is a central distinction for Deleuze and Guattari and so should also be for us as writers and you as reader. Referring to Canetti (1984), Deleuze and Guattari make a distinction between two types of multiplicity: 'mass ("crowd") multiplicities and pack multiplicities' (1987, p. 33). Whereas mass multiplicities work through 'large quantity, divisibility and equality of the members, ... one-way hierarchy, organization of territoriality or territorialization, and emission of signs', packs work through 'small or restricted numbers, dispersion, non-decomposable variable distances, qualitative metamorphoses, [and the] impossibility of a fixed totalization or hierarchization' (Deleuze and Guattari, 1987, p. 33). As will become clearer as we progress in the exploration of the qualitative differences of these two different forms of social organisation, there is a vast difference in the role of the individual in a herd or crowd and the same individual in a pack, with the individual in the pack afforded significantly more independence and autonomy. The pack requires individuals (of a kind) whereas the herd requires docile bodies that serve the needs of the master.

As we will discuss later, in Chapter 4, these differences are actualised through a number of societal practices including disciplinarian practices. It is in this context that ethics become central to our discipline, for there are a variety of positions that the discipline can take in relation to the knowledge it relates with. But at this point, prior to discussing this distinction further, it is important to address the elephant in the room: method.

References

Baker, J. 2013. Psychoanalysis and ecology at the edge of chaos: complexity theory, Deleuze/Guattari and psychoanalysis for a climate in crisis. *Psychodynamic Practice: Individuals, Groups and Organisations*, 19, 440–4.

Bateson, G. 1958. *Naven: a survey of the problems suggested by a composite picture of the culture of a New Guinea tribe drawn from three points of view.* Stanford, CA: Stanford University Press.

Bateson, G. 1970. Form, substance and difference. *In:* Bateson, G. (ed.), *Steps to an ecology of mind.* Frogmore: Paladin.

Bateson, G. 1973. *Steps to an ecology of mind: collected essays on anthropology, psychiatry, evolution and epistemology.* Frogmore: Paladin.

Bateson, G. 2002. *Mind and nature: a necessary unity*. Cresskill, NJ: Hampton Press.

Bell, J. 2006. *Philosophy at the edge of chaos: Gilles Deleuze and the philosophy of difference*. Toronto: University of Toronto Press.

Benjamin, J. 1987. The decline of the Oedipus complex. *In:* Broughton, J.M. (ed.), *Critical theories of psychological development*. New York: Plenum Press.

Bergson, H. 1922. *Creative evolution*. London: Macmillan.

Bowen, M. 1978. Toward the differentiation of self in one's family of origin. *In:* Bowen, M. (ed.), *Family therapy in clinical practice*. New York: Aronson.

Bradley, B. 2005. *Psychology and experience*. Cambridge: Cambridge University Press.

Braidotti, R. and Pisters, P. (eds) 2012. *Revisiting normativity with Deleuze*. London: Bloomsbury Publishing.

Brown, S.D. and Stenner, P. 2009. *Psychology without foundations: history, philosophy and psychosocial theory*. London: Sage.

Buchanan, B. 2008. *Onto-ethologies: the animal environments of Uexkull, Heidegger, Merleau-Ponty and Deleuze*. Albany, NY: State University of New York Press.

Burman, E. 2008. *Deconstructing developmental psychology*. London: Routledge.

Candland, D.K. 1993. *Feral childen and clever animals: reflections on human nature*. New York: Oxford University Press.

Canetti, E. 1984. *Crowds and power*. New York: Farrar, Straus and Giroux.

Deleuze, G. 1973. Five propositions on psychoanalysis. *In:* Lapoujade, D. (ed.), *Desert islands and other texts 1953–1974*. New York: Semiotext(e).

Deleuze, G. 1977. Four propositions on psychoanalysis. *In:* Lapoujade, D. (ed.), *Two regimes of madness: texts and interviews 1975–1995*. New York: Semiotext(e).

Deleuze, G. 1984. *Kant's critical philosophy: the doctrine of the faculties*. London: Athlone Press.

Deleuze, G. 1988. *Spinoza: practical philosophy*. San Francisco, CA: City Lights Publishers.

Deleuze, G. 1990. *The logic of sense*. London: Athlone Press.

Deleuze, G. 1994. *Difference and repetition*. New York: Columbia University Press.

Deleuze, G. 1997. *Essays critical and clinical*. Minneapolis, MN: University of Minnesota Press.

Deleuze, G. 2000. *Proust and signs: the complete text*. Minneapolis, MN: University of Minnesota Press.

Deleuze, G. 2001. *Pure immanence: essays on a life*. New York: Urzone.

Deleuze, G. and Guattari, F. 1986. *Kafka: toward a minor literature*. Minneapolis, MN: University of Minnesota Press.

Deleuze, G. and Guattari, F. 1987. *A thousand plateaus: capitalism and schizophrenia*. Minneapolis, MN: University of Minnesota Press.

Deleuze, G. and Parnet, C. 2006. *Dialogues II*. London: Continuum.

Deleuze, G., Bellour, R. and Ewald, F. 1988. On philosophy. *In:* Deleuze, G. (ed.), *Negotiations, 1972–1990*. New York: Columbia University Press.

Derrida, J. 1998. I'm going to have to wander all alone. *Philosophy Today*, 42, 3–5.

Dodds, J. 2011. *Psychoanalysis and ecology at the edge of chaos: complexity theory, Deleuze/Guattari and psychoanalysis for a climate in crisis*. Hove: Routledge.

Foucault, M. 2004. *The order of things: an archaeology of the human sciences.* London: Routledge.

Freud, S. 1977. *On sexuality: three essays on the theory of sexuality and other works.* Harmondsworth: Pelican Books.

Gould, S.J. 1981. *The mismeasure of man.* Harmondsworth: Penguin Books.

Holland, E.W. 1999. *Deleuze and Guattari's Anti-Oedipus: introduction to schizoanalysis.* London: Routledge.

Holland, E.W. 2013. *Deleuze and Guattari: a thousand plateaus.* London: Bloomsbury Publishing.

Jensen, C.B. and Rodje, K. (eds) 2012. *Deleuzian intersections: science, technology, anthropology.* New York: Berghahn Books.

Kratochwil, F. 2014. *The status of law in world society: meditations on the role and rule of law.* Cambridge: Cambridge University Press.

Lehrer, J. 2007. *Proust was a neuroscientist.* Melbourne: The Text Publishing Company.

MacGregor Wise, J. 2005. Assemblage. *In:* Stivale, C.J. (ed.), *Gilles Deleuze: key concepts.* Chesham: Acumen.

Maturana, H. and Varela, F. 1980. *Autopoiesis and cognition: the realization of living.* Dordrecht: D. Reidel Publishing Company.

Maturana, H. and Varela, F. 1998. *The tree of knowledge: the biological roots of human understanding.* Boston, MA: Shambhala Publications.

May, T. 2005. *Gilles Deleuze: an introduction.* Cambridge: Cambridge University Press.

Melville, H. 1853. Bartleby, the scrivener: a story of wall-street. *In:* Berthoff, W. (ed.), *Great short works of Herman Melville.* New York: Perennial library.

Morss, J.R. 1990. *The biologising of childhood: developmental psychology and the Darwinian myth.* Hove: Lawrence Erlbaum Associates.

Morss, J.R. and Nichterlein, M. 1999. The therapist as client as expert: externalizing narrative therapy. *In:* Parker, I. (ed.), *Deconstructing psychotherapy.* London: Sage.

Motzkau, J. 2011. Around the day in eighty worlds: Deleuze, suggestibility and researching practice as process. *In:* Stenner, P., Cromby, J., Motzkau, J., Yen, J. and Haosheng, Y. (eds), *Theoretical psychology: global transformations and challenges.* Toronto: Captus Press.

Nichterlein, M. 2013. Recasting the theory of systemic family therapy: reading Bateson through Foucault and Deleuze. PhD, University of New South Wales.

Obholzer, K. 1982. *The wolf-man sixty years later: conversations with Freud's controversial patient.* London: Routledge & Kegan Paul.

Pickering, A. 2010. *The cybernetic brain: sketches of another future.* Chicago, IL: University of Chicago Press.

Pickering, A. 2012. Cybernetics as nomad science. *In:* Jensen, C.B. and Rodje, K. (eds), *Deleuzian intersections: science, technology, anthropology.* New York: Berghahn Books.

Richards, G. 2002. *Putting psychology in its place: a critical historical overview.* Hove: Psychology Press.

Roazen, P. 1971. *Freud and his followers*. Harmondsworth: Penguin Books.

Semetsky, I. and Delpech-Ramey, J.A. 2012. Jung's psychology and Deleuze's philosophy: the unconscious in learning. *Educational Philosophy and Theory*, 44, 69–81.

Smith, D. 2012. *Essays on Deleuze*. Edinburgh: Edinburgh University Press.

Smith, D. and Protevi, J. 2013. Gilles Deleuze. *In:* Zalta, E.N. (ed.), *The Stanford encyclopedia of philosophy* (spring 2013 edition). Stanford University.

Spinoza, B.D. n.d. *Ethics*. London: Heron Books.

Stenner, P. 2009. On the actualities and possibilities of constructionism. *Human Affairs*, 19, 194–210.

Villani, A. 1999. *La guepe et l'orchidee: essai sur Gilles Deleuze*. Paris: Belin.

Zourabichvili, F. 2012. *Deleuze: a philosophy of the event together with the vocabulary of the event*. Edinburgh: Edinburgh University Press.

3
EMPIRICAL BECOMINGS

The problematic position of psychology's method

Is Deleuze a systemic thinker?

We have shown that Deleuze, with and without Guattari, challenges psychology to change its unit of analysis and we have pointed to the explicit alternative that Deleuze offers: an assemblage in motion as perhaps the best conceptualisation of actual life. This is a significant provocation in terms of the direction psychology has taken since its infancy. Yet in some ways this challenge is still a comparatively minor problem for psychology, for it is a problem that is only sitting at the surface of more – for lack of a better word – 'foundational' concerns. If the challenge of Deleuze is taken only to this limit, his contribution runs the risk of being reduced to a minor tweaking of systemic thinking as it is currently understood. There is indeed value in making direct connections between Deleuze's ideas and systemic ones and we believe some powerfully productive connections can be made at this level (Nichterlein, 2013). To start with, Deleuze himself acknowledges the value of systemic thought (Deleuze *et al.*, 1980, pp. 31–2) and many have read his contribution in the light of theoretical explorations on *open* systems as compared with earlier versions that based their research on the idea of *closed* systems. Yet such a take on the Deleuzian challenge runs the risk of his insights quickly being subsumed into 'a new and much improved' formula of what is already in place, a development that has little heuristic value in terms of what Deleuze's project has to offer. In fact, the evolution of systemic thought in psychology could be seen as a good example of what we do not want to happen with Deleuzian ideas, as innovation becomes routinised and bureaucratised.

The current challenges facing theorisation in current family therapy is a warning sign for an interpretation of Deleuze's ideas in psychology that adopts a systemic reading. In line with Deleuze's admiration of Whitehead's 'misplaced concreteness', the problem for family therapy is not that families and communities lack value or significance but that claims about their value are positioned as if they belong on a 'higher', 'transcendental plane' where questions of power and of the limits of institutions are left unexamined. Families are treated as unproblematically central to understanding the individual. Not to focus on this 'intimate' and 'natural' connection as central to systemic ideas is often considered a betrayal of the model. Furthermore, the complexities recognised by Bateson and others in the field of family therapy – complexities that perhaps would have been better honoured by a careful consideration of Tolstoy's famous opening to *Anna Karenina* – have been reduced to a few competing theories and a preoccupation with technique. The effect of this 'displacement of value' is that it lures the researcher – the apprentice, the thinker to be – away from the scrutiny of the more 'foundational' and critical aspects of the work at hand. The power of the social is captured in what could be defined as *conceptual stopgaps*, returning us to dogmas or 'images of thought'. In some ways, this is a replica of the concerns Deleuze and Guattari have with psychoanalysis in its forcing of the unconscious – as well as those attempting to understand it – forever back to 'mummies and daddies'.

Despite its radical promise, there is in the field of family therapy a return to defining principles, principles that, although different from the earlier ones – e.g. 'not the individual, but the family' – turn difference into a dialectics of sorts, a sparring to-and-fro. Family therapy loses its radical thrust as an alternative paradigm to conceptualise the human condition and turns into a collaborative partner with more traditional approaches that focus on individuals. In this new collaboration, the apparent difference between individual-focused and family approaches covers up the fact that although the contents change, the mechanism at the base is still the same. This is something that can best be summarised with the French saying '*plus ça change, plus c'est la même chose*'. This saying – less elegantly stated, the more things change the more they stay the same – was used almost like a type of 'mantra' by early family therapists to highlight what they believe was conservative mechanisms in place (Watzlawick *et al.*, 1974).

Perhaps a more progressive reading of this saying might serve as an introduction to a set of ideas in the philosophy of science that are allies in the project of Deleuze and Guattari. We are referring to some complementary aspects of the work of Thomas Kuhn (1996) and of Michel Foucault. For Kuhn, the macrohistory of science is not to be understood as a progressive line but in terms of continual shifts of paradigms that imply a reorganisation of what scientists, and hence the general population, claim to be knowledge. Kuhn's was a familiar name to 'drop' in the writings of the early systemic therapists who would assert that their insights were indicative and constitutive of a new paradigm within the social sciences. A Kuhnian reorganisation is a very different gesture to cohabitation, however. The promise offered by early systemic thinkers, when they stated that family therapy represents not merely 'a change of name [but] a change of game' (Haley, 2007, p. xiii), has turned into a comfortable yet paralysed 'background' position within the same paradigm they were hoping to challenge. Along somewhat similar lines to Kuhn, albeit in a more radical form, Foucault's critique of 'the order of things' (1973, 2004) also conceives knowledge as depending on the forms of social organisation rather than as bearing an objective nature as posited by positivism. Foucault focused on the discursive elements at the base of the practices of communities in confirming certain knowledges as relevant and credible. In a gesture of great irony, the attempted appropriation of Foucault by family therapy theorists – reading Foucault in terms of social constructionism (Gergen, 1994, p. 413; see also Gergen, 2009, p. 48) – has given rise to a rupture in family therapy, an abandonment of the early cybernetic insights on the significance of science. This rupture, while claiming to be informed by Foucault and indeed by the project of Deleuze, has estranged and ultimately reified not only the early insights of the field but also the insights of Foucault and of Deleuze. An easy alignment between current ideas in family therapy – ideas that are claimed to be systemic – and Deleuze, is just not possible. The ground will need to shake a little more, although some sketches of a new alternative can already be seen emerging (Barbetta and Nichterlein, 2010; Krause, 2012; Skott-Myhre et al., 2012).

Western reifications

The problem of reification is, however, not a problem that pertains just to psychology – or family therapy for that matter – but has permeated the Western search for knowledge for many centuries. Deleuze saw in Plato, Leibniz, Kant and Freud examples of great thinkers who backed away from the radical implications of their own insights (Protevi, 2010, p. 4), betraying those insights in favour of alternatives that were more familiar, more congenial with their times. This was not surprising for Deleuze, who saw the quest for engagement with knowledge as always in movement and aiming to maintain a maximum engagement with a truly abstract under-standing, an understanding that escapes reification. For Deleuze, plenary engagement is a utopian fantasy. Rather than a full and decisive description of 'what is out there', for him there is more value in seeing the waxing and waning in time of different theories – of different representational articula-tions – as part of the endless process of territorialisation–deterritorialisation–reterritorialisation by assemblages.

The search for knowledge has untimely elements that we often associate with gods and heroes when in fact they belong to this earth and to us all as equals. We are searching within a material world that we are, at the same time, collaboratively constructing through our daily activities. For the crux of any conceptual engagement for Deleuze is its materiality and a profound acceptance that there is no world that has a pre-established and transcend-ental order of which we aim to acquire accurate representations. The mis-leading understanding of concepts as representational – of thoughts representing images of an outside – comes to us from 'the classics'. Their claims provided a conceptual base that has become 'sedimented' as founda-tional to current thinking, defining what we take for granted in everyday life as well as informing critical attempts. Instead of Heraclitus, whom we mentioned above, insisting on the ebb and flow of reality, we have at the centre of the famous Raphael fresco *The School of Athens* the more familiar images of Plato and his student Aristotle. Adorning a wall in the Vatican, Raphael's scene gives pride of place to those two figures. It is true that there is a tension between them. While Aristotle has his outstretched hand palm downwards, as if to refer to earthly things, Plato points to the heavens (unless of course his gesture means 'up yours'). But there is between them a harmony that crosses the generations, even if daddy is slightly pompous and self-righteous and son is a little rebellious. They will be reconciled by the end of the movie. Indeed, master and disciple provide a horizon that quietly but relentlessly defines good and common sense in the Western mindset. And Aristotle was the teacher of Alexander who conquered the known world.

Visceral thinking

To think otherwise to what has been entrenched in our cultural sensibili-ties; to think outside this hegemonic frame of 'common and good sense' is a rigorous but necessary intellectual endeavour. It is difficult to enact, not just because of the conceptual rigour it requires but, perhaps more importantly, because of its affective demands. Spinoza felt this strongly and so did Nietzsche. For this endeavour is accompanied by 'profound distress', a distress similar to that Foucault experienced at the cusp of his work on discourse (2004, pp. xix–xx; see also Deleuze, 1988, p. 94). As Foucault explained, such distress alerts one to the limits of one's knowledge. This limit that can only be recognised if there is first a deep awareness that there is nothing outside of the knowledge we have that provides to such knowledge – and thus to our assertions – a transcendental and stable value. Such a type of knowledge shifts the ways in which we can evaluate, alerting us instead to an emotional – a passional (Morss, 2000) – component that is inherent to the pursuit of knowledge. Here, Deleuze brings in two writers who both, in their very different ways, remind us of the role language plays in these projects: the actor and playwright Antonin Artaud and the children's author, mathematician and logician known as Lewis Carroll (1990, thirteenth series). Deleuze points out an important and fundamental difference between the works of Artaud and Lewis Carroll. Deleuze uses Artaud to highlight limitations in what Artaud calls Lewis Carroll's 'perversity', a perversity that emerges out of engaging in 'puerile' language games and avoiding the deeper issues pertaining to language, 'namely, the schizophrenic problem of suffering, of death, and of life' (1900, p. 84). Such an approach to language, for Artaud and Deleuze, accepts the obligation to deal with a language that is intimately 'carved in the depth of bodies' (Deleuze, 1990, p. 84), calling for an engagement with knowledge that cuts across traditional dichotomies in Western science. *The School of Athens* is incomplete without, for example, some blood, some sweat, or some tears.

It is therefore not surprising that Deleuze's work will confront the science of psychology profoundly. Psychology's commitment to an unexamined and an impersonal empiricism is severely questioned by Deleuze's philosophy of difference and its critique of thought as representation. As James Williams comments, this is not to say that a recognition of Deleuze's project gives rise to a foolhardy denial of the presence and the value of structures and continuity (2008, p. 204). What Deleuze highlights is that successful manifestations of these elements often sediment into 'images of thought', creating obstacles to our ability to appreciate and engage with the fluidity inherent to life. Deleuze always calls for a more nuanced engagement with (critical) thought, one that not only affords the presence of the new – of the event (Bowden, 2011, p. 188) – but, ultimately, also facilitates movement and life. In this sense, critical knowledge is not separate from life – it is not a comment *on* life – but is an integral part of it, again confirming a monism (as compared with a dualism) in thought.

To summarise, what is central to Deleuze's project is not 'essences' to be identified and quantified, either objective or subjectively, but the movement present and nurtured by thought. As we hope will become clear as this chapter unfolds, more than a prescriptive method – which inevitably runs the risk of a representation of sorts – what Deleuze provokes us to embark on is a critical engagement with method so as to nurture a kind of play within the present structures. Experimentation then takes a very different meaning where science sits next to philosophy and art as activities where 'the brain becomes subject' (Deleuze and Guattari, 1991, p. 210), highlighting the importance of the subject not being taken for granted.

It is in this sense that we need to look at the empirical method informing contemporary psychology so as to explore the challenges that Deleuze presents to it. This exploration has strong resonances with what some critically minded psychologists have called 'deep empiricism' (Brown and Stenner, 2009; Stenner, 2008, 2009). Both highlight the fact that this new kind of empiricism is very different to the empiricism with which psychology is familiar. For better or worse, we will not be in Kansas anymore.

Thinking about method: the longevity of Rene Descartes

It was a particularly cold November night in Bavaria, about 400 years ago; about the Martinmas when (as the old ballad puts it) 'the nights are lang and mirk'. A footloose would-be military officer and would-be philosopher called Rene Descartes had found himself a nicely heated room in a farmhouse. His method was sound: feel cold, seek warmth. It is said that his daydreams that evening, and his nightdreams that night, both stimulated by the domestic warmth, laid out his life's work before him. This was a vision of a unified scientific philosophy, the inspiration for all his subsequent intellectual endeavours. This is, at least, a picturesque origin myth for the Cartesian worldview (Williams, 1978, p. 16). Descartes was possessed of an enquiring mind and he was puzzling about many things. Consistent with his military training, Descartes was an adept practical experimenter, for example investigating the structure and function of the eye using the eyes of dead oxen. He was an empiricist in the sense understood since Aristotle, which is to say that the world of extended matter, matter with weight, movement and resistance, was to be understood by direct engagement with it. But above all he was trying to identify the basic rules of sound method: rules of thinking that would minimise error, rules that could be clearly expressed and perhaps above all, rules that could be straightforwardly communicated to others, to be taught. For Descartes, as for Plato long before, philosophy was pedagogy (and as Whitehead commented, so much of Western philosophy has been footnotes to Plato). Descartes' training in military engineering, in the mathematics of ballistics and weaponry, provided his model, informing the method that was to emerge. What is often not noticed, however, is that his model informs the method in a number of ways that escape the notion of 'measurable data'. Even in the heat of battle it is possible to adjust and recalibrate the machinery of destruction, to change one parameter (angle? height? size of shot?) while keeping everything else as it was. Of course the design of the technology is geared – often quite literally – to enable such selective adjustment. (To use a more homely analogy, each variety of weight training apparatus at the local gym isolates a muscle group, everything else being constant.) And again the context is communication as commands to alter the settings can be efficiently given and implemented. The individual soldier is only part of a machine, as are those with higher ranks who position *that* soldier in *that* specific landscape to fight a specific moment of *that* equally unique war. But this is not the concern of Descartes. For him, the objective is clearly defined. The purpose is for this soldier to play his part in the war, or for that neophyte sapper to be taught his job. What is necessary is to define clearly the elements at play so as to be able to manage them effectively to achieve the desired purpose. It is all about control. For Descartes – and for we psychologists with him – this requires the isolating of factors, of dimensions, of forces. It requires taking processes apart, carefully naming the elements at play and putting them back together in ways that can thereafter be reproducible. One might call this methodology 'synthesis by analysis'. It is the method of systematic distrust. No surprise, then, that Descartes is perhaps best known for advocating radical doubt: science as paranoia.

Descartes was to come up with a number of specific ideas influential on the later development of psychology, including proposals about how the nervous system and visual perception work as well as more theoretical claims about the distinction between the mental and the material worlds. Only a few of these proposals were wacky – the identification of the pineal gland as the seat of interaction between mind and matter, for example. For it would be a mistake to underestimate Descartes in any of these areas of his thinking, and his synthesis of the experimental, the mathematical, the philosophical and the practical-military into a grand system was extraordinary. Descartes would feel at home in a modern neuroanatomical laboratory, in a missile development facility or in most psychology departments.

More than that, given his adoption of straightforward language for the expression and communication of his ideas – a secondary school understanding of French is enough to get the gist of his writings – and given his charming persona, one can imagine Rene Descartes as the presenter of popular TV programmes on science or math, warfare or the brain. This is all to say that it is difficult to grasp enough of the big picture bequeathed to us by Descartes, to pick it apart, to work out precisely where it went wrong. In many ways what was most wrong with Descartes was what he considered to be his greatest achievement, method. To put it in a slightly more nuanced way, Descartes was dead right about the significance of method, but dead wrong about what form method should take.

But we leave Descartes for a while – tucked up as snug as a bug in a rug in his Bavarian bivouac – to make some comments on method and on empiricism as method. Empiricism denotes an engagement with the world as it presents itself to us. Wikipedia opens its definition of empiricism with an apparently unproblematic statement: 'Empiricism is a theory which states that knowledge comes only or primarily from sensory experience.' Wikipedia is equally enlightening when explaining empirical research as:

> a way of gaining knowledge by means of direct and indirect observation or experience. Empirical evidence (the record of one's direct observations or experiences) can be analyzed quantitatively or qualitatively. Through quantifying the evidence or making sense of it in qualitative form, a researcher can answer empirical questions, which should be clearly defined and answerable with the evidence collected (usually called data).

These are definitions that most psychologists would recognise.

Histories of psychology tend to contrast empiricism, as the favoured orientation, with what they call 'rationalism', by which they mean the application of thinking or logic detached from contact with the real world. The empiricism/rationalism dichotomy is apparently clean and clear. 'Empiricism' is directly connected with experience, gathering knowledge by induction, whereas 'rationalism' is theoretical and establishes knowledge through a process of reasoning rather than from a connection with experience. In terms of this dichotomy – 'empiricism' versus 'rationalism' as guiding methods for psychological investigation – histories of psychology or accounts of the philosophy of psychology have tended to classify Descartes as one of the self-deluded and 'medieval' rationalists rather than as one of the enlightened, modern empiricists. Descartes' 'foreignness' – from the perspective of an English-speaking scientific and professional community – seems to play a part in his banishment from the comfort zone represented by the British philosophers, the ones historians of psychology identified as empiricists. But as we shall soon see, Descartes' approach to science was much closer to the dominant contemporary traditions within psychology than this typology suggests. This raises the question of the adequacy of the rationalist/empiricist distinction as made by orthodox psychology as it looks at itself, and as it looks at past contributions and at what are (from its point of view) distractions.

Psychology, we think, is correct to aspire to empiricism but it has mistaken what empiricism involves. Its treatment of the contributions to psychology of Locke, Berkeley and Hume – contributions seen as positive, if limited, in a tradition of empiricism – has been misconceived. Psychology's understanding of empiricism is, as mentioned before, to claim that experience is 'the origin *and* the source of validity of all possible knowledge' (Boundas, 1991, p. 6). Within psychology, Brent Slife has problematised this understanding of empiricism by the mainstream in psychology. He comments that the rebelliousness of 'the adolescent discipline of psychology' against its philosophical parent (2005, p. 5) has left it lacking the tools to realise that empiricism is 'a value system.... It asserts rather than describes' (2005, p. 2; see also Slife and Melling, 2009). Of course Slife's characterisation of psychology as an 'adolescent' discipline is something of a cliché and a contorted description given the role of psychology in constructing 'adolescence'. As Slife explains, what is often left unexamined by psychological researchers in the reading of data is the degree of variation in what is to be considered valid forms of experience (Slife and Slife, 2014, p. 571). For psychology's methodology to consider what has been left unexamined would make it put in question the very stability that it claims to represent. Another aspect that adds to the confusion as to the current use of the term 'empirical' in psychology, according to Slife, relates to qualitative methods in research. Qualitative methods attempt to deal directly with issues of meaning in data, whereas quantitative methods may be said to pursue meaning indirectly. According to Slife, qualitative methods are unhelpfully classified as a species of (positivist) empirical method when in fact their affinity is more with the phenomenological traditions (Slife, 2005, p. 3; see also Stenner, 2009). That is to say, the distinction between a science that aims to study what naturally presents itself to the mind to a study that claims that knowledge is inevitably mediated by a consciousness with intentionality. Of course it is important for adherents of qualitative research, in terms of status, to have their methodology recognised as empiricism, even if a 'soft' kind of empiricism. But the point here is not a competition of sorts. The question is not one of 'which one is best' for there are no tools – other than personal belief – that can evaluate this. It is an issue of conceptual clarity and of congruence.

Psychology's rejection of certain intellectual traditions as rationalist – as out of touch with reality – is correspondingly mistaken. If anything this rejection serves to cloak the similarities and continuities of modern psychology with Descartes (and others labelled as rationalists) as well as its limitations and its distorted understanding of empiricism. And if rationalism involves the mistaken adherence to presuppositions about a logical structure to reality, or the appeal to transcendent levels of reality, then orthodox psychology is rationalist not empiricist. There is then some value in looking more closely at what is meant by the notion of empiricism within psychology – the 'official' empiricism so to speak – so as to explore the contrast offered by a Deleuzian empiricism.

Reading psychology's reading of empiricism

A way to highlight these differences is by examining one of the paradigmatic forms that empiricism takes in contemporary psychology: the experimental testing of hypotheses central to quantitative research. This is a methodology that Descartes would recognise even though its statistical expression is a more recent development (Hacking, 1990, 2006). In one very influential formulation, encapsulated in contemporary psychology's statistical methodology, the researcher entertains the so-called 'null hypothesis' as a default until and unless she acquires evidence that forces a rejection of that null hypothesis in favour of a pre-defined alternative. In statistical terms, the null hypothesis states that two samples derive from one and the same population. Differences between the samples are superficial or trivial, mere appearance liable to mislead the naive. Only if the characteristics of the two samples are sufficiently distinct, as determined probabilistically, can these two samples be identified with two corresponding, distinct populations such that a true underlying difference has been discerned in the world. In other words, the null hypothesis is a landscape containing no effects or differences, a kind of white noise or blank slate of explanation, a soup. Each posited site of possible effects or differences is to be experimentally manipulated, one by one, by reference to appropriate samples. All effects and differences in the world that are in some way taken for granted are undermined and put into question by a post-Cartesian, bureaucratic form of doubt. For even a successful finding of difference – of the bifurcation of populations – is only ever provisional. Even the rejection of a null hypothesis is only grudging and tentative. The rejection is constituted by the statistically estimated unlikelihood of an experimental result falsely representing a null reality – that is to say of a positive result, a result that seems to demonstrate a difference, an effect, arising from a background in which no such difference or effect 'really' exists. The criterion has conventionally been set at a 5 per cent likelihood of an experimental (sample) effect being associated with an absence of effect in the population, what one might call a false positive. And the 'bureaucratic' dimension of this methodology is not to be overlooked. Many psychology journals will not consider a submitted article for publication if the effects it claims are not demonstrated at that 5 per cent level, if not better. Notwithstanding the enthusiasm of psychological researchers for effects that are statistically significant in that sense – and their enthusiasm is entirely understandable in the context of workplace expectations, peer esteem and career aspirations – these findings are but ephemeral bumps and wrinkles in a surface that is thought of as basically featureless, pristine. The findings, strictly speaking, are at best only as good as the next experiment, an experiment that in many cases never takes place. In the meantime, the results have 'become proof' of something; they acquire a positive and affirmative status in an 'evidence-based' economy of professionalised knowledge.

For Descartes it is both possible and necessary, as a philosophical or experimental scientist, to identify and to isolate one factor at a time, to accept, reject or suspend each factor individually according to their own 'merit'. As we mentioned earlier, this is the Cartesian method of doubt. In each case the status of his knowledge can be assayed: 'I accept this – I reject that.' An analogy used by Descartes himself is taking apples out of a barrel one by one and checking the soundness of each. More formally, Descartes' method is to 'reject all merely probable knowledge, and only to trust to what is perfectly known and cannot be doubted' (Descartes in Williams, 1978, p. 33). This is what becomes central in his method. Having visions in his overheated room, Descartes feels that he can choose what objects to look at, what objects to overlook. He can choose which features of any of those objects to pay attention to. The world for Descartes becomes a world made of wax; a malleable world that can be not only picked up and analysed (Stengers, 2011, p. 348), but can also be the subject of communication of a military precision. In some ways, for Descartes thinking is easy if one is disciplined to open one's eyes to see what is already there. It is this gesture that Deleuze sees as the base of good and common sense becoming a philosophical base for much of what we take for knowledge (Deleuze, 1994, pp. 37–8).

Isabelle Stengers takes this point a step further and comments on how Descartes is, in a sense, like a judge in the European Civil Law tradition, subjecting nature to interrogation and 'demanding an explanation' point by point (or we might say that he is like TV's 'Judge Judy' Sheindlin in her arbitration show). He is the boss. For Stengers, Descartes' mistake, or his false claim, is to assert that the physical and social conditions in which he operates can be suspended in this piecemeal fashion. As Stengers observes, 'Descartes' doubt *requires* the specialized social environment which ... it undertakes to judge' (Stengers, 2011, p. 259, emphasis added). Similarly, Stengers notes, the meaning that a psychologist may read into an item of animal 'behaviour' – such as the peck of a pigeon at a coloured disc – is a meaning dependent on 'a hybrid social environment intermingling the pigeons and the psychologists who undertake to pass judgment on the pigeon's capacity to judge' (2011, p. 261).

One reason for emphasising this aspect of Descartes' method is the way in which contemporary psychology reproduces it. It is not merely the experimental testing of hypotheses that relies on the supposed holding constant of 'everything else' while one factor is manipulated. This approach to method can be found in forms of psychology far removed from this traditional quantitative experimental research method. Here we include (as mentioned above) phenomenologically oriented qualitative methods even though we believe that such methods are an improvement on the scope and depth of psychological research. These methods manifest a more socially just orientation to the practice of research – the subject researched is not just a passive object of examination but is actively engaged in the construction and the consideration of the researched meaning. Yet despite these 'democratic' advances, the observer(s) involved are still considered 'stable' and 'reliable' in their observation and so is the content observed. Whether facts or meanings, research implies a transcendental unity and stability – an *identity* – of the elements at play, elements that include the researcher.

Equally so, there is a direct connection between Descartes and the psychologists of our time who identify as 'social constructionists', influenced by the writings of Kenneth Gergen, John Shotter and others. This is surprising for several reasons. Social constructionists, along with adherents of other radical movements in psychology, are emphatic about rejecting certain components of Descartes' scheme, especially the version of mind–body dualism that Descartes articulated. But for social constructionism, it seems to be thought possible to suspend everyday life and re-imagine one's social and political world in a voluntary manner (McNamee and Gergen,

1992). Forms of narrative therapy that endorse a social-constructionist framework encourage clients to see their personal circumstances in this way too (White, 1995; White and Epston, 1989). This Cartesianism of social constructionism should be carefully noted. Like Descartes himself, social constructionists pick and choose between the available elements or alternatives. As Stengers writes, there is an abdication of responsibility and of engagement in this 'ironic and disenchanted equivalence of all explanations' (Stengers, 2011, p. 261). There is no more than a 'sad relativism' in play, a rather pathetic gesture a little like re-writing a Jane Austen novel so that it is about zombies or werewolves. If Descartes had popped outside once in a while in that long night, into that biting Bavarian Martinmas eve, he might have been reminded of the world outside his cell and outside his doubting, hallucinating self. But his doubting, self-conscious self remained, instead, a rock on which he built his system. As Descartes might have said, 'method begins with me!'

To focus exclusively on mind–body dualism as Descartes formulated it, and triumphantly to reject it, is not to fix the Descartes problem. This was recognised in Descartes' own times especially by Spinoza. Social constructionism misunderstands the responsibility involved in thinking, in what Stengers calls (from Whitehead) 'thinking under the constraint of creativity' (2011, p. 254). Creativity, central to experimentation and so strongly emphasised by Deleuze, is a heavy burden. It is a burden that Descartes, for example, was not prepared to take up. With its mathematical precision Descartes' alternative to creativity was hardly an easy option, yet so far as his legacy for psychology is concerned, it is a selling out. And in many ways the Cartesian approach is the paradigm for that variety of science that dominates modern-day psychology, the variety that Deleuze calls 'royal science'.

Deleuze's empiricism and the appropriation of David Hume

But prior to examining the important Deleuzian formulation of royal science, it is helpful to consider Deleuze's understanding of empiricism in more detail. Deleuze's offering to psychology at the level of methodology is nothing short of perplexing. For in a somewhat surprising turn of events, Deleuze can be said to agree with modern psychology in celebrating Hume (and empiricism) and rejecting Descartes (and rationalism). But his reasons for these evaluations are very different from the rationale of psychology as we currently know it, thus inviting psychology (once more) to rethink its methodological practices. This is required because the version of empiricism in mainstream psychology that we have briefly discussed is profoundly misleading. It is thus essential to note that in guiding us to alternatives, Deleuze is not rejecting empiricism but re-defining it. Deleuze's empiricism is materialistic through and through. This is not to exclude the abstract – the conceptual and the virtual – but to say that these aspects of experience need to be explained in intimate relation to the actual, to the material. The world with which we engage is not being set aside in favour of a world of ideas or a higher level of reality. If anything, Deleuze invites us to engage with the world with more directness. The intervening, transcendent membrane of Cartesian doubt is to be pushed aside, *Matrix*-like, to focus on actual processes. (In the words of Richard Crossman, 'There must come occasions on which the drapery is whisked aside, and the reality of power revealed' (Bagehot, 1963, p. 54).) As Deleuze would say, 'We do not recognise, we encounter' (1994, p. 139). Similarly, neither we nor Deleuze reject method in science. What is rejected is, as Slife indicates, an *unexamined* method, a method that naively takes for granted the possibility of establishing a direct connection with a stable and integrated reality as well as an equally stable (self) identity pertaining to the researcher and, in the case of psychology, to the research subjects. In relation to these points, Deleuze states that he worked in a way that avoids 'everything that makes up the world of the subject and of the object' (2001, p. 25). In doing so, Deleuze took a critical position in relation to the conservative triumphalism ubiquitously present in contemporary science in terms of its consequences in society, and to the naive political orientation of mainstream science.

As Smith has pointed out (2012, p. 19), Deleuze continually returns to the history of philosophy, in particular to its traditions of empiricism. As discussed in Chapter 1, Deleuze's commitment to empiricism is present throughout his work, running parallel to an equal commitment to a form of metaphysics. This is a strange combination that, in some ways, might present as 'paradoxical' to our common and good sense. Rajchman comments on this when he states that Deleuze 'was an empiricist, a logician. . . . It is a shame to present him as a metaphysician and nature mystic' (2001, p. 7). Rajchman wants to highlight Deleuze's 'lightness, his humour, his naïveté, his practice of philosophy as "a sort of *art brut*"'. These two styles – empiricism and metaphysics – seem to be in conflict because the openness of empiricism is usually juxtaposed with a metaphysics that assumes an understanding of nature as consisting of clear and definable entities. Given the latter perspective, the work of science, and of thought, is to re-present a good copy, a copy with clearly enunciated parts interacting in a precise and predictable way albeit within a respectable margin of error. This account of metaphysics and of empiricism is the worldview, however, that

Deleuze deeply critiques in *Difference and Repetition*, in a critique that frees both empiricism and metaphysics to renewed ways of engaging with each other.

In one of his strongest anti-Hegelian moments, Deleuze reads empiricism as an emphasis on openness versus the closure of dialectics with its 'mobilization of negation for the sake of allegedly superior synthesis' (Boundas, 1991, p. 8). What Deleuze challenges in Hegel is the idea that reasoning through dialectics – reasoning through an interplay with negatives – will get us to a superior knowledge of truth. Deleuze is not antagonistic to the concept of complexity and a special kind of dualism plays a central role in his reading of empiricism (Deleuze, 1991, p. 108). But he is critical of Hegel's assumption that such reasoning leads to a superior type of knowledge, perhaps to a type of knowledge that is 'sublime' in Kant's sense. Deleuze's dualism does not aim at higher understanding – a synthesis – but at the constitution of the stability we experience. What is transcendental in his empiricism is not an ultimate reality but a confirmation that what is real is processes and a constant becoming of identity, of both subjects and objects.

In the rehabilitation and redefinition of empiricism, as in his other projects, Deleuze looked for allies. He saw a useful ally in the Scottish philosopher of the Enlightenment, David Hume. Deleuze saw in Hume 'something very strange which completely displaces empiricism, giving it a new power, a theory and practice of relations' (Deleuze and Parnet, 2006, p. 11). For a renewed psychology to start with Hume might also perhaps be a good idea. Deleuze comments early in the first chapter of his first book *Empiricism and Subjectivity* that 'Hume proposes the creation of a science of humanity' (1991, p. 21). This would seem to be a study of human nature. But Deleuze continues some lines later, as if deliberately to perplex us, stating that 'Hume is a moralist and a sociologist, before being a psychologist; the *Treatise* shows that the two forms under which the mind is *affected* are essentially the *passional* and the *social*' (Deleuze, 1991, p. 21). These are fascinating terms that adumbrate central themes in the rest of Deleuze's writing and which mark critical questions for our discipline. These are ethical and socio-political themes, themes that are often considered of secondary relevance for a science of psychology but which, as we hope will become clear as the book progresses, are in fact of primary significance.

Key to understanding this different trajectory, Deleuze invites us to consider, is that he reads empiricism as a 'critical but nontranscendental philosophy' (Boundas, 1991, p. 8). That is to say that in Deleuze's version of empiricist philosophy, the position of the subject and of the given –

perceptions – are turned upside down. Instead of starting with a subject that uses method to access certainty of the world – a world that is out there, a transcendental world – Deleuze sees in Hume's empiricism a very different problematic. The question is 'how a subject is constituted inside the given' (Deleuze, 1991, pp. 86–7). In posing the problem this way, what is challenged is the very stability of what is understood to be immutable in nature.

As Millican (2009a, 2009b) explains in a (fairly traditional) introductory class on Hume at the University of Oxford, Hume can be seen as building on the works of both Newton and Locke. Hume was writing in the middle to latter part of the eighteenth century when the influence of Newton in science, and of Locke in political philosophy and psychology, was still very significant. As Millican sees it, Hume took from Newton a reorientation of science from 'understanding' into 'systematization' and from Locke – opposing Descartes – a move away from the pursuit of 'certainty' (through the use of doubt) into a recognition of 'probabilities'. For Hume, intelligibility comes not out of an external natural order to which we have access, but from an active systematisation of one's experience. Experience, in turn, is a result of perceptions, yet its actual presence in the mind has (following Locke) more to do with the operations of the mind than with the characteristics of an outside order. For Hume, all that there is is a multitude of impressions, what Deleuze would call pre-individual singularities – chaos in the strictest sense of randomness. As Millican explains, what Hume 'wants to say is that there is no real glue in nature or that there is nothing at all that we could remotely understand' (2009a, 4:32–4:41). Furthermore, for Hume there needs to be a strict separation between impressions and identity – of ourselves or of things. For Hume, identity needs to be constantly constituted and reaffirmed. As for Deleuze, change and difference are primary, identity is secondary.

For Deleuze, what is 'at work in Hume's philosophy [is] the problem of how a multiplicity of ideas and impressions in the mind comes to constitute a subject with beliefs that go "beyond what is immediately present to the senses"' (Bell, 2009, p. 6). Instead of the synthesis by analysis that Descartes promotes, what Deleuze admired in Hume was his synthesis of 'the biggest of all fictions – Subject, World, and God' (Boundas, 1991, p. 9). Science for Hume, then, is not an activity of discovering what is 'out there' but about understanding how those things 'out there' are perceived by a 'subject' without the need of a God who could account for such stability, as Berkeley had suggested. Hume, after all, was a contributor to the Enlightenment with its celebration of the ability of humans to engage with their existence on their own merits. And Hume, as Deleuze states, is quite clear as to how this is carried out. For Hume, in the words of Deleuze, 'Belief and invention are the two modes of transcendence' (1991, p. 132). This helps us to see what Deleuze means by transcendence. It is certainly a 'going beyond' but not in the sense of making contact with a higher reality; it is more like a leap in the dark.

For Hume, this multitude or multiplicity constitutes experience through a double process, the first being a process of selection and the second one of reflection. Hume approaches this argument in *A Treatise of Human Nature* by stating two types of activities of the mind – impressions and ideas – that differ in terms of their degrees of 'force and liveliness, with which they strike upon the mind, and make their way into our thought or conscious- ness' (1969/1739, p. 49). Impressions strike the mind more forcefully than ideas which, in turn, emerge as copies – reflections – of the earlier ones. Here we can already identify the two processes at play. Deleuze clarifies that in terms of the first process, 'within the collection [multiplicity], the principle elects, chooses, designates, and invites certain impressions of sen- sation among others' (1991, p. 113). Deleuze comments that there are two central groupings of principles, each carrying out a different role: the first selective and the second constitutive. Thus 'the principles of passion are those that choose the impressions of pleasure and pain'. On the other hand 'the principles of association … choose the perceptions that must be brought together into a composite' (Deleuze, 1991, p. 113). Hume called this first process or role *atomism* which, as a process, appears the more famil- iar to psychology since it is at the base of so much that is core to our research. It is through the principle of atomism that 'objects' are distin- guished as impressions to the mind. Yet a Humean atomism is not a reduc- tion to a genesis or a beginning of sorts – a primal world of atoms – but rather it refers to an active and selective process of perception. In this sense, much is already determined by the selections that are thus made. These 'constitutive' determinations are often left unexamined and, if they are, it is often only in terms of instrumentality, of effectiveness, marginalising issues of ethics and of choice. The definition of a particular problem (and not others) to be subjected to research, as well as the way in which the research is to be carried out, is not neutral but affirms a certain order of things. And as for identity in general, such orders have the appearance of stability, and of being consistent across time, 'only by a fiction of the imagination' (Hume, 1969/1739, bk I, part IV, sn II, p. 251).

Selecting and associating

This Humean point is central to Deleuze's thought and is of considerable importance in terms of challenges to psychology. Given that identity is established by belief and imagination – by creative acts of the mind – and given that mind and body are not two separate realms but are closely interrelated, Deleuze focuses on how one's body engages with the world, on what a body can do. For Deleuze, just as the body is not a component of a combination made up of body plus mind, the body itself is not meaningfully divided into stable parts. The body is 'a body without organs', without pre-defined characteristics. Such an orientation afforded Deleuze and Guattari considerable liberty in terms of the unit of analysis, as we have explained. Expanding on what we discussed in the previous chapter, assemblages are a composite of available bits and pieces as understood in terms of traditional units of analysis. This idea can be traced in psychology to some extent, especially in certain versions of psychoanalytic theory. Melanie Klein, who was writing in the middle decades of the twentieth century, explored novel ways of articulating psychic reality in terms of 'partial objects' (Deleuze and Guattari, 1983, p. 44). For example, 'the child-nipple' constitutes an identity that has more reality than 'a child and a mother interacting'. These proto-Deleuzian formulations of assemblage survive in psychoanalysis only to the extent that child psychoanalysts influenced by Klein continue to think of such structures as primitive developmental stages, to be replaced or transcended by integrated selves with a clear identity. Deleuze and Guattari were sympathetic with versions of psychoanalysis that recognise the fragility of wholeness, yet in many ways they followed instead in the steps of Gregory Bateson in seeing every element of the individual in constant relation to an ecology:

> Consider a man felling a tree with an axe. Each stroke of the axe is modified or corrected, according to the shape of the cut face of the tree left by the previous stroke. This self-corrective (i.e., mental) process is brought about by a total system, tree-eyes-brain-muscles-axe-stroke-tree; and it is this total system that has the characteristics of an immanent mind.
>
> *Bateson, 1971, p. 288*

The shift to this Humean kind of atomism requires a significantly different gaze at what is researched and the way research is done.

Yet despite the value that Deleuze saw in the first process – the selective process pertaining to atomism – his admiration seems to have been tilted towards the second of the processes in which '"Certain" impressions of sensation are called upon to be that from which impressions of reflection proceed' (Deleuze, 1991, p. 113). It is again through belief and imagination that relations are established between the impressions so as to articulate a systematisation of ideas. Here, the principle of *association* so much admired by Deleuze explains the emergence of reflections as ideas. Here is where we can understand that, for Deleuze as for Hume, an identity cannot exist without external relations (Bell, 2009, p. 13) because identity is an idea that results from such systematisation. Associationism in this sense therefore highlights a point that is central to Deleuze: the externality of relations. If atomism 'selects', out of the multitude of elements present at any given time, some that are to be recognised, association 'constitutes' them within a larger frame of meaning. In this process both the world as a complex net, and the subject as the one that renders the world intelligible, are constituted as two sides of the same coin. Here, one can see elements of what Deleuze, with Guattari, describe in *Anti-Oedipus* as the three syntheses of the unconscious. Here, too, the subject, as well as the objects, is the result of the activities of the mind. Deleuze and Guattari discuss what they call the synthesis of the unconscious to mark that these processes take place *prior* to consciousness. Indeed these processes construct consciousness. Hume was clear in stating that what facilitates such associations are *habits* that afford the presence of a certain strength and power to evoke ideas (Deleuze, 1991, p. 114). In other words, it is repetition – a function so much admired by Deleuze – that, under the name of habit, affords the emergence of a certain stability that we then associate with identity. This is why Hume was so sceptical with respect to laws of cause and effect. For Hume, all that experience provides are *habits* of thought, that is, associations between experiences. One can use these habits to extrapolate assumptions as to what will happen next, yet these associations cannot affirm anything about what will *actually* happen in the future.

Hume's ideas were controversial in their time. They seemed to constitute an attack on Judaeo-Christian ideals that, as well as proposing a celestial and earthly order, positioned humans as having a superior status to animals, rational and closer to God. Berkeley's proposals about perception had been radical and shocking but they were coupled with the celebration of the role of God in guaranteeing the veracity of human experience. One hundred years before Charles Darwin, Hume put human knowledge alongside that of animals, as part of the natural world, a gesture that Deleuze was to follow with his interest in reading human behaviour in ethological ways, as we will discuss in Chapter 4. The later work of Kant was in part a response to and a critique of this gesture of Hume. Kant's search for a way to maintain a certain human supremacy led him to postulate the presence of necessary, a-priori conditions, the human faculties. As Millican comments, Kant's human-centred claims were to be countered over the centuries not only by Darwin's contributions to biological science in the nineteenth century but also by quantum mechanics in the twentieth, both developments being very much consistent with Hume's insights (Millican, 2009b). In some ways Deleuze is the Hume of the twentieth century and his philosophical formulations bring to bear the scientific contributions of the intervening centuries as well as the conceptual ups and downs of those times.

Jeffrey Bell calls attention to the fact that the double process identified by Deleuze mirrors a second more profound process for Hume. This second level refers to the relations we have briefly described earlier between, on the one hand, the processes associated with the passions and, on the other, the principles of association (Bell, 2009, p. 17). Against mainstream traditions that locate cognition – the cogito – as central to knowledge and science, Deleuze reads Hume as giving clear primacy to the passions. Passions 'are absolutely primary' (Deleuze, 1991, p. 120), a priority that will become manifest in his later emphasis on the desiring machines of *Anti-Oedipus*. For Hume, morality is founded in sentiment, in a particular kind of sympathy for other humans (Millican, 2009a, 11:45–11:54) rather than on a rational basis. Rather than laws, Hume pointed to institutions as articulations of this general connectedness.

Deleuze's thought is full of examples of double processes, of parallel processes constituting the reality we experience. Another significant example is the idea of *double articulation*. Deleuze and Guattari examine this idea of double articulation in Plateau 3 of *A Thousand Plateaus*. Where Hume's distinctions were about humans – their passions and institutions – and the ways their subjectivity and their knowledge is constituted through certain principles, in these later writings of Deleuze and Guattari the focus moves to the vital process of the creation of forms as the central activity of life. Pushing Hume's positioning of humans as equals to animals to the limit, Deleuze and Guattari saw these processes present, at least in some way, in all life on earth. Human expression and knowledge is but an example of larger processes. Resonating with what we have said in Chapter 2 regarding changes to the unit of analysis in psychology, Deleuze states that the subject is not an individual – an autonomous entity with a clear identity – but is part of a larger plane wherein both the subject and the plane are constituted through a double articulation. Deleuze and Guattari teasingly portray this double articulation as 'God is a Lobster' (1987, p. 40). Life articulates itself through a double articulation whereby the first 'chooses or deducts [*sic*], from unstable particle-flows ... *(substances)* upon which it imposes a statistical order of connections and successions *(forms)*'. The second 'establishes functional, compact, stable structures *(forms)*, and constructs the molar compounds in which these structures are simultaneously actualized *(substances)*' (Deleuze and Guattari, 1987, pp. 40–1). One approximation to this for our human condition is that the first of these articulations constitutes the individual and other elements are constitutive of the assemblage – *the molecular* of Deleuze and Guattari – while the second refers to *molar* forms of social organisations such as the State and minorities. Both of these forms operate in the context of an infinity that overflows at both levels, energising ongoing transformations.

Engaging with the world

We will continue exploring this idea of double articulation as we progress through the remaining chapters. In particular this will help us to articulate the intimate interplay between the individual and larger organisations. Prior to this, however, there is value in returning to the point raised above concerning knowledge being based on 'belief' rather than on information. Rather than a passive reception, knowledge is constructed both in terms of 'subjects' and 'objects'. Knowledge, then, is personal inasmuch as it does not refer to a correlation with what is 'out there' but to a 'capture', a seizing of a territory or *habitus*. Science – like any activity that implies knowledge – is thus not a detached rational exercise but one that is highly personal and, as such, it is a life commitment of sorts, a vocation. This is a critical element to consider in a world that is known for cynical disbelief and for a poorly understood irony; a world whose major concern is how to deal with disillusionment and disheartedness. As Deleuze states:

> The modern fact is that we no longer believe in this world. We do not even believe in the events which happens to us, love, death, as if they only half concerned us. It is not we who make cinema; it is the world which looks to us like a bad film.... The link between man and the world is broken. Henceforth, this link must become an object of belief: it is the impossible which can only be restored within a faith.... Whether we are Christians or atheist, in our universal schizophrenia, *we need reasons to believe in this world....* Because the

point is to discover and restore belief in the world, before or beyond words.

Deleuze, 1989, pp. 166–7

For Deleuze, this belief needs to come from an engagement of our bodies with 'this world' (1989, pp. 166–7). This is the domain of existential issues, but an existential engagement that is very different in nature to that of traditional humanistic approaches. It is a visceral engagement that emerges in and from our bodies like an Artaudian cry and, as Deleuze says, lays 'before or beyond words' and consciousness.

What is Philosophy? was the last book published under the joint names of Deleuze and Guattari. It is a book that Deleuze wrote in its entirety but had published as a co-authored book to honour his long friendship with Guattari (Dosse, 2010, p. 456). Deleuze starts the Conclusion to *What is Philosophy?* ('From Chaos to the Brain') with a direct reference to the experiential dilemma of knowledge: 'We require just a little order to protect us from chaos. Nothing is more distressing than a thought that escapes itself' (Deleuze and Guattari, 1991, p. 201). The echoes of the Humean invitation to systematisation can be heard in these words as well as the distress to which we have made reference in relation to Foucault earlier in the chapter. The distress one feels in such a situation is profound and is the reason 'why we want to hang on to fixed opinions so much' (Deleuze and Guattari, 1991, p. 201) including the 'more sophisticated' opinions we call good and common sense. Opinion is a line of protection, an 'umbrella' Deleuze would say, that protects us from chaos. In some ways, it is an effective protection for it establishes simple direct connections with the world, connections that afford a 'recognition' – an association – with past memories. Yet the strength of opinion is also its weakness for the extension of such protection and engagement is limited to local and highly transitory experiences that, if left unexamined, lead to totalising and oppressive assumptions. More times than not, as Deleuze indicates in *Difference and Repetition*, instead of supporting the diversity constitutive of life, opinions of good and common sense end up doing the opposite.

Science, art and philosophy

It is here that the value of art, philosophy and science becomes relevant for Deleuze. These disciplines offer no comfortable reduction or representation of chaos, or barrier to chaos, as so many religions and philosophical systems do 'in order to paint a firmament on the umbrella, like the figures of an

Urdoxa from which opinions stem' (Deleuze and Guattari, 1991, p. 202). Rather, they embrace chaos and live to tell the tale.

This critical distinction gives us some further insight into the problems that Deleuze sees in phenomenological investigations, for the challenge is not a subjective (re)connection with a fundamental, experiential type of knowledge – *Urdoxa* for Husserl. Instead, what Deleuze sees as important is to challenge and transcend the opinions that constrain existence and, in a gesture of infinite construction, establish newness and confirm life. Science, philosophy and art stand as equal in this attempt. As Deleuze explains, 'philosophy, art, and science come into relations of mutual resonance and exchange' (Deleuze *et al.*, 1985, p. 125) and they must be considered as 'sorts of separate melodic lines in constant interplay with one another'.

Philosophy, art and science want us to plunge into the chaos because it is through this act that the 'real' emerges through a true newness – a new system of belief, a new plane of reference – that affirms life. And, as we have stated, it is life and vitality in one's life – what we might call 'health' – that is central to psychology. This plunging is not a 'reproduction' of sorts – a representation – but a constructive and affirmative activity that can perhaps be best described as an ordering; as a capturing of a piece of the infinite chaos so as to create an order. As Deleuze says, instead of 'a being of sensation' – a being that can recognise sensations – what is of importance is to establish 'a being of the sensory' (Deleuze and Guattari, 1991, p. 203), a being that emerges out of the sensory and that opens up to the infinite, to an oceanic sea of possibilities of existence. It is as if Deleuze is telling us that in order to achieve a much sought after freedom or wellness, one needs to engage in this relation with the chaos so as to constitute a *chaosmos*: neither preconceived nor predicted, instead a 'composed chaos' (1991, p. 204). As Nietzsche put it, 'One must have chaos in oneself/To give birth to a dancing star.'

This constructed chaosmos is what Deleuze and Guattari call 'a plane of immanence' or, using Bateson's concept, a plateau (Bateson, 1958). A plateau is 'a piece of immanence' (Deleuze and Guattari, 1987, p. 158) that holds a certain organisation, a material extension where life can take place through self-production – the formation of chaosmos. Needless to say, these fields are neither totalising not transcendental, but the result of con-certed living activities. We would like to say 'human' activity but, against humanistic definitions, Deleuze argues that this process also takes place at other levels of life activity on earth, including the tectonic plates. It is in this sense, as Delanda says, that Deleuze and Guattari refer in Plateau 3 to 'geology' so as to establish a material play of difference with the more familiar discursive 'genealogy' (Delanda, 2004; see also Goodchild, 1996, pp. 147–8).

Deleuze calls for us to live the life of an artist of sorts, which is to say life as a creative thinker. The life of the artist, however, like that of the scientist and of the philosopher, does not come easy. The experience is intense, not just because such a person has to deal with chaos – by seizing the complexity and establishing an existential territory – but also because it requires a breaking away from opinion, from the grid of social definitions that, more than the law, regulate everyday life. As James Joyce put it, not without a touch of cosmopolitan arrogance, 'You talk to me of nationality, language, religion. I shall try to fly by those nets' (Joyce, 1964, p. 203). Deleuze talks about the 'originals' and the 'prophets' (1997) to identify different positions in relation to these becomings of the artist. We will return to this point in Chapter 5 when we discuss the clinical and the critical.

At this point, however, we want to discuss a little further the critical position of science in society. Deleuze is clear that science stands on a par with the arts and philosophy in performing similar social functions. As he states, these activities provide a 'plane over the chaos'; a new relationship with chaos that, in its newness, establishes a direct relationship with what is real. The image Deleuze employs – the need of an umbrella as protection, and the painting of the firmament on its inside – helps to articulate the ambivalence present in 'images of thought' such as *Urdoxa*, the notion of a grounded experience. These images of thought are at times adequate to deal with the (Foucaultian) distress that has framed this chapter, when so to speak it is raining or when we are in search of shade. But the umbrella proves quite limited in other meteorological situations – on a pleasantly sunny day, a windy one or in a hurricane. Like umbrellas, all knowledge is useful to some extent and in some circumstances. This applies to our sense of self also. The difference between a Deleuzian umbrella and the umbrella we use in everyday life is that the latter is one that we can open and close at will since we are separate from it. It is a tool of our conscious decision-making. Deleuze's umbrella, on the other hand, is an assemblage – a composite that we could call 'us–umbrella' – that emerges out of the chaos, not knowing or quite unable to differentiate between climates. Another analogy could be found in the character of Truman Burbank from the Weir movie *The Truman Show*. Like Truman, we are entirely surrounded by this world; we are part of it to the point where the notion of a conscious negotiability is simply an illusion. All we have is the opportunity to cut across the screen, to create a rupture so as to engage somehow with what is *actually* out there; with a bit of the chaos. Deleuze says that this is what art, philosophy and science do. The ways they do it, however, differ. The plane that artists create is of affects and percepts, where philosophy creates concepts and science creates 'functives' (Deleuze and Guattari, 1991, ch. 5). Each of these creative activities engages in different ways with the chaos that we existentially confront, producing different effects. Each constitutes a temporary rupture of the images of thought that 'protect' us from the chaos. Yet, as a rupture, they are transitory and will eventually disappear without leaving much trace or, on the other hand, may become the source of a new dogma, a new image of thought. This may be how to think of Copernicus or Einstein. As Kuhn explained, their ideas were revolutionary at the time but now they are at the base of much that we consider well-informed opinion, what Kuhn calls a paradigm (1996). And opinion – more than science – is the 'real' enemy. As Deleuze observes, the struggle is not so much with chaos as such as with opinion. This is the profound struggle, 'for the misfortune of people comes from opinion' (Deleuze and Guattari, 1991, p. 206).

There is a continuity between the insights we discussed above regarding Hume's interest in systematisation, and the use of 'functives' to define the essential scientific activity. For Deleuze, 'functives' are the elements of functions that display themselves 'as propositions in discursive systems' (Deleuze and Guattari, 1991, p. 117). The role of functions is to establish regularities in the relationships of different elements so as to produce a (relational) plane of reference. Functions are different to 'objects' and here lies a powerful distinction. As explained when discussing Hume, the establishment of functional relationships is the closest science can get to the idea of identity. It is in this sense that Deleuze talks about science 'slowing down' the speed of life – freezing a moment – so as to be able to identify, not 'things' but states of affairs: '[S]cience takes a bit of chaos in a system of coordinates and forms a referenced chaos that becomes Nature' (Deleuze and Guattari, 1991, p. 206). Here we find another crucial point in the concept of 'becoming'. Unlike Descartes, the idea of science for Deleuze is not to establish control but to foster complexity. Nature is not there to be discovered and mastered, but life is there to engage and to create with. The state of affairs articulated by science according to Deleuze aims to describe a unique relationship between the elements researched, but instead of a search for a certain identity (of the elements at play), what is important in research is to develop an acute awareness that 'the thing [itself] is always related to several axes at once according to variables that are functions of each other' (Deleuze and Guattari, 1991, p. 122). In short, good science does not show 'things', it shows 'variables'; ever-varying variables. It is in this sense, and once more counterintuitively to good sense, that Deleuze claims that science does not unify the referent but rather generates 'all kinds of bifurcations' (Deleuze and Guattari, 1991, p. 123). This is so because science, once again, is more interested in the engagement with chaos and complexity than in establishing a 'true' nature of essences. As Deleuze says, 'Science would relinquish all the rational unity to which it aspires for a little piece of chaos it could explore' (Deleuze and Guattari, 1991, p. 206).

It is in this subtlety of orientation where a pivot is established for a profound bifurcation in terms of the role of science, of its uses both to the community and for future scientific work. Given its tendency to 'slow down' – to freeze the intensity of life – by the creation of a plane of reference, science opens itself up to regulation. Take, for example, these statements: 'the body has an average temperature and out of its range we have pathological presentations'; 'there are such things as *healthy* and *unhealthy* food'; 'exercise has effects on our body and on our mind'. These are assertions that claim to have scientific standing. They are at the same level as the responses received by the alien in opening Chapter 2 when in search of knowledge of us as human beings. Yet this kind of knowledge is of a different type to that of which we have been speaking. Something has taken place in the activities of the scientist that has made difficult the distinction between science, norms and regulation. Science morphs subtly, as Foucault has pointed out, from an engagement with chaos into an instrument for government and politics (2003, 2008, 2009). It is at this point that there is value in looking at Deleuze's comment about 'the brain becom[ing] subject' (Deleuze and Guattari, 1991, p. 210) for what is often left out of psychology is the social element in any subjectivity, an element that necessarily brings forth issues of politics in the form of governance and governmentality. This connects with the subtle yet important distinction between an animal in a herd and an animal in a pack. It is at this level, and in resonance with Foucault, that Deleuze and Guattari have their own line of analysis in terms of the relation of science with politics. In *A Thousand Plateaus* Deleuze and Guattari make a distinction between 'minor' and 'royal' science by relating these types of science to two very different socio-political organisations.

Royal and minor science

In Plateaus 12 and 13 of *A Thousand Plateaus*, Deleuze and Guattari discuss the relation of the 'war machine' and the State. According to Smith and Protevi (2013), 'the former is a form of social organization that fosters creativity (it "reterritorializes on deterritorialization itself"), while the latter is an "apparatus of capture" living vampirically off of labor (here Deleuze and Guattari's basically Marxist perspective is apparent)'. Deleuze and Guattari define a kind of science that they label 'royal' or 'State' science which they contrast to a form of science that they at different times label 'minor', 'vagabond', 'nomadic', or 'ambulant'. The variety of terms used for this second type of science gives a hint about its diversity and plurality and about its relationships with the centralised, masterful character of the first type. As they state, these 'are two formally different conceptions of science' (Deleuze and Guattari, 1987, p. 367) that are in constant tension, with royal science continually appropriating the material of the minor science and the latter undermining – 'cutting loose' – the knowledge(s) affirmed by royal science.

Some of the features of the two types of science will suggest themselves from the two sets of terms noted above. It seems obvious that at least in some respects, mainstream psychology would be classified as State science, for psychology plays an important role in the regulation of modern populations. Psychology has been used for at least a century to select immigrants and to screen military recruits, to subdivide school students on the basis of aptitude and to ration resources for mental health in a strange mixture of social welfare and workforce management. Sciences including many aspects of what has been called the 'psy-complex' (Pulido-Martinez, 2014; Rose, 1985) are straightforwardly identifiable as State science. Psychology seems like a deferential, efficient servant and supervisor of more lowly servants. But there is more that is needed than a simple critique of mainstream psychology. As Barney puts it in the context of mental health,

> Since the 1960s, the body of critical literature has been steadily expanded and now provides an even more impressive deconstruction and debunking of the medical model. . . . [But it has] made little difference in either the language or the basic operations of the mental health system.
>
> *Barney, 1994, pp. 19–20.*

Before discussing whether psychology as we currently know it is a royal or State science, and in what sense, it is important to be clear about what is meant by this term and what is meant by the contrasts drawn between the two forms of science identified by Deleuze and Guattari.

Royal science is characterised by an all-pervasive formalisation and by the search for lawful relationships between postulated entities. Here lies a subtle yet powerful point of distinction, for, as we have seen, relationships are central to science but in royal science these relationships are subordinated to arrangements that are lawful, i.e. 'strict' or 'rigid'. In minor science relations are contingently and variably defined. This distinction concerns itself with 'the ideal' and 'the required' in the natural universe. Whereas the former relates to a specific order, the latter refers to the conditions of emergence and to unique combinations that require an *ordinal* rather than a *numerical* analysis; the first reduces choices to fit within normative guidelines, the second focuses on conditions that could vary from case scenario to case scenario. It is this reduction to 'an ideal' that turns Deleuze's plane of reference into (unexamined) opinion. It is at this point, we believe, that such knowledge – a plane of reference that has turned into opinion – becomes most effective as a State mechanism of external regulation. 'Like gravity' is perhaps the royal prototype for aspects of our world that we take for granted: the market economy, or inequalities between genders, races and classes. To treat such systems as 'natural' and inevitable – realities to which there is no alternative – is to treat them as law-bound and as essential, granting them a certain type of power that can then be used for the maintenance of the State. Royal science has a close connection with the interests of the State: 'the concern of a man of the State [is] to maintain a legislative and constituent primacy for royal science' (Deleuze and Guattari, 1987, p. 367). As an institutionalised practice, royal science relies on sharp distinctions between the governed and those who govern and between the intellectual and the labourer. The royal sciences 'surround themselves with much priestliness' (Deleuze and Guattari, 1987, p. 373) and they take a contemplative form in which assumptions are made about a fixed external point of view that makes possible 'watching the flow from the bank' instead of an engagement with the chaos that Deleuze so much advocates. In this, science's activity betrays empiricism and turns it into a type of secular religion where humans observe and seek knowledge of a transcendental and unified order (Deleuze and Guattari, 1991, p. 125). Minor science, instead, in its contingency, nourishes multiplicity and differentiation.

Consistent with its detached, transcendental style, royal science emphasises predictability, reproduction and iteration. The same conditions will give rise to the emergence of the same consequence. In the teaching of mainstream psychology, much emphasis is placed on the 'replication' of results rather than on a search for difference. One of the 'official' reasons for the detail provided in published reports of research in psychology is to enable other scholars to reproduce the conditions and manipulations in which case, it is held, the same results should emerge. This notion of replication turns out to be more a matter of faith – thus confirming its 'ideal' status – than a matter of tangible practice, for it is uncommon that experiments are replicated and when they are, it is common that results show variations (Open Science Collaboration, 2015). The 'failure' of a replication – the emergence of different results from the original report – is typically explained away on the basis that some aspect of the conditions has in fact differed. This can be blamed on incomplete, misleading or occasionally on lazy or fraudulent reporting of original findings. If these excuses don't help, there is always a 'trump card' at hand: unknown differences in samples that require further investigation. The presupposition embodied in the practice of replication – the reliance on the stability of underlying effects, so long as everything is done in exactly the same way – is saved. The story is a comedy of sorts as in the classic sense of an order that has been restored, in stark contrast to the tragedy Deleuze admired so much in Nietzsche. Nature is supposed to have stayed as it was when the first experiment was carried out, while attention was transferred to other questions. Science then confirms its role as representing what Nature 'really' is instead of looking at a more complex, empiricist exercise of an encounter with the chaos out there so as to bring forth novel ways to deal with our human existence. Royal science works in line with State mechanisms of control and works effectively because of its intimate relation with opinion and 'good and common sense' that afford, as we mentioned earlier, an unexamined approach to empiricism.

In contrast, Deleuze and Guattari sketch the outlines and the history of a rival (empirical) orientation. Characteristically this form of science concerns itself with multiplicities, with '[r]hizomatic multiplicities that occupy space without "counting" it and can "be explored only by legwork"' (Deleuze and Guattari, 1987, p. 371). This idea of 'exploration by legwork', as elsewhere repeated by Deleuze, is a sign for the groundedness of the alternatives to royal science. They are experimental, empirical sciences in the sense understood by Deleuze and by Guattari. They involve what might be called detective work, work that can in several senses be thought of as 'plodding', as 'doing the hard yards'. Where royal science works with sets of points that all form relationships, where every point is a point on a preestablished yet indeterminate line and every line is a line on a plane, minor science treats points as scattered 'singularities' drawn fresh from the outside chaos and where lines articulate novel ways of systematisation. Royal science seems to want to build from the plane of reference rather than taking the untimely risk of continuously (re)engaging with the chaos constitutive of life and our human condition.

Minor science, in contrast, is science on the move, hence 'ambulant'. Its path is not fixed or predictable, hence (one meaning of) 'nomadic'. This is not to say that it lacks rigour. It has its own form of precision which is not the precision of State science. Its precision emerges from a detailed and disciplined work in the delimitations of functives and the establishment of relationships between them. Its rigour comes not from the examination of a stable outside reality, but from the constructive definition and examination of the elements and processes that constitute what is observed. In this sense, as Deleuze and Guattari state, the methodology of minor science is to 'extract from things a determination that is more than thinghood (choséité), which is that of corporeality (corporéité), and which perhaps even implies an esprit de corps' (1987, p. 367). As we have said, minor science establishes 'points' as it goes as markers of what has been explored. It is in this sense that Deleuze and Guattari are interested in cartography, not as a tracing exercise but as map making (1987, p. 12). That is to say, they are interested in the conditions of emergence of a phenomenon – conditions that cannot be taken for granted – rather than in delineating the characteristics of phenomena. In this, Deleuze is finely attuned to Foucault. Thus science that is vague, vagabond, nomadic, minor or ambulant challenges the orthodoxy of royal science.

Importantly, the two rival forms of science always coexist. But the coexistence is, not surprisingly, tense and contested. From the point of view of royal science, nomad science is 'portrayed as a prescientific or parascientific or subscientific agency' (Deleuze and Guattari, 1987, p. 367), as a practice that is not 'up to scratch', often being the practice first to be excluded when funding is tight unless it can prove to be 'useful' to royal science. In fact, the State always 'finds it necessary to repress the nomad and minor sciences' (Deleuze and Guattari, 1987, p. 368) and 'contain' them for, ironically, they impress the royal scientist as 'being soft', inexact and vague. One feature of this repression is the treatment of individual scientists. 'There is a type of ambulant scientist whom [sic] State scientists are forever fighting or integrating or allying with, even going so far as to propose a minor position for them within the legal system of science and technology' (Deleuze and Guattari, 1987, p. 373). As we have already stated, Gregory Bateson is a good example of the tribulations and power of scientists of this kind within the social sciences (Pickering, 2010, 2012). This process is reminiscent of the idea of so-called 'soft money' as short-term, grant-based support for the salary of the researcher. Any contemporary scientific institution or industry therefore manifests an admixture of the royal and the alternative forms of science. As noted above, there are many aspects of psychology that fit in closely with the Deleuzian idea of royal science, but the minor and resistant role already played by other forms of science needs to be recognised. It is also important to note that the power of psychology as a State science should not be exaggerated for this would be to collaborate in the repression of the alternatives and to believe psychology's own publicity, so to speak. In some respects and in some circumstances psychology itself represents a minority science struggling against bigger forces, such as the multinational royal science of the pharmaceutical and military industries.

(Re)thinking psychological method

The recently published *Encyclopedia of Critical Psychology* has no entries for science, for the philosophy of science or for the sociology of science. It has an entry on *Methodologism/Methodological Imperative* which is defined as a tendency that 'overemphasizes methods and neglects ontological, epistemological, practical and political considerations' (Gao, 2014, p. 1176). Yet there is no entry for method in itself. Science is the 'big bad wolf' in critical approaches and even Foucault hesitated to tackle it. Foucault was clear that he was not against method and science in themselves. What he was against was positivism and the construction of a specific type of science: human science (Foucault, 2004).

What we have attempted to do in this chapter is to show that avoiding science and method is not an option. As Ben Bradley states 'A psychology whose primary rationale is to promote social justice need not throw away its scientific aspirations. Indeed, the things it studies will be *more* rigorously arrived at' (Bradley, 2005, p. 3). There is much to gain by engaging fully with science, in particular with the philosophy of science and empiricism. For Deleuze this is central. His insights into a 'minor' use of science, of a science that runs counterintuitively to representation and to common and good sense, is an important ally for the project of critical psychology. Of course, the main problem – as well as the main opportunity – lies in the fact that a critical position cannot sit still, for science has this internal tension between the royal and the minor counterparts, a lively tension that resembles the ongoing struggles between a royal sovereignty and a life in difference and multiplicity. Deleuze's invitation to psychology is to see science not as 'the big bad wolf' but one of the pack. The wolf is only a danger for the owner of the herd.

If we are to be succinct after a long chapter, as to the important challenges that Deleuze presents to methodological aspects of psychology, these can be summarised in three main points. First, psychology needs to let go of its timidity and take up empirical research in its pure and radical forms. To do so, it needs to grow out of its 'adolescence' and establish a more reflexive relationship with the philosophy of science in which it is grounded rather than leaving such foundations unexamined. Empiricism – as distinct from positivism and phenomenology – is a good place from which to start for psychology. Here, as we indicated earlier in the chapter, the work reconnecting with Whitehead and 'deep empiricism' might prove to be of value.

Second, and in line with current neurophysiological insights, psychology needs to let go of the idea of representation and of reproduction. Science is an activity that is essentially transformative and psychology needs not only to look at the world in terms of how it presents to our senses but also to the possibilities and responsibilities that surround such knowledge – both in terms of the world and of us as observers and participants in this world. Deleuze's comment that, in his interest on psychology, Hume was 'a moralist and a sociologist' is a good reminder that what is important in our field is an active engagement in understanding not just the pathos – the clinic – of our condition but, more importantly, its health. In order to do so, we must understand that what is of foremost importance to a science of psychology is its ethical dimension as an exercise of evaluation of the type of world it is involved in constructing. There must be a shift from reproduction to transformation. Such a shift needs to start with psychology, as a science, letting go of the idea of knowledge as a cognitive and neutral exercise that takes place in the mind of a passive observer, an exercise of recognition of a stable natural order, and needs to consider the full implications implied in the awareness that in the activity of the researcher there are far more profound elements at play. The researcher is establishing – either confirming or creating – a certain state of affairs that has significant effects on issues of governance. This realisation refers not only to a shift concerning the people 'out there' who are 'researched', but also concerning the researcher her- or himself, observing the people 'out there', people who – as Maturana would say – could be themselves. The self of the scientist is inextricably connected to the knowledge it produces and it needs to take responsibility for the choices being taken.

Finally, if psychology wants to avoid the dangers of nurturing a type of knowledge aiming to normalise our human condition – norms that transform our subjectivity into docile bodies – then the challenge that this presents to us is how to creatively engage with the heavy burden of creativity. We need to find critical and novel alternatives to what presents as 'for granted' to us, as deeply determined and inevitable in our human condition, so as to honour both the infinite possibilities that escape such 'states of affairs' as well as 'the people to come' (Deleuze and Guattari, 1991, p. 218).

We will return to these dynamics in the next chapter when we look at what a more fully Deleuzian psychology would look like. This chapter, however, closes the first part of the book in which we have attempted to introduce Deleuze's ideas to a psychological audience through a critical analysis both of psychology's unit of analysis and its method. It would be betraying Deleuze's project to stay forever in the realm of critique, however, in the 'comfort zone' of the detached intellectual. Transformation comes only with the active engagement with an alternative.

References

Bagehot, W. 1963. *The English constitution*. Glasgow: Collins.

Barbetta, P. and Nichterlein, M. 2010. (Re)learning our alphabet: reflecting on systemic thought using Deleuze and Bateson. *Human Systems: The Journal of Therapy, Consultation & Training*, 21, 399–419.

Barney, K. 1994. Limitations of the critique of the medical model. *The Journal of Mind and Behaviour*, 15, 19–39.

Bateson, G. 1958. *Naven: a survey of the problems suggested by a composite picture of the culture of a New Guinea tribe drawn from three points of view*. Stanford, CA: Stanford University Press.

Bateson, G. 1971. The cybernetics of 'self': a theory of alcoholism. *Psychiatry*, 34, 1–18.

Bell, J.A. 2009. *Deleuze's Hume: philosophy, culture and the Scottish Enlightenment*. Edinburgh: Edinburgh University Press.

Boundas, C.V. 1991. Deleuze, empiricism, and the struggle for subjectivity. *In:* Deleuze, G. (ed.), *Empiricism and subjectivity: an essay on Hume's theory of human nature*. New York: Columbia University Press.

Bowden, S. 2011. *Priority of event: Deleuze's logic of sense*. Edinburgh: Edinburgh University Press.

Bradley, B. 2005. *Psychology and experience*. Cambridge: Cambridge University Press.

Brown, S.D. and Stenner, P. 2009. *Psychology without foundations: history, philosophy and psychosocial theory*. London: Sage.

Delanda, M. 2004. Deleuze and the use of the genetic algorithm in architecture. *In:* Columbia University, Art and Technology Lecture Series.

Deleuze, G. 1988. *Foucault*. Minneapolis, MN: University of Minnesota.

Deleuze, G. 1989. *Cinema 2: the time image*. London: Athlone Press.

Deleuze, G. 1990. *The logic of sense*. London: Athlone Press.

Deleuze, G. 1991. *Empiricism and subjectivity*. New York: Columbia University Press.

Deleuze, G. 1994. *Difference and repetition*. New York: Columbia University Press.

Deleuze, G. 1997. *Essays critical and clinical*. Minneapolis, MN: University of Minnesota Press.

Deleuze, G. 2001. *Pure immanence: essays on a life*. New York: Urzone.

Deleuze, G. and Guattari, F. 1983. *Anti-Oedipus: capitalism and schizophrenia*. Minneapolis, MN: University of Minnesota Press.

Deleuze, G. and Guattari, F. 1987. *A thousand plateaus: capitalism and schizophrenia.* Minneapolis, MN: University of Minnesota Press.

Deleuze, G. and Guattari, F. 1991. *What is philosophy?* London: Verso.

Deleuze, G. and Parnet, C. 2006. *Dialogues II.* London: Continuum.

Deleuze, G., Descamps, C., Eribon, D. and Maggiori, R. 1980. On a thousand plateaus. *In:* Deleuze, G. (ed.), *Negotiations, 1972–1990.* New York: Columbia University Press.

Deleuze, G., Dulaure, A. and Parnet, C. 1985. Mediators. *In:* Deleuze, G. (ed.), *Negotiations, 1972–1990.* New York: Columbia University Press.

Dosse, F. 2010. *Gilles Deleuze & Félix Guattari: intersecting lives.* New York: Columbia University Press.

Foucault, M. 1973. *El orden del discurso.* Mexico: Tusquets editores.

Foucault, M. 2003. *Society must be defended: lectures at the Collège de France, 1975–1976.* New York: Picador.

Foucault, M. 2004. *The order of things: an archaeology of the human sciences.* London: Routledge.

Foucault, M. 2008. *The birth of biopolitics: lectures at the Collège de France 1978–1979.* New York: Palgrave Macmillan.

Foucault, M. 2009. *Security, territory, population: lectures at the Collège de France 1977–1978.* New York: Palgrave Macmillan.

Gao, Z. 2014. Methodologism/methodological imperative. *In:* Teo, T. (ed.), *Encyclopedia of critical psychology.* New York: Springer.

Gergen, K. 1994. Exploring the postmodern: perils or potentials. *American Psychologist*, 49, 412–16.

Gergen, K. 2009. *An invitation to social construction.* London: Sage.

Goodchild, P. 1996. *Deleuze and Guattari: an introduction to the politics of desire.* London: Sage Publications.

Hacking, I. 1990. *The taming of chance.* Cambridge: Cambridge University Press.

Hacking, I. 2006. *The emergence of probability: a philosophical study of early ideas about probability inductions and statistical inference.* Cambridge: Cambridge University Press.

Haley, J. 2007. Foreword. *In:* Nichols, M.P. and Schwartz, R.C. (eds), *The essentials of family therapy.* Boston, MA: Pearson.

Hume, D. 1969/1739. *A treatise of human nature.* Harmondsworth: Penguin Books.

Joyce, J. 1964. *A portrait of the artist as a young man.* New York: Viking.

Krause, I.-B. (ed.) 2012. *Culture and reflexivity in systemic psychotherapy: mutual perspectives.* London: Karnac.

Kuhn, T.S. 1996. *The structure of scientific revolutions.* Chicago, IL: University of Chicago Press.

McNamee, S. and Gergen, K. (eds) 1992. *Therapy as social construction.* London: Sage.

Millican, P. 2009a. 3.1 Introduction to David Hume. *General Philosophy.* University of Oxford. www.youtube.com/watch?v=q6SYJpPNty8

Millican, P. 2009b. 3.2 David Hume: concluding remarks. *General Philosophy.* University of Oxford. www.youtube.com/watch?v=PID9VsjJCCk

Morss, J.R. 2000. The passional pedagogy of Gilles Deleuze. *Educational Philosophy and Theory*, 32, 185–200.

Nichterlein, M. 2013. Recasting the theory of systemic family therapy: reading Bateson through Foucault and Deleuze. PhD, University of New South Wales.

Open Science Collaboration, 2015. Estimating the reproducibility of psychological science. *Science*, 349, n.p.

Pickering, A. 2010. *The cybernetic brain: sketches of another future.* Chicago, IL: University of Chicago Press.

Pickering, A. 2012. Cybernetics as nomad science. *In:* Jensen, C.B. and Rodje, K. (eds), *Deleuzian intersections: science, technology, anthropology.* New York: Berghahn Books.

Protevi, J. 2010. Preparing to learn from difference and repetition. *Journal of Philosophy: A Cross-Disciplinary Inquiry (Nepal)* 5, 35–45.

Pulido-Martinez, H.C. 2014. Psy-complex. *In:* Teo, T. (ed.), *Encyclopedia of critical psychology.* New York: Springer.

Rajchman, J. 2001. Introduction. *In:* Deleuze, G. (ed.), *Pure immanence: essays on a life.* New York: Zone Books.

Rose, N. 1985. *The psychological complex: psychology, politics and society in England 1869–1939.* London: Routledge and Kegan Paul.

Skott-Myhre, K., Weima, K. and Gibbs, H. 2012. *Writing the family: women, auto-ethnography, and family work.* Rotterdam: Sense Publishers.

Slife, B.D. 2005. Philosophy of science considerations in the EST controversy. Paper presented at the meeting of the American Psychological Association, Washington, DC.

Slife, B.D. and Melling, B.S. 2009. The ideology of empiricism. *Edification: Journal of the Society for Christian Psychology*, 2, 44–8.

Slife, B.D. and Slife, N.M. 2014. Empiricism. *In:* Teo, T. (ed.), *Encyclopedia of critical psychology.* New York: Springer.

Smith, D. 2012. Deleuze and the history of philosophy. *In:* Smith, D. and Somers-Hall, H. (eds), *The Cambridge companion to Deleuze.* Cambridge: Cambridge University Press.

Smith, D. and Protevi, J. 2013. Gilles Deleuze. *In:* Zalta, E.N. (ed.), *The Stanford encyclopedia of philosophy* (spring 2013 edition). Stanford University.

Stengers, I. 2011. *Thinking with Whitehead: a free and wild creation of concepts.* Cambridge, MA: Harvard University Press.

Stenner, P. 2008. A.N. Whitehead and subjectivity. *Subjectivity*, 22, 90–109.

Stenner, P. 2009. On the actualities and possibilities of constructionism. *Human Affairs*, 19, 194–210.

Watzlawick, P., Weakland, J. and Fisch, R. 1974. *Change: principles of problem formation and problem resolution.* New York: Norton.

White, M. 1995. *Re-authoring lives.* Adelaide: Dulwich Centre Publications.

White, M. and Epston, D. 1989. *Literate means to therapeutic ends.* Adelaide: Dulwich Publications Centre.

Williams, B. 1978. *Descartes: the project of pure enquiry.* Harmondsworth: Penguin Books.

Williams, J. 2008. *Gilles Deleuze's logic of sense: a critical introduction and guide.* Edinburgh: Edinburgh University Press.

PART II

Putting the assemblage to work

4

THE ACTUALITY OF MULTITUDES

On the limits of democracy

How do we then start to engage with Deleuze and psychology? How do we make this encounter work? After some consideration, we thought that the best entry to this alternative world might be through this bold statement by Deleuze and Guattari:

> [E]very democrat ... finds him or herself not responsible for Nazism but sullied by it. There is indeed catastrophe, but it consists in the society of brothers or friends having undergone such an ordeal that [they] can no longer look at each other, or each at himself, without a 'weariness', perhaps a 'mistrust'.... Nor is it only in the extreme situations described by Primo Levi that we experience the shame of being human. We also experience it in insignificant conditions, before the meanness and vulgarity of existence that haunts democracies, before the propagation of the modes of existence and of thought-for-the-market, and before the values, ideals, and opinions of our time.... We do not lack communication. On the contrary, we have too much of it. We lack creation. *We lack resistance to the present.*
>
> *Deleuze and Guattari, 1991, pp. 106–8*

It might be surprising to begin with a quotation that provokes us to question the virtue of democracy and to look at the possible dangers that contemporary democracy brings to our human condition. Isn't democracy a good system of government, perhaps the best we know of? And what has democracy to do with psychology after all? Psychology, it may be said, is a profession of the individual and, as such, it stands independent of political trends. But Deleuze would question this assertion. As we have already discussed, the claims of a science and discipline of psychology to being 'objective' no longer stand in a Deleuzian world. Instead, psychology – as any other type of science – needs to be evaluated according to the type of science, royal or nomad, that is practised. Equally so, claims regarding the presence of 'natural, determined and determinable' elements in our 'essence' as human beings need to be questioned so as to include not just a context but the conditions of possibility for such a context. Furthermore, we also have to come to terms with the Deleuzian claim that such a context – and our 'nature' within it – is but one of the possible ways of arranging and engaging with the chaos surrounding our existence. It is in this context that the political element must be included in the analysis of the discipline; not just because politics is a foundational element to one's individuality as a social animal, but also as an evaluative tool to assess the effects of the types of social organisation in which we participate. Such an evaluation engages with these effects not as manifestations of a 'natural order', but as a possible type – among many – of organisation and of governance.

It is within these parameters that democracy needs to be put to the test not just by politics as a specific science but by all sciences, including psychology. Within psychology the ideas we hold of the concept of democracy need to be scrutinised according to the affects that see their emergence as well as the effects its claims have in the actuality of everyday life. The democratic desire is that of treating each other as equals, as brothers and sisters – as members of a pack – rather than belonging to a hierarchical order, where a master manages its flock or herd. It is in this domain that much thought still needs to take place, for the ideal of democracy is at great risk when such an ideal is put into practice. This is where the quote opening this chapter becomes meaningful and speaks to psychology, demanding an examination of our claims and a more direct engagement with our practices. The ways in which we betray such an ideal are numerous, including the ways in which we treat fellow human beings in their difference. As Foucault says: 'We have yet to write the history of that other form of madness, by which men, in an act of sovereign reason, confine their neighbors, and communicate and recognize each other through the merciless language of non-madness' (Foucault, 2004a, p. xi).

This political dimension calls for an evaluative, ethical dimension that Deleuze would argue is a dimension that is inherent to any human activity, including scientific observation. As we discussed in the previous chapter, for Deleuze and Guattari the political presents itself within science through the distinction between minor and royal science, not as an ideology or as a distinction between party lines but as a manner of doing science. Along with the arts and with philosophy, Deleuze values science and the productive engagement that it entails yet, in line with his approach to all topics, his take on it makes empirical science almost unrecognisable to our current understanding. Deleuze does not claim neutrality in the observation – objectivity – as central to science but portrays a very different engagement between science and politics. His project goes beyond traditional party lines to look at the ontological dilemmas that present to the human condition in ways that force us to think on our condition beyond the limits and definitions that are easily available. A good example of how he goes beyond party lines can be seen when he reflects on the effects of May'68 (Deleuze and Guattari, 1984). As we discussed in the first chapter, this event was 'crushed' by all political parties at the time, 'on the left as much as on the right' (p. 235), yet it had a force of its own that forged the emergence of a new type of subjectivity. This is the vitality that we believe a Deleuzian science of psychology would be interested in, a science that calls for a re-evaluation of all of our 'standard' practices in the discipline.

The political element continues being central when we move to a more concrete level of consideration of Deleuze's ideas within psychology. Yet, as with Foucault, the type of political thought that Deleuze calls us to consider is of a different kind to what has been considered so far in psychology. Deleuze does not call for a psychological study of those involved in political activities, as study subjects: an individualised engagement with politicians and with political decision-making. As we have been repeating, in an untimely refrain, one of Deleuze's major critiques is of transcendental explanation, of claims to have a privileged understanding of what is taking place. Instead, he proposes that a 'transcendental' field is established through synthetic and productive acts. As such, politics needs to refer not to something that happens 'out there' but to something that is intimately related with one's attempts to engage with the actual process of construction and synthesis of one's reality. Such politics is not an observation but a reference to a core aspect of the constructive nature of life. Equally so, it is not reflexive but recursive: it does not attempt to evaluate in a detached and, once again, transcendental way but to inform and evaluate practice in an ongoing manner.

For Deleuze, as for Guattari, an engagement with politics is inevitable if we are to consider the social nature of ourselves. As we discussed in Chapter 2, a central concept for Deleuze and Guattari's metaphysics is what Holland terms 'Intra-Species Social Organization', where the individual emerges out of the social. If there is a 'nature' for the individual, it is that of having a position within a group. Human beings are not solitary entities, which is not to say that some individuals may choose solitude as part of their differentiation within society, a classic example being people choosing monastic life.

Given the 'intrinsic' social element present in our selves as humans, issues of governmentality are central to all of our activities. Although it is perhaps not surprising, it is a matter of concern that the discipline of psychology has given so little attention to this dimension. It is not surprising because, as we indicated in the last chapter, the discipline has taken the scientist *out* of the research equation and has assumed a stable nature of both the researcher and the object researched (Law, 2013). Deleuze's revision of what empiricism entails has drawn attention to the role of the researcher being central to scientific observation despite its claims of objectivity. In this, he has not been alone but in the company of a number of other scientists, such as Maturana and Varela, of philosophers of science, in particular Isabelle Stengers (1997, 2000) and of sociologists of science like Bruno Latour (Duff, 2014, pp. 35, 83). This turn brings with itself an interest not only in the 'facts' but also in the communities of researchers involved in the research. Facts then get entangled with other motivations and assumptions shared by the scientific community in which the research takes place. Furthermore, as Brown and Reavey explain regarding the types of research that take place around memory (2015, ch. 2), research activity and the knowledge so constructed is not neutral but defines social and material pathways of understanding that, in turn, inform further research as well as the general opinion of the community at large. It is at this level that the distinction Deleuze and Guattari make between minor and royal science becomes central in the ethical evaluation of scientific disciplinarian practices. This distinction is a powerful reminder that the social activity of science-making is not neutral but has power effects within the community in which such practice takes place: they actively inform the elements that build the social – the community, the nation – in which such a researcher in psychology acquires status and participates as a citizen. It is at this point that a new dimension of analysis becomes relevant when reflecting on the limitations of the knowledge that the alien introducing Chapter 2 could acquire from books on mainstream psychology. Such an alien would have not just missed the limitations and inconsistencies present in the psychological discourse; it would have also missed out on the power effects that such knowledge recursively has on social life.

A further political element of analysis is also required when looking at the power effects of psychological definitions not just within one's community but also the movement of psychological concepts on a global scale and the power effects of this movement. It is important to notice the inequalities involved. In line with critical analysis of the flow in economic markets in terms of what is exported and imported between so-called developed and developing countries, much can be said for example about which books in psychology are translated and which are not, and which criteria are used to define psychological phenomena within comparative research in psychology. This dimension is of particular importance for, as Ethan Watters comments, it is increasingly unnerving how 'American culture pervades the world' (2010, p. 1). In line with our concerns regarding psychology turning into a type of King Midas, Watters comments that 'the visual landscape of the world has become depressingly familiar.... Our golden arches [a reference to McDonald's] do not represent our most troubling impact on other cultures; rather it is how we are flattening the landscape of the human psyche itself' (Watters, 2010, p. 1). Like the deforestation of large areas of the globe – deforestation in the name of facilitating required agriculture – the flattening Watters refers to is intimately connected with issues of governmentality. Psychology has to come to terms with the political aspects of its practices and come to terms also with the effects of its wishful and triumphalist dreams of an objective science to better the human condition. Such a realisation might help it to perhaps gain some caution and modesty in the face of the complexity of its working within life's web.

On sheep, wolves and the dangers of 'stupidity' in human activity

These are considerations that provide an important opening for the second part of this book and our attempts to look constructively at Deleuze's proposal – how we read and comprehend his ideas – so as to put them to work in the production of *a* psychology. Deleuze liked the indeterminacy of the article 'a' for it stands in stark contrast with the violence of 'the'. If we are to look at a productive articulation of Deleuze's ideas in the working of psychology, the first step is to move away from claims of transcendental certainty. When it comes to psychology, such claims are wrapped in representational claims and present an abundance of good and common sense yet, by the timidity of their internal structure – which includes a concern with error – reduce psychological knowledge to 'a kind of radio quiz' obsessed with 'artificial or puerile situations' (Deleuze, 1994, p. 150) rather than substantive knowledge regarding the human dilemma. Deleuze made this reference when commenting on the dangers of a focus on error as the threat or the opposite to thought, for error can only be identified where the answer is already known. As discussed in Chapter 3, Deleuze and Guattari saw only psychoanalysis, among the available versions of psychology, as a force to be reckoned with. Deleuze's concern is with the more familiar forms of psychology – what is often thought of as composed of empirical and behavioural psychology. His words in this respect are sobering when challenging common sense assumptions of habit:

> How are we to explain the fact that … we feel ourselves in effect so close to the mystery of habit, yet recognise nothing of what is 'habitually' called habit? Perhaps the reason lies in the illusions of psychology, which made a fetish of activity. Its unreasonable fear of introspection allowed it to observe only that which moved. It asks how we acquire habits in acting, but the entire theory of learning risks being misdirected so long as the prior question is not posed – namely, whether it is through acting that we acquire habits … *or whether, on the contrary, it is through contemplating?* Psychology regards it as established that the self cannot contemplate itself. This however, is not the question. The question is whether or not the self itself is a contemplation, whether it is not in itself a contemplation, and whether we can learn, form behaviour and form ourselves other than through contemplation.
>
> *Deleuze, 1994, p. 73*

Deleuze's take on psychology needs, first and foremost, to assert thought and the constructive and complex nature of life as it is experienced in a chaosmos. This is to say, it needs to assert the active engagement of a life in the process of production: in the process of making sense and producing a response to the problem of living. Deleuze's take on psychology will also acknowledge the plurality of possible sustainable responses to the human dilemma. There is no *one right* way in life but an ever expanding number of possibilities. Here, we can start to appreciate a 'darker' side to psychology's timidity and its preoccupation with error.

For Deleuze, more than error, it is 'stupidity [*bêtise*]' that is of concern. Stupidity 'haunts' thinking (Deleuze, 1994, p. 151) in ways more disturbing and more foundational than error, for stupidity is a state of thought 'where we possess the simple *possibility* of thought, but do not yet think' (Zourabichvili, 2012, p. 8). Zourabichvili extends this definition by explaining that in stupidity, people negotiate the actualities – the pre-existing possibilities – 'and the relative truths and falsities that came to be inscribed within them' (2012, p. 8) without any disturbance of the status quo. In stupidity, movement and differentiation are taken out of the equation of life. Once this happens, what is left is in close resemblance with Foucault's notion of 'docile bodies' (1991): bodies that do not present resistance to the present as Deleuze would say. What is missing in stupidity is not error – a mistake or distortion in thought as a representation – but a lack of individuation (Deleuze, 1994, p. 151). Here we also see a connection between stupidity and (lack of) life itself for Deleuze because, as we have explained, for Deleuze 'Life exists only in being differentiated' (Zourabichvili, 1996, p. 195). This connection, then, between stupidity, life and individuation, affords a shift to the social and to the importance for psychology to focus on identifying what is not only 'important' but also 'singular' (Deleuze, 1994, p. 190) in the constitution of the individual. Deleuze referred to stupidity in three of his early books: *Nietzsche and Philosophy*, *Proust and Signs* and *Difference and Repetition*. The concept went underground since then, but is very much present in his constant focus on differentiation through singularities and through a resistance to what is taken for granted in life.

   In the writing of this book, we have tried to keep as a central thread Holland's question as to the type of social organisation we are supporting through our activities as citizens within societies. This question can be used to engage with the ethics of our activities as researchers and as practitioners in psychology. Are we, through our actions, engaging with a society that can be recognised as a herd or are we individuals within a pack? In other words, one of the key questions we must address in our discipline if we are to perform this turn into what is important and what is singular, is how seriously is the discipline addressing issues of diversity and complexity? We have little doubt that psychology has to some extent recognised the value of diversity and of respect for difference, yet we would argue that the timidity that we have referred to has hindered significantly this desire and has stupefied our pursuits. As we have explained, such timidity manifests itself in a return to predefined patterns of thoughts – it folds back into itself and, by relying on common and good sense, finds what is already known and familiar. Deleuze's proposal challenges psychology to move away and differentiate out of this timidity. It challenges psychology to have the courage to look at its own stupidity and plunge into the uncertainty of dealing with the unknown so as to explore and support newness and complexity in terms of the possibilities of existence available to us humans. In attempting to answer the critical question regarding the kind of world we are living in – a question that must be asked in tandem with the question of what kind of world is *worth* living in – a critical distinction needs to be established. Both the question and the method used in such a quest does not refer to 'a world as it is' but to 'an empirical world we construct through our actions'. We are aware that the 'world as it is' is a concerning state of affairs. Terrorism, warfare, financial crisis and climate change go hand in hand with increased social inequity, even destitution, with breakdowns in community life and an increase in stress and 'mental illness'. In many ways, it is seductive to give in to the temptation of taking a judgemental position and making claims as to what has gone wrong. If arrogance permits, we could even make claims as to how to resolve it with the proviso that this would only be possible should we have the 'power' to make such changes or, a variation of the same, if the leaders in power were to follow 'our' judgement. There is indeed nothing wrong in looking for solutions. The problem is the form – the structure of thought – in which this search takes shape, for such a judgement often has the implied corollary that we, the citizens who are 'different' from the sovereign, the one who has power, have little capacity to effect change. In a transcendental world, change – and responsibility – lies elsewhere. This process of 'judging' according to Deleuze is part of the problem. We do not need more rational judgement but an engagement with an ever-increasing multitude of activities moving 'against the grain' of totalising practices. It is not the 'world out there' that Deleuze invites us to 'judge' but to an engagement with ways to make 'our world' more real and more honest to its life, which is to say, more complex and diverse.

There is some value at this point in returning to Deleuze and Guattari's reference to the Wolf-Man for it invites a number of further considerations relevant to these issues and how Deleuze defines a way forward. This return is already sketched by Deleuze himself when discussing *bêtise* and *bête*, which are translated respectively as 'stupidity' and 'stupid'. Yet, as Derrida accurately noted, these are words that cannot be translated adequately (2007, p. 37). Even in French, Derrida continues to clarify, 'there is no stable semantic context that could univocally guarantee a safe translation from one pragmatic use ... into another' (2007, pp. 37–8). Derrida himself uses the word *bête* in his studies regarding political issues of governance (2009). It is interesting to note that in the case of Derrida, the word *bête* is translated as 'beast', making a useful connection with animals. But Deleuze is quick in clarifying that 'Stupidity [*bêtise*] is not animality. The animal is protected by specific forms which prevent it from being "stupid" [*bête*]' (1994, p. 150). In his anti-humanism, Deleuze saw a continuity between humans and animals, whereas Derrida was more concerned with the differences between animals and humans, in particular when considering the law. Deleuze, in his desire to break away from 'all too human' forms of organisation, saw value in the idea of 'becoming-animal' (Deleuze and Guattari, 1987, Plateau 10). By himself and in conjunction with Guattari, Deleuze worked through the similarities and the differences we have with animals. As will become clear later in the chapter, stupidity has to do with the latter, with the differences. Prior to moving to the singularity of our human condition, it would be worth pausing to consider the value Deleuze and Guattari saw in working from the similarities that humans have with animals, in particular the distinctions that emerge with the Wolf-Man.

Deleuze and Guattari offer a critique of psychoanalysis' reading of the dilemmas that the Wolf-Man presented. Among their main observations is that the wolf is not a dog, it is not a domesticated animal that establishes a, for the lack of a better word, 'one-to-one' relationship with a household and a master. It is neither a cow nor a sheep, herd animals which, like the dog although in a less privileged manner, have a docile relationship with a master. The wolf moves in packs: it hunts, plays, rests and lives in constant relation, not to a master, but to the pack. This is to say, wolves live among equals, organising themselves in relation to the tasks at hand. This is not to say that they have the same tasks, not even the same status, but that the differences are not inherent as characteristics of 'special' wolves nor as hereditary privileges. The characteristics of the pack are in constant negotiation. This is of importance to Deleuze. As we have been exploring throughout this book, there are some consistent elements in the sometimes bewildering complexity of Deleuze's thought. One of these is the primacy of a 'differing difference' and another is the claim that the social organises itself immanently, with phenomena – the 'things' we observe – and individual subjectivity being results that 'emerge out' of productive processes. As productions, they all possess an equal status. Their manifestations might vary, but they are all equal in terms of substance and status. What differs is their functionality and relevance in different settings. This is, however, not a reason for privilege – and thus inequality – but for discernment as to what is relevant when and for what purposes. It is in this sense that for Deleuze, there is no right or wrong way of doing things but the presence or absence of well-posed problems. Having a lack of understanding of these conditions is often at the base of dismissive judgment. Discernment does not refer 'just' to a type of theoretical calculation – a type of logical formula – that affords a reasoned judgement, but to an existential engagement with the life we live, an engagement that calls forth modes of living. It is in this sense that what is at stake for Deleuze is not morality but an evaluative ethics, an ethics that helps us engage with problems not only in meaningful but also honourable – that is to say, non-stupid – ways. As he writes,

> it is the solution that counts, but the problem always has the solution it deserves, in terms of the way in which it is stated (i.e., the conditions under which it is determined as problem), and of the means and terms at our disposal for stating it. In this sense, the history of man, from the theoretical as much as from the practical point of view is that of the construction of problems. It is here that humanity makes its own history, and the becoming conscious of that activity is like the conquest of freedom.
>
> *Deleuze, 1988a, p. 16*

An evaluative ethics then confront us with the fact that life is not a static process but an existential and constructive call; for not taking for granted the state of affairs but proactively to engage in the construction of the world. If we are to go back to the wolf and its pack, the actions of the wolves need to be considered in the context of their activity within the pack. Their position and the activities they engage with – for example, hunting – cannot be fully described as instinctual, as pertaining to some internal stable essence, but include an evaluative engagement with their circumstances – the geographical conditions in which the hunt takes place as well as the nature of their prey – as well as their role in the pack. Holland summarises these ideas well when he writes 'At the limit, packs form multiplicities that resist totalization, unification, and reduction to a homogeneous mass' (2013, p. 95). To consider the nature of the wolf's movements without these 'external' relations would be to miss it in the same way that such understanding would also be lost if one attempted to read their behaviours in terms that are so general they position 'the pack' at the same level as 'the herd'. For Deleuze, this type of analysis calls for an 'ethology of a new order' (Buchanan, 2008, p. 155).

Ethological considerations on (human) life

There is indeed a connection between Deleuze's interest in ethology and modern psychology's approach to human beings through the study of their behaviours. But, as with the transformations we have seen Deleuze exerting in the concept of empiricism – transformations that have left this methodology almost unrecognisable to psychology – Deleuze's approach to (animal) behaviour leads to unfamiliar conceptual landscapes. This is so because behaviour is seen not 'in itself' or in connections with individual cognitions but through particular ethological conceptualisations. Deleuze saw in the ethology of Jakob von Uexküll the application of many of Spinoza's ideas (1988b, p. 124). Deleuze and Guattari did not make direct reference to von Uexküll in *Anti-Oedipus* even when it is hard not to see a connection between their reference to the 'stroll' of a schizophrenic (1983, p. 2) and von Uexküll's work, starting with the title to his book – *A Stroll Through the Environments of Animals and Humans* (1934). In this book, von Uexküll critically investigates mechanistic understandings of animals and men, as '*mere* machines' (1934, emphasis added, p. 5). His critique was not against machines[1] but against mechanistic approaches that 'pieced together the sensory and motor organs of animals, like so many parts of a machine, ignoring their real functions of perceiving and acting' (1934, p. 6). Earlier than better known ethologists like Konrad Lorenz and his studies on 'imprinting' in geese, von Uexküll's ethology introduced what Buchanan would describe as 'a new way of thinking about reality' and von Uexküll was one of the 'first to really push for the subjective experience of the animal' (2008, p. 2). Buchanan uses the word *onto-ethology* to refer to this new type of ethological thinking. Explaining this idea from von Uexküll, Buchanan writes: 'The being of the animal unfolds through its behaviour and we catch a glimpse of this from within its own environment, its bubble-like *Umwelten*.'

Umwelt – and its plural *Umwelten* – is German for 'environment' or 'surrounding'. In explaining von Uexküll's *Umwelt*, Deely describes it as

> the physical environment as filtered by the given organism according to what is 'significant' to it. . . . *Umwelten* are thus species-specific: No two types of organisms live in the same objective worlds, even though they share the same physical environment.
>
> *Deely, 1986, p. 269*

It is easy then to understand why such a concept is so appealing for a materialist Deleuze. In line with an appreciation of life as an ordering of chaos promoted by Deleuze, and with Maturana and Varela's idea of 'structural determinism' (1998), for von Uexküll 'organisms are selective *interpreters*; they are perceiving and acting subjects that do not respond to external effects in a causal-mechanical way, but rather with specific, autonomous responses' (Bains, 2006, pp. 61–2).

This reorientation of ethology has three relevant aspects for Deleuze. The first is a reorientation of the definition of bodies away from essences – away from identity – into capacities and activities: 'you do not know beforehand what a body or a mind can do' (Deleuze, 1988b, p. 125). Rather than a (hypothetical) essence, *actual* capacities. Capacity for Deleuze refers to what affects the organism and, in turn, what is affected by the organism: what can the body hear, smell? What is it that moves it and what is moved by it? It is in this sense that an animal is always seen in its relation with its world. In direct reference to von Uexküll, Deleuze uses the example of the tick and its specific *Umwelt*. The tick has an environment that is defined by three particular affects:

> the first has to do with light (climb to the top of a branch); the second is olfactive (let yourself fall onto the mammal that passes beneath the branch); and the third is thermal (seek the area without fur, the warmest spot).
>
> *1988b, p. 124*

This orientation towards capacities brings forth an interesting transformation of our traditional definitions of the living world. Deleuze can claim, for example, that 'there are greater differences between a plow horse or draft horse and a racehorse than between an ox and a plow horse' (1988b, p. 124). We can appreciate here, once again, the resonances between Deleuze's work and Foucault's insights on the power of discourse, insights that Foucault owed to his reading of Borges' *The Analytical Language of John Wilkins* (Foucault, 2004b, p. xvi). In this essay, Borges questions the merits of the work done by the Anglican clergyman and natural philosopher John Wilkins (1614–72) in developing a universal language. Referring also to Hume, Borges comments that '[w]e must go even further, and suspect that there is no universe in the organic, unifying sense of that ambitious word. If there is, then we must speculate on its purpose; we must speculate on the words, definition, etymologies, and synonymies of God's secret dictionary' (Borges, 1942, p. 231).

The second aspect inherent to this approach to ethology refers to these capacities being realised – being fulfilled – not according to a logical consequence of their internal structure, but according to their relationships with their circumstances. Again in reference to Spinoza, the affects of an animal – the relation that such an animal establishes with its *Umwelt* – can either 'sadly' diminish its powers or 'joyfully' increase them. It is here that the evaluations of what is good or bad – the ethical dimension – becomes visible. Deleuze calls for unique and immanent rather than transcendental assessments, which is to say that what is good for one animal can be bad for another. Even more so, what is good for an animal in one set of circumstances may no longer be in another. 'Goodness' and 'badness' are relational terms rather than normative ones. This is a powerful warning for psychology as we will discuss later, in particular in relation to the semiotic complexities proper to human life and to the psy-complex.

The final aspect relevant to this ethological approach is that it 'studies the compositions of relations or capacities between different things' (Deleuze, 1988b, p. 126). In other words, this approach to ethology explores and tries to give an account of the presence of increased complexity in life. It is here that Deleuze and Guattari's concept of *assemblage* becomes relevant. Such a study brings to the fore a number of questions for Deleuze. As he writes:

> How do individuals enter into composition with one another in order to form a higher individual, ad infinitum? How can a being take another being into its world, but while preserving or respecting the other's own relations and world? And in this regard, what are the different types of sociabilities for example? What is the difference between the society of human beings and the community of rational beings?
>
> (1988b, p. 126)

The composability of individuals into higher individuals is central to our social nature. It is here that the question of herds or packs emerges as both genuine and relevant. Prior to addressing this question, however, there is value in exploring in more detail the issue of composability, for it is here that a claim for a 'radically reenvisioned' ethology lies (Buchanan, 2008, p. 159). It is here that ethology shows that it 'has less to do with the study of behaviour per se than it does with the continual becomings that compose different bodies' and that, as Deleuze and Guattari state elsewhere, 'the notion of behaviour proves inadequate, too linear, in comparison with that of the assemblage' (Deleuze and Guattari, 1987, p. 333). Rather than behaviour, what is important for Deleuze and Guattari is 'the exchange of actions and passions so as to participate in the 'composing of a more powerful body' (1987, p. 257) – the assemblage and the construction of territories.

The refrain and territorial assemblages

This move to ethological considerations of behaviour brings to the fore an important concept for Deleuze and Guattari, a concept that is intimately connected with the notion of assemblage: the territory, or perhaps more accurately, the process of territorialisation. Before getting into the practicalities of this concept, there is value in discussing briefly the concept of the refrain, a translation from the Italian word, ritornello. The refrain is the title of Plateau 11, where the notion of territory and territorialisation is explained. This plateau continues the explanations of Deleuze and Guattari's alternative metaphysical chaosmos by looking in more detail at the more complex self-emerging elements of chaosmos. As Holland explains, this plateau 'picks up where the Geology plateau left off, exploring in further detail the alloplastic stratum' (2013, p. 66). Borrowing from Ferenczi, and possibly Freud, 'alloplastic' is the name Deleuze and Guattari use to describe the third and last stratum of chaosmos composition, with inorganic and organic being the first two. Alloplastic provides a characterisation of human behaviour but is not exclusive to humans. It refers to those animals that 'bring about modifications in the external world' (Deleuze and Guattari, 1987, p. 60). In this stratum, 'expression becomes linguistic rather than genetic; in other words, it operates with symbols that are comprehensible, transmittable, and modifiable from the outside' (Deleuze and Guattari, 1987, p. 60). As perhaps expected, the passing from the organic stratum into the alloplastic one is the passing from animals living in a certain milieu – a certain ecological niche – to animals establishing a territory.

Giving the refrain the status of the title of a whole plateau in *A Thousand Plateaus* confirms the centrality of this concept in the thought of its authors. In fact, Deleuze once commented – perhaps jokingly – that the refrain in philosophy is 'the new' concept they have created (Deleuze and Eribon, 1991, p. 381). Their use of the refrain serves two functions. First, it once again moves thought away from visual representations into the domain of music – in particular, musical variation – where a (Bergsonian) duration becomes central. Second, it articulates the idea present in *Difference and Repetition* that it is in repetition that identity is established. A refrain – a word that also means a bird's song in French – is defined by the *Oxford Dictionary* as 'a recurring phrase', a type of musical chorus. The function of this repetition is to highlight the central themes or dilemmas articulated in the musical piece. This is a critical difference from our modes of representation based on the visual for, instead of measures, music is based on *rhythm*. As Holland states, 'Rhythm is utterly distinct from meter (in the same way that smooth space can be distinguished from striated)' (2013, p. 67). Meter is a standard tool of measurement, created artificially – as other such tools – for purposes that serve closely the interests of the State (e.g. the measure of the land for tax and rent considerations), whereas rhythm, as Holland – following Deleuze and Guattari – states, is

> 'the Unequal or … Incommensurable' relation of difference between milieus. 'Meter is dogmatic', as Deleuze & Guattari put it, 'but rhythm is critical: it ties together critical moments, or ties itself together in passing from one milieu to another'. The wing-span and flapping tempo of a fly are metrical, as are the circuits of a spider spinning its web and the dimension of the resulting mesh: the relations between the two set up a rhythm. 'It is as though the spider had a fly in its head.' … In this case the rhythm is predatory (the mesh-span is 'designed' to be smaller than the wing-span); in others it is symbiotic, as with snapdragons and bumblebees, orchids and wasps. In their complex networks of relations with the surrounding environment, milieu components (such as wing-span or mesh-size) become 'melodies in counterpoint, each of which serves as a motif for another: Nature as music.'
>
> *Holland, 2013, p. 67, emphasis and references omitted*

Deleuze and Guattari use the refrain across the realm of their metaphysics to account for the layers of composition present in chaosmos. Milieus – the non-organic environment out of which living emerges – is composed in a rhythmical way. Having this central idea in mind – of 'Nature as music' – the emergence of complexity takes place through the repetition of motifs, repetition or constancy. The difference between 'a milieu', in which animal behaviours are functional, and 'a territory' is marked by the presence of a 'temporal constancy and a spatial range' (Deleuze and Guattari, 1987, p. 315). In this sense, the territory is a more complex presentation of a milieu, one that – due to its constancy – affords the emergence of new qualities in particular, the emergence of the assemblage.

We have examined the concept of assemblage in Chapters 1 and 2. There is, however, value in exploring assemblages further by focusing on their activity. As we have indicated, for Deleuze and Guattari, ethological considerations provide a good understanding of our human way of functioning. It is particularly in the context of the last of the three considerations discussed above – regarding the composition of larger bodies – that we can more fully appreciate Deleuze's articulation of the notion of assemblage. Assemblages can be regarded as compounds made up of a number of elements, some material and some symbolic or semiotic. This distinction moves us out of the domain of simple milieus and individual *Umwelten* and refers instead to more complex systems. It is in this sense that assemblages are not contained within the individual – they are not a possession of an individual – and escape traditional definitions of self. Assemblages transverse through individuals, radically transforming traditional conceptualisations of individuals; bodies are no longer the loci of individual subjectivity but are at the crossroads of a multitude of assemblages. Furthermore, in a way that actualises the openness of the system, assemblages are in movement; they are the result of a process of *territorialisation* of space.

There is a temptation here again to revert to traditional systemic conceptualisations, and the classical image of 'animals creating their ecological niches' might appear to be a simpler way of describing this. As expected, however, as with all of Deleuze's concepts, there is a twist that is meaningful. As Holland comments, although all animals belong to a certain environment and have a specific *Umwelt*, not all animals have a territory (2013, p. 67). A certain milieu – an ecological niche – becomes a territory when such a space 'ceases to be merely functional (e.g., predatory or symbiotic) and become expressive instead. And what they express first and foremost is territoriality itself' (Holland, 2013, p. 68). Deleuze and Guattari explain this transition by stating that 'There is territory precisely when milieu components cease to be directional, becoming dimensional instead' (1987, p. 315). This is not to say that they don't fulfil a functional aspect. They still do but they do more than that: expression transcends the function and, recursively, starts to determine function. So, what was initially a functional response determined by a certain set of either internal or external conditions, now becomes a distinct and consistent trait in the context of a specific territory. Birds' songs are prime examples of this process of territorialisation for Deleuze and Guattari. A bird's song is usually related to courting but it can become more than that, such that birds sing or emit sounds resembling their environment, such as the lyre bird. When a territory is established by the bird, its song becomes an element of courtship only within their specified territory. In this context, expression acquires a certain autonomy in relation to function. It is in the expressivity of the territory that art emerges, giving rise to one of Deleuze and Guattari's most famous sayings: 'art [does] not wait for human beings to begin' (1987, p. 320). It is also in this sense that Holland talks about 'onto-aesthetics' for it is art – the aesthetic dimension – rather than the genetic, the instinctual or the learned in itself that defines the parameters of existence for territorial animals.

Deleuze and Guattari clarify that the territory must be seen as referring to the assemblage rather than to the animal. Although the animal performs the territorialisation – the act of creating a territory – the territory, once established, becomes larger than the animal, which then becomes only one of its parts. This change in the order of things is similar to the change that takes place when a certain behaviour expands into a territorialising behaviour. Here, function becomes subordinated to expression once the function takes expressive qualities. The territory – as an emerging quality – has a life of its own that exceeds the individual. It is in this excess, this surplus, that territories takes precedence over behaviours as commonly understood and this is where it makes sense for Deleuze and Guattari to state that 'the notion of behaviour proves inadequate, too linear, in comparison with that of the assemblage' (1987, p. 333). In line with Batesonian insights on logical categories of learning (Bateson, 1964), behaviour cannot be seen as independent of its context. With territory, the notion of context is further articulated and is connected to a constructive act. Behaviour and context are not separate things but emerging qualities of a complex system.

Deleuze loved animals like the tick and disliked domesticated ones, in particular cats (Boutang, 2012, A for animal). This a gesture that is not only consistent with his project but again reminds us of another relevant advantage to psychology of the conceptualisation of human behaviour in terms of ethology. Deleuze and Guattari valued the ability of ethologists to 'have retained the integrality of a certain undivided "terrain"' (1987, p. 328). They saw in this approach 'a great advantage over ethnologies [because] they did not fall into the structural danger of dividing an undivided "terrain" into forms of kinship, politics, economics, myth, etc' (1987, p. 328). This is not to say, however, that Deleuze and Guattari overlooked the social. We have already commented how Deleuze and Guattari reversed the explanatory framework through what Holland aptly described as the ISSO (Intra-Species Social Organization) and we have talked also about the dangers of stupidity and the importance of differentiation within a pack. It is in this context that structure needs to be seen in interplay with geopolitical circumstances and turned into a type of tragic condition where we – as humans – are left with the task of creating an existence of sorts. It is in this sense that Deleuze and Guattari see great value in the concept of (a fluid) territory rather than (a stable) structure. As they state, 'How very important it is, when chaos threatens, to draw an inflatable, portable territory. If need be, I'll put my territory on my own body' (1987, p. 320).

Prior to moving into specific dilemmas proper to living a human life – dilemmas we will expand on in the next chapter – it is important that we examine a distinctive element pertaining to the human condition: the symbolic. As Holland states, 'there is also something distinctive about human behaviour: it is mediated not just through territories and refrains, but also through the Symbolic Order or semiotic stratum' (2013, p. 76). It is in fact at this level that distinctions between packs and herds can be established in our human condition because, as perhaps it is redundant to state, humans are not wolves, cows or birds. Deleuze, however, uses the notion of *becoming-animal* as a key concept to put to work the idea that what constitutes reality is not essences but processes. In this sense, and as we will expand on in the next chapter, rather than a humanistic approach to becoming – where 'what becomes' is our true human nature – for Deleuze becoming is a moving away from the position in which we find ourselves. Rather than 'becoming one-self', one becomes 'other'. Furthermore, and in line with Nietzsche's *Human, All Too Human*, one becomes something other than (an-other) 'human', one becomes initially *animal* and eventually *imperceptible*. We will discuss further the implications of Deleuze's take on the concept of becoming in the next chapter. First, it is important to return to the role of the symbolic or semiotic order for Deleuze and Guattari.

Semiotics and regimes of signs

It is through the understanding of the central role that the refrain – and ultimately music – plays in Deleuze and Guattari's metaphysics that we can start to grasp how semiotic elements connect with territories and with individual animals. As Deleuze and Guattari explain 'As matters of expression take on consistency they constitute semiotic systems' (1987, p. 334). Once again, the anti-humanist approach is confirmed because the semiotic element is not exclusive to humans even though it certainly is core to human activity. Even more so, humanistic assumptions often conceal Western ethnocentric assumptions regarding the human condition for, as we discuss below under 'faciality', 'The face is not universal ... the face is the typical European' (Deleuze and Guattari, 1987, p. 176).

Semiotic considerations of a kind have been circulating in psychology for some time. Discursive and social constructionist ideas in the field have emphasised the role of language in the formation of subjectivity and have had some success in introducing the value of diverse methodologies within the discipline of psychology, particularly in relation to qualitative research. Furthermore, Gergen has particularly emphasized that psychology, as a discipline, should be transformative (1985). These insights, however, have only partially explored symbolic issues if we are to read them in the light of Deleuze's insights. This is partly so because social constructionism relies significantly on phenomenological and humanistic assumptions. In doing this, and in line with the concerns we have already discussed in Chapter 3 regarding methodological limitations, social constructionism stops short of realising the radical implications of a fully articulated philosophy of difference.

Deleuze and Guattari provide an interesting expansion on semiotic and discursive aspects familiar to the discipline, an expansion that we can only cursorily refer to in this book, for an appropriate treatment of Deleuze's work on language and its implications for psychology merits a book on its own terms. For the purposes of this book, however, we will focus on the critical issues highlighted by Deleuze and Guattari in *A Thousand Plateaus* by articulating a nuanced material and ethological understanding of the elements participating at the semiotic level, namely language, 'faciality' and 'money'.

Language

In order to understand Deleuze and Guattari's take on language, we must understand their concerns regarding the taken for granted. Deleuze is against unreflective approaches to language and against considering communication as unproblematic and as a necessarily good thing. As Colombat indicates, 'Deleuze's entire work rebukes the notion of sign as it was defined by theologians (St Augustine) and by linguists (Saussure)' (2000, p. 14). For the purposes of this book, we will look at language mainly through what Deleuze and Guattari write on language in *A Thousand Plateaus*. With respect to language Deleuze and Guattari make reference to two levels: on the one hand, there is what we often associate with linguistics, that is, the study of language; and, on the other, there is what they call the 'regime of signs' which partly resembles the idea of discourse in that it connects language to wider socio-political issues. Plateau 4 of *A Thousand Plateaus* – *November 20, 1923: Postulates of Linguistics* – deals with their concerns regarding the often accepted assumptions found in linguistics regarding the way language operates. In this plateau, Deleuze and Guattari overturn four fundamental linguistic postulates. The first postulate – 'Language Is Informational and Communicational' (1987, p. 75) – is questioned through highlighting that language is not used to communicate information but to order and to compel obedience to a certain form of organisation, primarily, to the State: 'The compulsory education machine does not communicate information; it imposes upon the child semiotic coordinates possessing all of the dual foundations of grammar (masculine-feminine, singular-plural, noun-verb, ..., etc' (1987, pp. 75–6). In line with structuralist insights, language is not a neutral (individual) expression but a positioning of individuals within 'regimes of signs'. In this sense, 'Language is not life; it gives life orders. Life does not speak; it listens and waits. Every order-word ... carries a little death sentence – a Judgement' (1987, p. 76; see also Skott-Myhre, 2015, p. 310). The transformations expressed in language are not related to the variations in life but to what is convenient and desirable for the established order. This is the context of Deleuze and Guattari dating this plateau to the day in 1923 that the German Mark was pegged so as to stop hyperinflation. Rather than its internal grammar, the emphasis they give to language then is in its use and its effects. Aligning themselves with aspects of early systemic insights (Watzlawick *et al.*, 1967), Deleuze and Guattari consider pragmatics to be 'the cornerstone of linguistics, rather than an ancillary or marginal sub-discipline' (Holland, 2013, p. 79; see also Deleuze and Guattari, 1987, pp. 77–8).

The second orthodox linguistic postulate can be paraphrased as 'Language can and should be understood separately from "extrinsic" factors' (Holland, 2013, p. 77; see also Deleuze and Guattari, 1987, pp. 85–91) and the third 'There Are Constants or Universals of Language That Enable Us to Define It as a Homogeneous System' (Deleuze and Guattari, 1987, p. 92). The critiques of these postulates offered by Deleuze and Guattari are usefully considered together. Traditional linguistics studies language as a system following an internal structure. Such a study is, in some ways, counterintuitive to our common experience. In everyday life, we see words as having a direct and unproblematic relationship with external 'things'. Things are, it seems, what we perceive. It was Saussure who proposed that word meaning can be understood as having two interplaying elements – signified and signifier – which need to be understood within the larger context of language as a whole system. From Saussure onwards, there has been an increasing interest in looking at the interplay *between* signifiers, at times – particularly in so-called postmodern approaches – questioning the value of 'the signified' altogether. As Bogue explains, for Deleuze this is inadequate for at least three reasons: the problem of reference is either subsumed within a logic of representation or simply bracketed, and hence ignored; the signifier dominates the signified and ultimately effaces the sign as an object of analysis; and the reign of the signifier encourages a textualism that either makes the real coextensive with language or closes language in on itself, thereby assigning pragmatics a secondary function outside linguistics.

Bogue, 2004, p. 110.

The materialist approach of Deleuze questions this approach in interesting ways. Finding a nuanced alternative to an unproblematic relationship between a word and a thing and to the notion that language needs to be considered only in terms of its internal organisation, Deleuze and Guattari conceive language and material elements as conjugating into productive assemblages that constitute the social field. In assemblages, as Holland states, 'corporeal practices and effects take place in reciprocal presupposition with the discursive practices and vice versa' (2013, p. 79). The critique then is twofold. At one level that runs in parallel with Saussurean and systemic conceptualisations, it is emphasised that it is inadequate to think in terms of isolated words relating with individual things 'out there' – with individual 'things' with clearly distinct separate elements, language and materiality. Words must be thought of instead as emerging out of material fields and within complex material-semiotic systems. At another level the critique is against the positioning of language as a commentator on the corporeal or material. As Deleuze and Guattari say, 'Representations are bodies too! ... Expressions are inserted into contents, in which we ceaselessly jump from one register to another' (1987, pp. 86–7). The evocative power of memory in one's behaviour – Proust's madeleine – is a simple example of this dynamic. Another, perhaps more complex, example can be found in the clinical work with the systemic notion of 'reframe', where the careful use of different words can bring forth significantly different bodily and systemic responses (Watzlawick *et al.*, 1974). Language, in this sense, is poorly served if it is only evaluated in its internal (grammatical) form, needing instead to be considered in its material dimension. Language is also equally poorly served if such evaluation is through standardised and predictable patterns.

To explore Deleuze and Guattari's critique of the fourth and last postulate, we need to return to the distinction between royal and nomad sciences, in particular the different positions that language has within these sciences. This postulate states that 'Language Can Be Scientifically Studied

Only Under the Conditions of a Standard or Major Language' (Deleuze and Guattari, 1987, p. 100, emphasis added). For Deleuze and Guattari, this orientation in linguistics leads linguistics to establish an unexamined alliance with dominant forms of power; an alliance that has significant deleterious effects for difference and processes of differentiation. As they write, 'the scientific model taking language as an object of study is one with the political model by which language is homogenized, centralized, standardized, becoming a language of power, a major or dominant language' (1987, p. 101). To express the point more fully, they add a little later in the paragraph that 'The scientific enterprise of extracting constants and constant relations is always coupled with the political enterprise of imposing them on speakers and transmitting order-words.' This critique has strong resonances with concerns about the scientific and disciplinarian practices within psychology which we will discuss a little later. At this point, however, we would like to expand further in the alternative that Deleuze and Guattari propose: an alternative that builds on and illuminates the distinction between royal and nomad science. As they write,

> Must a distinction then be made between two kinds of language, 'high' and 'low,' major and minor? The first would be defined precisely by the power (*pouvoir*) of constants, the second by the power (*puissance*) of variation. We do not simply wish to make an opposition between the unity of a major language and the multiplicity. Rather, each dialect has a zone of transition and variation; or better, each minor language has a properly dialectical zone of variation.
>
> (1987, p. 101)

For Deleuze and Guattari, rather than language being judged by its integrity with respect to an original purity, these 'kinds' of language point more to the movement that takes place in a language, the differentiation into a different type of language altogether. Of course, differentiation is central to Deleuze but, as discussed in Chapter 1, it is a focus on conceptualisation in movement – in experimental thought – that is key. The distinctions of language made by Deleuze and Guattari are not distinctions that set these types of language in competition with each other. It is not a matter of 'either/or' but of different uses of language or of languages. As they explain, 'there is no language that does not have intralinguistic, endogenous, internal minorities' (1987, p. 103). The relation between major and minor language calls, then, for an appreciation of its dynamics and transformations; of how each informs and participates in the construction of the other. As Deleuze and Guattari say, 'the more a language has or acquires the characteristics of a major language, the more it is affected by continuous variations that transpose it into a "minor" language' (1987, p. 102). It is in this sense that Deleuze and Guattari call for a recognition of science as being able to accommodate different treatments of the same language: 'either the variables are treated in such a way as to extract from them constants and constant relations or in such a way as to place them in continuous variation' (1987, p. 103). As we will explain in more detail in the next chapter, Deleuze favoured the latter − continuous variation − for it is in this orientation that the affirmation of multiplicity and of difference takes place. It is easy to see the focus on major language by linguistics as a form of royal science, which helps in turn to identify the connection between nomad science and a minor linguistics. This difference of treatment can also be applied to the discipline of psychology.

Faciality

'Faciality' is the second semiotic structure of relevance for Deleuze and Guattari. It is analysed in two of the plateaus of *A Thousand Plateaus*, one of which is entirely dedicated to this issue: *Plateau 7. Year Zero: Faciality*. In some ways, faciality is their response to the idea of subjectivity. Reference has been made above to Deleuze and Guattari's concerns with the *Urdoxa* present in phenomenological conceptualisations, by which they mean a doxa that affirms a transcendental human individuality through taken-for-granted universal structures of experience. Deleuze and Guattari question the concept of a transcendental subjectivity or human essence. Here the distinction is nuanced because Deleuze and Guattari do not question the presence of subjectivity but the validity of claims regarding a transcendental or universal subjectivity. In some ways, it could be argued, Deleuze and Guattari problematise the concept of subjectivity. They do so by adding a new element − faciality. This development will have significant implications when considering processes of individuations and strategies against *la bêtise*.

A simple way of describing faciality is to say that it refers to aspects of subjectivity that are socially recognised, perhaps even taken for granted: 'At any rate, you've been recognized, the abstract machine has you inscribed in its overall grid' (Deleuze and Guattari, 1987, p. 177). Monty Python's *The Life of Brian* presents a more humorous example when Brian was 'preaching' to the crowd, saying that 'they were all individuals' and the crowd replies, 'yes, we are all individuals' with a sole voice saying 'no, I'm not'. We will talk more about that lonely voice in the next chapter − about what Deleuze calls 'originals'. At the moment we want to focus on subjectivity as an articulation of a certain regime of sign. It is the face that 'crystallizes' the regime of sign, confirming a further refrain in the territory, a further solidification of a certain order of things. Regimes of signs, then, are not exhausted in language. Language goes hand in hand with a certain faciality: with a certain form of subjectivity that presents itself as common and good sense. As Deleuze and Guattari state, 'the signifier is always facialized. Faciality reigns materially over the whole constellation of signifiances and interpretations.... The mask does not hide the face, it *is* the face' (1987, p. 115).

An important consideration regarding facialisation is that it does not refer to just one face but the articulation of a semiotic system with multiple elements. The face is not individual but is a function of the assemblage. Each of the faces in the system, then, is in a position defined by the system and in intimate relationship with the other faces that complete the system and thus completes the initial face. Facialisation implies closure of the system and, through repetition, the creation of ever-increasing expansion of the territory by the incorporation of new elements into the familiar and predictable. As Deleuze and Guattari write,

> The complete system, then, consists of the paranoid face or body of the despot-god in the signifying center of the temple; the interpreting priests who continually recharge the signified in the temple, transforming it into signifier; the hysterical crowd of people outside, clumped into tight circles, who jump from one circle to another; the faceless, depressive scapegoat emanating from the centre, chosen, treated, and adorned by the priests, cutting across the circles in its headlong flight into the desert. This excessively hasty overview is applicable not only to the imperial despotic regime but to all subjected, arborescent, hierarchical, centered groups: political parties, literary movements, psychoanalytical [and psychological?] associations, families, conjugal units, etc.
>
> *1987, p. 116*

Deleuze returns to this double-headed symbolic presence in his later writings when he discusses philosophical concepts going hand in hand with certain *conceptual personae* (Deleuze and Guattari, 1991, ch. 3). This is not to say that the two – the facialisation of regimes of signs and the conceptual personae – are one and the same. Quite the contrary, they belong to opposite poles of human responses to the dilemmas of life. But they are good reminders of the underlying structures in Deleuze's thought.

Language is not of static entities but of systems in movement. Faciality crystallises assemblages, totalities, whereas the conceptual personae refer to the articulation of originals in thought. In this, the conceptual personae is an example of resistance to regimes of signs, an example of creative acts and an 'untimely' reminder that life is never exhausted in any process of territorialisation. It is in this sense that, for Deleuze and Guattari, more important than the familiarity we encounter in a recognised – or perhaps recognisable – subjectivity, is the counterintuitive movement of de-personalisation – of becoming imperceptible, of escaping the grid of significations whose familiarity comes at great cost.

Deleuze and Guattari's notion of faciality carries significant heuristic power for psychology and becomes very helpful in developing a more nuanced evaluation of psychology as a professional practice. The concept of faciality affords this because it connects subjectivity not with unique and autonomous individual phenomena but with complex participation in larger systems, in particular semiotic systems of interpretation. This nuanced evaluation brings forth a critical question regarding the uses and the effects of psychological practice and creates a distinction between normative psychology and the processes of individuation that Deleuze sees as central to all living activity. Life, health and our becomings in life stand in ongoing tension with the forces that Deleuze would call forces of sedimentation – of rigidification or ossification – that a too established regime of signs implies. In this sense, the distinction between the faciality available in a certain society, and the path of becoming 'originals', is central to understanding the distinction between a royal – State-like – and a minor psychology. This is a path that requires a painful dis-membering of the imposed set of normalities in one's life, a path full of pathos. Prior to discussing this distinction, we want to refer to the last of the semiotic structures identified by Deleuze and Guattari: money.

Money

Money, for Deleuze and Guattari, is a powerful element in the apparatuses of capture often associated with the State, and other masters in society. Money, like faciality, pertains to larger regimes of signs. Unlike faciality, money seems to belong to a level of analysis very distant from what is taught in psychology. Money as a phenomenon surely belongs to economics. It affects us – especially when there is not enough of it – but the idea of conceiving it as a semiotic system rather than as an economic unit seems somehow 'out of place', perhaps as much 'out of place' as politics or even religion. This sense of 'displacement', Deleuze and Guattari would perhaps argue, is due to the difficulties emerging out of unexamined assumptions in common and good sense in the Western world: assumptions that, in turn, facilitate certain types of government, even when these regimes are not desirable.

Money is perhaps the most material articulation of the productive flow constituting society and also perhaps the best way through which one can appreciate the effects of different types of circulation of surplus, of wealth, in modern societies. For Deleuze and Guattari, money is particularly important because it is a central piece within the structural mechanisms of capture implied in different regimes of signs, and has a particular role within despotic regimes as well as within capitalism. For Deleuze and Guattari, 'money' as a concept must be differentiated from 'exchange' because of the often unexamined implications of both concepts. Indeed, at face value, money facilitates exchange and disentangles value assumptions from different commodities. Although at many levels this is desirable – and thus, so the argument goes, the success of capitalism as an economic system – what is often left unexamined in this observation is the operations that afford such a move: operations that, Deleuze and Guattari would argue, hide more insidious mechanisms of capture of our becomings as human beings. For Deleuze and Guattari, money as we currently understand it emerges in the Greek city – the Corinthian tyranny in particular – where a general equivalence is established between money and goods and service. Money 'derived not from exchange, the commodity, or the demands of commerce, but from taxation' (Deleuze and Guattari, 1987, p. 442). As they explain,

> In the case of Corinth, metal money was first distributed to the 'poor' (in their capacity as producers) who used it to b[u]y land rights; it thus passed into the hands of the 'rich,' on the condition that it not stop there, that everyone, rich and poor, pay a tax, the poor in goods or services, the rich in money, such that an equivalence money-goods and services was established.
>
> (1987, p. 442)

Money then does not operate as a free-floating 'neutral' tool for exchange of commodities but serves – for lack of a better word – 'ulterior' motives serving the organisation of classes in society and, perhaps more importantly, it enables 'activities of the "free action" type ... to be compared, linked, and subordinated to a common and homogeneous quantity called labor' (Deleuze and Guattari, 1987, p. 442). More than money as a material object, what is important to note is the *circulation* of such money, where this type of circulation – more than money in itself – serves regulatory functions within a society.

These considerations might seem to exist in a kind of 'liminal zone' for psychology and to be of secondary importance to the discipline. We believe that such an understanding has more to do with taboos in our profession rather than with the actuality of the discipline. Suffice to notice the differences of salaries – between a medical professional, a psychologist, a therapist, a social worker and a counsellor – to quickly reveal the practical power that such definitions have in real life and the powerful elements of psychological practice that are left unexamined in mainstream considerations. Another powerful example of how money is an active participant in the systems in which we operate is the differences of provision of services when engaging in private versus public practice, differences that are far more profound than a simple exchange of money. The alleged psychoanalytic practice of charging clients for sessions that they know they will miss (not cancel) raises a number of questions about the role of the exchange of money between professional and client.

Psychology revisited: the psy-complex or a sheep in wolf's clothing

We believe that these critical clarifications – regarding an ethological approach to the human condition with notions like territory, language, money and regimes of sign – give us some powerful insights into the discipline of psychology; into its potentials and its dangers. Through these clarifications we are now in a position to look in more detail at what a Deleuzian psychology might look like and how it might work. We have already discussed the impact of Deleuze's ideas on two central elements of scientific psychology – its unit of analysis and its method. This encounter is, however, only one possible use of Deleuze's ideas: a reading that is fairly constrained, if not reactive. As we have discussed above, a more profound problem confronting psychology is that of stupidity, which is to say, a danger of being subsumed by normative State-like processes. These centralised and centralising processes are identified by Deleuze and Guattari as 'apparatus[es] of capture' (1987, Plateau 13). As we have clarified, stupidity does not pertain to animals per se because only those animals – in particular humans – who are able to get caught in regimes of signs face stupidity as a problem to be reckoned with.

It should be emphasised that Deleuze and Guattari are not calling for popular resistance to regimes of signs or for a world free of society or of apparatuses of capture. They are more likely to be humming songs from *The Rocky Horror Show* than from *Les Mis*. They are not even claiming that regimes of signs are not desirable (perhaps regimes of signs are, precisely, that which we desire); or that territorial spaces are 'bad things'. We cannot but exist in territories and within certain regimes. Refrains are central in providing a certain solace in the face of the anguish of chaos. 'But we should not confuse these ... assemblages ... with organizations such as the institution of the family and the State apparatus' (Deleuze and Guattari, 1987, p. 242). Deleuze and Guattari comment that professionalism is a territorial gesture of sorts (1987, p. 321); a way of defining a social identity, of establishing a certain territory wherein our behaviours acquire a certain meaning and purpose. The question is more subtle than just a simple rejection. For Deleuze, 'the question has always been organizational, not at all ideological' (Deleuze and Parnet, 2006, p. 109). It is exactly because the issue at stake is not ideology that organisation needs to be separated from – needs to be seen as distinct from – regimented or prescriptive modes of life. Certainly organisation of chaos – chaosmos – is the mechanism by which certain orders become regimented and despotic. But this is seen as an excess of organisation, an excess with significant consequences, in particular *la bêtise*.

For psychology to deal with stupidity means that psychology, as a discipline, needs to look at how its knowledge participates in the complexity of society as we live it. At the same time psychology needs to affirm a (critical) differentiation within the systems in which we participate. Here, psychology proves lacking. As a discipline, psychology demonstrates a general lack of reflexivity: a certain unwillingness to apply its insights to its own functioning so as to inform its practice. A 'foundational' belief that what psychology addresses are objective entities that are present in a stable manner in the world has somehow 'excused' the discipline from investigating the effects not only of what it does but also of its own definitions and reflections into what it does. The discipline has concerned itself with defining and promoting how it can help society. But it has been partially blind to, or at best has not addressed with equal zeal, the investigation of what has not worked and, what is perhaps more concerning, the damage that its knowledge and its practice has produced (iatrogenic effect). In this respect, psychology can again be recognised in Slife's formulation: as an adolescent discipline of sorts, keen to embrace its privileges but struggling to accept its responsibilities and the consequences of its actions.

These foundational concerns are sharply delineated when we look at psychology with a Deleuzian conceptualisation. One way to explore these issues more deeply is by re-engaging with psychology's timidity, a timidity that, as we argued in Chapter 2, constantly returns psychology to what is familiar. We can now say that the familiar is what is predictable, not necessarily as particular behaviours or events, but more so as logical consequences of certain regimes of signs. Here, the distinction between royal science and minor science is once again central, with royal or mainstream science often inadvertently confirming and affirming a certain representation of what it is to be human. This orientation within the discipline ends up having powerful effects in society, two of which we believe are central. First, such timidity – with its implied return to what is familiar – has the effect, as we discussed in Chapter 3, of transforming certain planes of reference into opinions. This return does not help the process of differentiation central to life and does not help with the more concrete yet equally complex engagement with the chaos in which life takes place. What it does instead is to rigidify and reify modes of lives that, notwithstanding their success at some point, are then normalised and set as standards of what it is to be human. It is in this context that the globalisation of a certain image of thought – of Western individuated white man – becomes the yardstick to measure not only 'normality' but also 'health'. Gatens has made reference to this effect in a more general manner when she states that 'As part of the discursive construction of human society, the human sciences do not simply describe but also serve to organize bodies, their powers and their capacities' (1996, p. 163). It is in this sense that when describing elements common to critical psychology, Parker comments that 'psychology pretends to merely describe human activity, but this description requires a degree of declared or surreptitious interpretation that prescribes a correct version of events' (2015, p. 4).

Stenner advances this argument further when he comments that

> psychologists have tended to push prematurely towards a parody of Kuhnian normal science achieved, not through genuine consensus, but by way of a combination of fiat and a dogmatic denial that there are important facets of human existence that are not expressed in terms of its own primary concepts (whether those be 'behaviour', 'information processing', 'natural selection' or 'connectionism').
>
> *2009, p. 196*

It is in this context that there is a connection between the contribution of Deleuze and a concept well known in critical circles within psychology: the psy-complex (Burman, 2015, p. 73; Haaken, 2015). In many ways, this is an easy connection to make because, although the concept is often associated with the work of Foucault (Parker, 1999), it is also connected with that of Deleuze (1988c). As Pulido-Martinez states, 'The psy-complex is delineated as an *assemblage* of diverse elements that frame and make possible the place and the operations of psychology in contemporary societies' (2014, p. 1598, emphasis added). We suggest that what is conveyed by the notion of the psy-complex is perhaps the best available description of psychology as a royal science, as a science that serves the purposes of the powers that be to define a grid of understanding that helps to position people into a certain system of governability. This aspect of the uses of a science has been amply explored and articulated by Foucault (1974, 1979). But the contribution of Deleuze helps us to improve on the over-ideological notion of psy-complex which after all relies on Marx as well as on Foucault.

What is important to note from a Deleuzian perspective is that the reification underlying the construction of the psy-complex supports in turn a second important effect of royal psychological practice. Consistent with Deleuze's comments in *Difference and Repetition* on the status of difference in a philosophy of identity, the question emerges as to the role played by difference. What is the effect of differing descriptions of the human condition when put in relation to the yardstick already established? In other words, how does psychology in practice deal with what presents as different? One answer is 'management'. Boundas reflects on what he refers to as 'theories of management' which are described as 'theories that mobilize instrumental rationality for ends which they do not choose to dispute' (1996, p. 327). For Boundas these are to be contrasted with theories 'which, being unwilling to operate with entrenched ends, raise issues of substantive rationality, as they aim to replace old objectives with a set of new and hopefully better ones'. The former type of theoretical enquiry, focused on instrumental rationality at the cost of questioning unexamined assumptions is, we believe, the type of theoretical frame prevalent, yet in an unexamined manner, in psychology training and research. Parker comments on the political dimension here by stating that, in taking this orientation,

> psychology's gaze is directed at those outside the discipline who are assumed to be non-psychologists and who are routinely deceived and misrepresented.... [T]here is a deep problem in the way that relations between those 'inside' the discipline are separated from those viewed as being 'outside'.
>
> *2015, p. 3*

A mirror process of increasing inequality and external regulation can also be described within the emerging sense of regulation of the profession itself, of what counts as valid knowledge and credible practice (e.g. Postle, 2007).

These are all reflections on a discipline that, in the name of science, is reducing the repertoire of possibilities available to us and that, in the name of normality and of health, is also increasingly investing in ways of fomenting a type of subjectivity that is not diverse but docile – a herd-like stupidity. In some sense, this is a direct reference to the quotation that opened this chapter, a quotation that in its full form includes a revealing detail, that 'The ignominy of the possibilities of life that we are offered appears from within' (Deleuze and Guattari, 1991, pp. 106–7). Psychology, in this sense, can be seen as suffering the consequences of the breakdown of the foundational fraternity that should guide its endeavours and, without the presence of such constraints (Stengers, 2000), is increasingly focused on providing mechanised solutions, solutions that systematically exclude consideration of their consequences for the social and for life.

It is in light of these concerns that Deleuze's philosophy can be seen as bringing to the fore a critical and productive approach to psychology, different from what we have seen in the past. Deleuze's critique has often been associated with post-structural gestures of 'decentring the human'. This is a valid although partial reading of what Deleuze has to offer. Indeed, Deleuze decentres the human because his ideas move away from naturalistic approaches to a human essence and favour a reading of human life as participating in larger vitalistic processes. Such an approach affords a different relationship with the discipline of psychology. But there is more in Deleuze's project that invites us to reconsiderations within this discipline. It is here that his concern for *la bêtise* becomes central, in particular in the context of differentiation as central to philosophy as a critical activity.

The role of Deleuzian critique as a new direction in psychology

Consistent with his considerations on *la bêtise* and his admiration of Nietzsche, Deleuze thought of philosophy as having an active role in evaluating the health of society. For Deleuze and for Nietzsche, the philosopher is like a doctor, and the philosopher's first task is to make a diagnostic evaluation of its patient – society. In this sense, philosophy's task is 'clinical' as well as critical in as much as it aims to provide a reading of the types of life that a society engenders. Such a reading not only provides commentaries on the current state of affairs – the health of the system – but also, as good diagnosis ought to, identifies ways forward through *noble* solutions to the current social dilemmas. In this sense, this 'clinical' aspect of philosophy implies a political element as well. Deleuze had an ongoing commitment to working in this clinico-critical dimension within philosophy, a commitment that perhaps explains the promise of his ideas for the discipline of psychology. It is in the context of this commitment that we understand Deleuze's relentless critique of psychoanalysis – the only real 'contender' in psychology – as well as his more pointed critique of traditional etiological distinctions (e.g. sado-masochism). We will explore these issues in more detail in the next chapter. What is important to remember at this point, however, is that this critical aspect does not relate only to concrete elements of what we traditionally understand as clinical work – the therapist, the client and the clinic. It also refers to the health of the whole ecology of ideas and practices constitutive of a society, an ecology within which an understanding of the world, of clinical practice and of our selves – as citizens, clinicians, clients and so on – takes place. This is of central importance for it is a source of significant transformations of the role and position of clinical work, reminding us that pathos and therapy are not part of an exclusive language, a language detached from everyday life – a language that invites us to think in terms of 'us' and 'them' – but rather a particular way of engaging with everyday life. It represents a commitment to engage in *noble* and *joyful* ways of living. Such a transformation also moves conceptualisations of clinical practice away from the common understanding as an independent and deeply private practice, located in a safe place where consciousness can express itself freely and from thence search for better ways to be in the world. Instead, clinical practice is seen to be a practice that, like all other social practices, emerges and makes sense within particular societies.

From this angle, clinical practice needs to be understood in terms of the unique and useful purposes it serves in society at large. It is in this sense that the clinico-critical has to do not just with the clinical world but with the social and political dimensions of our human condition. It has to do with the diagnosis of societies, which is to say, with the evaluation of the types of social production in which we participate. It is in this sense also that we can perhaps more fully understand Deleuze's earlier comment: 'we do not lack communication. On the contrary, we have too much of it. We lack creation. *We lack resistance to the present*' (Deleuze and Guattari, 1991, p. 108). The resistance that Deleuze with Guattari calls forth is not a 'partisan' critique, a critique that stems from a specific ideological position pointing at the limitations of different aspects of society while rescuing or valuing others. As we explained in the previous chapter, such an attitude would fall into the 'Cartesian' fallacy that invites us to believe that we could 'pick and choose' as we like. Perhaps more importantly, Deleuze's call for resistance is not an endorsement of the popular version of Hegelian dialectics often underlying critical work.[2] Such a dialectics – often characterised as a clear-cut process of thesis, antithesis and synthesis – is what Deleuze 'most detested' (Deleuze, 1973a, p. 6). And he did so because it perhaps is the best example of a type of knowledge that Deleuze and Guattari call *fascicular* (1987, p. 5) – a knowledge that claims to engage with diversity only to subsume it back into totalitarian and universal themes.

In this sense, Deleuze and Guattari would not see a problem with a critical psychology that is constantly diversifying (Parker, 2015, p. 2). This is so because the resistance that is called for by Deleuze is resistance against such totalitarian or universal regimes. Deleuze and Guattari are striving against the all-too-available and ready-made descriptions regarding how the world and ourselves tick. The resistance that Deleuze calls for is not of individual entities, protesting that 'I like assertiveness but I dislike aggression' or 'I like empowerment but I dislike manipulation'. Instead it stands against complex systems of knowledge and of opinion that stop short our becomings, that capture and hold captive the untimely process of differentiation. Deleuze refers to large systems, to regimes of signs of Foucaultian *dispositifs*. These are complex articulations that work a little like Kesey's 'Combine' as it is portrayed by Dale Harding in *One Flew Over the Cuckoo's Nest* (1973). The Combine is an ecology of might, red in tooth and claw, and might is right. Natural subservience to overwhelming power, like the rabbit's to the wolf, is at the same time rational and above all, in Orwellian mode, no other way is even thinkable. Possibility is itself dragooned.

The resistance that Deleuze calls for stands against the regimes of sign that constitute and confirm not just opinion but also the subjectivities to which we have access. It is in the passive acceptance of this set of assumptions – assumptions that, following the example of the Combine, would claim a 'naturally' aggressive and competitive human nature – that the artistic becomings lying ahead of our existence are restrained and one's existence is transformed into that of docile and domestic animals, sheep in a flock.

We must be careful not to fall into the mistake of believing that the problem is one of identity: that where we have gone wrong is in believing we are scared sheep when in reality we are assertive wolves. If unchecked, such a claim can easily turn out to be an invitation to a different set of opinions. Nothing 'in itself' will suffice. As Deleuze and Guattari clarify,

'What interest us [...] are precisely the passages and combinations' (1987, p. 500). What Deleuze is calling for is a resistance against the reification and rigidification of (social) structures. This is not to say that structure is not necessary, but that there is a constant flow between structure – organisation – and chaos. The fact that we require some structure in order to exist – that we cannot avoid the fact that we constantly find ourselves involved in the construction of territorial spaces – does not imply that we require totalising structures, transcendental and, for Deleuze and Guattari, despotic spaces. As quoted previously, we only need 'small rations of subjectivity in sufficient quantity to enable you to respond to the dominant reality' (1987, p. 160). Deleuze's critique – a critique with profound implications for the clinic – is a critique of the prevalent tendency to define and normalise all spaces of our existence.

For Deleuze, rather than the search for 'the nature of the human condition', what is central is the ongoing process of evaluation and of creation that is inherent to the construction of scientific and other types of knowledge and of life itself. Deleuze's 'clinical' process recursively demands, like the mythical Ouroboros, a constant return to diagnosis of the effects of its earlier recommendations. Such circularity affords a different engagement with the constitutive forces shaping societies as well as selves. In terms of the self, rather than engaging with the well-known dichotomy that reads such forces as individual or internal manifestations of the dynamic tension either between genetic and learned aspects – the interminable nature–nurture debate – or between consciousness and unconsciousness, for Deleuze (and Guattari), these forces transcend the individual and are at the base of the constitution of one's modes of living as social animals, as animals of the pack. Our sense of self – our modes of living – are not stable but are in ongoing construction and so are the institutions and the world around us. This is not a social constructionist-style construction – where the conscious mind of the individual purposefully constructs and plays with options for reality – but a constitutive force that is not only larger than one's consciousness but also, recursively, shapes such consciousness.

In this sense, Deleuze's proposal resonates intimately with Kierkegaard's famous comment: 'life can only be understood backwards, but it must be lived forwards'. There is a double movement implied in this. On the one hand, we are left to make sense of what has happened (Deleuze and Guattari, 1987, Plateau 8). This part of the formula – this attempt to understand backwards – needs to be informed by the insights of Spinoza, in that such constitutive forces need to be understood not in terms of their 'essences' but in terms of their capacities. This is to say, understanding has to be of the power these forces have to affect the assemblage in the same way that the assemblage needs to be understood in its ability to affect. Rather than stable categorisations, an active engagement with these forces focuses on a genealogical or, as Deleuze clarifies, geological understanding of these forces so as to allow the philosopher or thinker to position him- or herself as a good player in the face of fate and of the unique dice-throw, the unique living conditions, that they are trying to understand and work with. On the other hand, and despite such an understanding, we are still left with the untimely task of 'living a life': with the infinite task of engaging in a noble way with the singularities that shape us and give our life expression, through 'a life'. Such labour is informed not only by our understanding but also by our will to stand firm in spite of the ever-present banality of a life already defined by myriad mechanisms of capture (Rajchman, 2000). In this sense, in this creative search for individuality, life is best grasped as flux, and 'to live' (May, 2005, ch. 1) requires the evaluation of and negotiation with the mechanisms of capture implied in those regimes of sign from which we emerge. These mechanisms, like Ulysses' Sirens, often provide false solace in terms of the task at hand.

If psychology as a science is challenged to undertake the impossible task of working out regularities in our human condition, it needs to approach this task in a very different manner from the current search for essences where variation – difference – is read as variables of such essences. The work instead needs to be topological and must attempt to point to the continuous flux experienced by assemblages as they are traversed by forces, forces that cause them to move and to be in constant (trans)formation. This movement is between what Deleuze and Guattari term 'striated' and 'smooth' spaces (1987, Plateau 14). Striated space is sedentary space, the space instituted by the State and other regimens of signs. Striated space is 'a space riddled with lines of divide and demarcation that name, measure, appropriate and distribute space according to inherited political designs, history or economic conflict' (Conley, 2005, p. 258). A striated space is a well-defined space that captures (nomad) becomings into stable identities; into an interiority that is often confused with subjectivity but, in fact, constitutes a sophisticated mechanism of continuous control (Deleuze and Negri, 1990; Deleuze, 1990b). Striated space is the space of State apparatuses and, as such, they have an implicit danger of over-codification and totalisation. Smooth or 'nomad' space, on the other hand, is a space with no grid of measurement. It is a space that is 'boundless and possibly oceanic, a space that is without border or distinction' (Conley, 2005, p. 258). Deleuze used the images of the sea or of the desert to refer to this type of space.

Assemblages live between these spaces and change is possible because *'you will never find a homogeneous system that is not still or already affected by a regulated, continuous, immanent process of variation'* (Deleuze and Guattari, 1987, p. 103). Resonating with the dynamics between a major and minor language, Deleuze and Guattari describe this flux by stating that

> Smooth space and striated space ... are not of the same nature. No sooner do we note a simple opposition between the two kinds of space than we must indicate a much more complex difference by virtue of which the successive terms of the oppositions fail to coincide entirely. And no sooner have we done that than we must remind ourselves that the two spaces in fact exist only in mixture: smooth space is constantly being translated, traversed into a striated space; striated space is constantly being reversed, returned to a smooth space. In the first case, one organizes even the desert; in the second, the desert gains and grows; and the two can happen simultaneously.
>
> *1987, pp. 474–5*

To see either smooth space or striated space as desirable or undesirable in themselves misses the point that what is at stake is not identities but relational variation and their expression in the constitution of a life.

Deterritorialisation and the war machine

This awareness of the ongoing variation and flux of life raises awareness that critique – as well as understanding – is only part of the set of considerations at hand. Another crucial part has already been preempted when talking about the interplay between striated and smooth space. Movement in life is not unidirectional; it is not a predictable line from a smooth chaos to totalising and highly striated regimes of signs. The untimely creation and affirmation of new possibilities of life – what Deleuze would call 'the people to come' – is a relational engagement in the variations and complex combinations present between such poles. In order to understand how this variation and flux works, we need to address further concepts in Deleuze and Guattari's proposal.

In their metaphysical project, Deleuze and Guattari see an ongoing establishment of form and identity through repetition and variation. This interplay affords the emergence of ever more complex living processes out of molecular inorganic particles. For Deleuze and Guattari, this set of assumptions is present at all levels of what we observe in this world, from the strata of the inorganic world where steppes and other geological formations demonstrate a certain rhythm in their constitution and life, to the milieus of organic life. It is also present in the territories, ever-growing in complexities, established by certain types of animals, including humans. This set of explanations, however, can lead to a dead-end. Foucault experienced this impasse in his conceptual work for a significant time when investigating similar processes in relation to power (Deleuze and Maggiori, 1986, p. 92). This is not surprising, for increasing complexity, as Deleuze and Guattari explain, always runs the risk of leading to an increase in the rigidity of systems, a rigidity that creates a grid that fixes and determines the form and the activities of all its elements. This is observable in the animal world, with colonies of ants or bees as a good example of a complex system with set roles for all its members. There is something, however, within our condition that generates a certain dislike of such systems of organisation, a dislike that is similar to the dislike we feel about conditioning. This dislike reminds us that there is more to life than what we have already discussed. For indeed, as Zourabichvili states, 'There is an oppression that coincides with this striation' (2012, p. 175).

Deleuze and Guattari warn us against the idea of liberation or emancipation, as traditionally understood, as the solution to this problem. For them the solution is in art and in the resistance to *la bêtise* through the ongoing process of differentiation. In order to understand Deleuze's argument here, two central elements should be emphasised. First, and in many ways anticipated throughout the previous chapters, the emergence and growth of complexity does not follow causal relationships.[3] This is contrary to the predominant assumptions in mental health. In other words, it is not the case that depression is straightforwardly due to the lack of a specific neurotransmitter. The type of phenomena Deleuze and Guattari are interested in describing fall into the category of what von Foerster would describe as non-trivial machines (Goujon, 2006, p. 209) or Prigogine as systems out of equilibrium (Prigogine and Stengers, 1984). In such systems, difference, multiplicity and unpredictability are core to the phenomena observed.

The second element relates to two important notions for Deleuze and Guattari: *deterritorialisation* and the *war machine*. We have already introduced the idea of striated and smooth space as possible spaces of existence for assemblages. With this distinction we also need a further refinement of assemblages and their activities of territorialisation. Deleuze and Guattari clarify that, if striated space is created by activities of territorialisation (activities that constitute an assemblage), smooth space is the result of activities of deterritorialisation executed by a different type of apparatus: the war machine. War machines are 'not "machines for war"' (Bonta and Protevi, 2004, p. 136). They 'tend much more to be revolutionary, or artistic, rather than military' (Deleuze *et al.*, 1980, p. 33). Deterritorialisation 'is the movement by which "one" leaves the territory' (Deleuze and Guattari, 1987, p. 508). As Deleuze and Guattari explain,

> [w]henever a territorial assemblage is taken up by a movement that deterritorializes it (whether under so-called natural or artificial conditions), we say that a machine is released. That in fact is the distinction we would like to propose between *machine* and *assemblage*: a machine is like a set of cutting edges that insert themselves into the assemblage undergoing deterritorialization and draw variations and mutations of it.
>
> *1987, p. 333*

It would be a mistake to consider deterritorialisation to be in simple opposition to territorialisation – a kind of antithesis – because it refers to a different kind of activity altogether. As May says, 'Deterritorialization is the chaos beneath and within the territories' (2005, p. 138). It is a potential for difference and an ongoing reminder of our intimate connection with chaosmos. Deterritorialisation is 'always multiple and composite' (Deleuze and Guattari, 1987, p. 509). Very much like using the clutch in a car to disengage the workings of a specific gear, deterritorialisation, 'unhinges' the state of affairs, affording a smooth place to emerge and for the possibilities of altogether new combinations to take place. When the clutch is used, there is no assumption that 'the next move' will be to go to third or second gear. What the clutch affords is to open the engine for difference. In doing this, it could be said that the clutch acts through increasing the manoeuvrability of the car, it increases its options. Deleuze and Guattari chose the specific name of 'war machine' to describe one of the two 'great alloplastic and anthropomorphic assemblages' (1987, p. 513) (the other such assemblage is the State apparatus). The distinction between assemblage and machine noted above highlights a distinction that is, in some respects, arbitrary, for machines – war machines – are assemblages too, but they work in a different way. Deleuze and Guattari establish an association between the war machine with the nomads and dedicate their twelfth plateau to talk about nomadology and the war machine. They date this plateau to 1227, making reference to the death of Genghis Khan. This again is Deleuze and Guattari being playful for, as they explain,

We thought it possible to assign the invention of the war machine to the nomads. This was done only in the historical interest of demonstrating that the war machine as such was invented ... the nomads do not hold the secret: an 'ideological', scientific, or artistic movement can be a potential war machine, to the precise extent to which it draws ... a line of flight, a smooth space of displacement.

1987, pp. 422–3

War machines are the space where nomad becomings take place. For Deleuze, becoming – nomad becoming – is the alternative to essences and identity. Becoming is a critical and material concept that has direct significance for psychology. We will discuss this concept in detail in the next chapter. At this point, however, we want to maintain the focus on the interplay between regimes of signs – regimes that are most clearly articulated in the shape of State apparatus – and war machines, in particular, on the power that deterritorialisation and the war machine have over life. And here we come to the second to last of the Deleuze and Guattari concepts we will use in this book: the line of flight. Deleuze and Guattari denote the operation of deterritorialisation with this, perhaps one of their best-known concepts. The line of flight is a creative movement that displaces the territorialised space. Lorraine describes the line of flight as 'a path of mutation precipitated through the actualisation of connections among bodies that were previously only implicit (or "virtual") that releases new powers in the capacities of those bodies to act and to respond' (2005, p. 145). This formulation points up the connection with Spinoza. In the movement of an assemblage, lines of flight are those aspects that result in the assemblage being unhinged in some unexpected ways and thus able to transform and engage in new and unpredictable possibilities. Nomads are for Deleuze and Guattari the example par excellence of people living in deterritorialised space. They do not 'possess' a territory but are in constant movement, constantly engaging with their circumstances in new, and renewing, ways. Art, in turn, is the activity that is most commonly associated with this process because art, as Parr explains, 'at its most creative mutates as it experiments, producing new paradigms of subjectivity' (2005, p. 147). And, as we have explained, movement and experimentation are central to conceptual work for Deleuze. Encounters and newness also – hence the stroll of the schizophrenic in the park. Deleuze and Guattari were, however, aware of the dangers inherent in the line of flight both as concept and as event. The risks are not merely the risks of the precipitate. Lorraine describes the dangers identified by Deleuze and Guattari (1987, pp. 205–6) by stating that lines of flight 'can become ineffectual, lead to regressive transformations, and even reconstruct highly rigid segments' (Lorraine 2005, p. 146). An ageing hippie, a clinical case of schizophrenia and a failed revolution are respective examples of each of these possibilities. The risk of betrayal lies at the heart of every flight, as Icarus found out.

The rhizome

The last concept we will employ is one that has become even better known within some psychological circles than the line of flight: the 'rhizome' (Hoffman, 2008; Kinman, 2012a, 2012b; Morss and Nichterlein, 1999). It has been said that 'War machines are "roughly synonymous" with the rhizome' (Bonta and Protevi, 2004, p. 136). The rhizome is a concept central to Deleuzian thought. It is the concept Deleuze and Guattari chose as the first plateau in *A Thousand Plateaus*. Rhizome 'is the best term to designate multiplicities' (Deleuze, 1990a, p. 362). The rhizome characterises the type of knowledge proper to nomadic thought. Indeed, Deleuze and Guattari stated that 'the brain's [sic] organized like a rhizome' (Deleuze *et al.*, 1988, p. 149).[4] Perhaps more importantly, for Deleuze the rhizome is precisely one example of an open system (Deleuze *et al.*, 1980, pp. 31–2).

In botany, the rhizome refers to a type of plant that instead of having the lineal and centralised distribution of a tree (roots, trunk, branches and leaves), grows by extending itself through and on the surface of the ground and developing both roots and offshoots when it finds a nurturing environment. Rhizomic knowledge, correspondingly, is a type of knowledge that is essentially decentralised. Instead of constructing itself 'vertically' – ever deeper into an interior or ever higher into a parallel, ever-increasing totalitarian regime of signs – rhizomic knowledge grows 'horizontally', constantly expanding in unpredictable yet highly complex ways. Instead of being a stable form of thought, it is highly contingent and contextual.

The rhizome is central to Deleuze because as an image of knowledge it does not attempt to represent an image of the world, but is fundamentally connective and productive (Deleuze, 1976, pp. 44–5). It establishes experimental connections with the outside, an outside that is – in itself – also shifting. This is thought in movement – a war machine – that engages with the world in an empirical way, creating spaces of existence; populating 'desert islands' (Deleuze, 1950s) with different entities that are, themselves, continually changing.

In line with the influence of the rhizome, as an image, in popular readings of Deleuze's ideas, it has extensively informed the writing of this book. We must, however, state our mischievousness at this point and declare that we have purposefully used a very different image to approach Deleuze. As Holland says, the rhizome is a botanical image of Deleuze's thought and the wolf-pack is its ethological counterpart (2013, p. 94). A reminder that all images of thought have limited validity, this interplay enables us to look at how the being of the pack can be best understood not in the most familiar way, as a pack with established roles, but also as a pack in movement, moving without property although with ever-changing territories.

We have now covered the central aspects of Deleuze and Guattari's metaphysical proposal and we are also in a position to look at a positive way forward for psychology. Psychology must face the difficult question that emerges out of understanding Deleuze and Guattari's challenge as to the validity of its claims and its orientation. We have discussed the limitations both of psychology's unit of analysis and of its methodology. We have also examined the dangers of a psychology that allies itself too closely to a State apparatus and works in the construction of a herd-like mentality where health is made synonym with normality. What, then, is left for psychology as a discipline? Is psychology to 'admit' or 'confess' that it is trapped? Does it need to admit that, since its first claim of being a sci-entific laboratory practice, as a discipline, psychology made a big mistake? One of Deleuze's best-known articles is his rather passionate response to a critic when he was cornered to 'admit it' (Deleuze, 1990a), reminding us that any response needs to include a personal, a passional engagement. The questions posed – such a confrontation – are perhaps indicative of the affec-tive engagement that psychology needs to start with, to work out its own line of flight.

As with any line of flight, this path commences with a recognition of the problematic circumstances in which a solution emerges. Psychology needs to understand the problems that a science with its timidity faces, and needs to find a way to move away from this state of affairs. We have little doubt that the psychologist confronted with such a provocation will feel not only 'misrepresented' (here again that word 'representation' that Deleuze disliked so much) but, perhaps more importantly, insulted. Psy-chologists most likely will feel that their genuine attempts to serve human-kind – a service that often implies less remuneration than other professions, thus a 'double sacrifice' – have been distorted. The problem of stupidity, as Derrida had indicated before in relation to psychoanalysts, is not a problem with psychologists as people but a problem of their engagement with a psy-chology that is mechanised, that is lacking in thought. Foundationally, psychology as a discipline needs to own up to the realisation that its problem is not one of essences, of identities, but one of definitions and of practices. As a discipline, psychology calls for a unique combination of human practices. It calls for a unique mixture of science, of philosophy and of art. As a discipline, it invites a certain reflexivity in its studies: some of us within the community feel an interest in understanding what we – as human – are. Such reflexivity has to maintain a critical position where it takes into consideration its effects as a body of knowledge *while still maintaining a position of a peer – a fraternal position – within the community*. Here, Parker's comments regarding critical aspects in psychology are important to bear in mind (2015).

For Deleuze, however, there is a more important role for human activity: the creation of the new (and thus the different) so as to facilitate the endless affirmation of life. It is this productive dimension and how it applies to psychology that we will discuss next. Here, the question that psychology needs to face is that of considering not 'what human nature is' but, as Deleuze would say, what 'human nature can do'. In particular, it must face the recursive question of *what is psychology doing to support the becoming of a humane – rather than human – collective?*

Psychology's positive dimension: unleashing the becomings of a wolf through a call for a minor science

Boundas comments that 'the presence of subversive tendencies is unmistaken [*sic*] in Deleuze's work (especially in those that he co-authored with Félix Guattari) [including his] attempt to summon those who are in a position to stand against the State's capturing forces' (2006, p. 21). This subversiveness – which others call perverse (Zourabichvili, 2012, pp. 177–8) – is at the base of Deleuze and Guattari's (not unqualified) preference for smooth space. They value smooth space because 'the struggle is changed or displaced in them, and life reconstitutes its stakes, confronts new obstacles, invents new paces, switches adversaries' (Deleuze and Guattari, 1987, p. 500). Smooth space is, however, inextricably connected with striated space and, ultimately, these relatively desirable effects of smooth space only acquire meaning in relation to the stability inherent to the regularity provided by the regime of signs that constitutes the grid striating the space. If we tear up a square metre of cobblestones to reveal the beach beneath, what we have is a square metre of beach. 'Of course, smooth spaces are not in themselves liberatory…. Never believe that a smooth space will suffice to save us.'

Other than a recapitulationary Conclusion, these are the last words of the last plateau of *A Thousand Plateaus*. With these words, Deleuze and Guattari remind us with great power that 'the trick' is to keep focused at the level of process and of transformation. It is in this sense that for Deleuze, this 'clinical' approach does not provide a stable system of critique – as perhaps was attempted by Marx and by Freud. Deleuze invites us instead to the construction of 'the dawn of a counterculture' (1973b, p. 253). Evocative words, each with a precise meaning. With 'dawn' Deleuze makes reference to the importance of the half-light dimension of this activity, that is, to the fact that what is pursued as the outcome of this activity is a time and space of emergence rather than of plenitude; of becoming rather than of being. 'Counterculture', on the other hand, is equally salient because, for Deleuze, philosophy as a human practice draws its particular *puissance* from the act of 'going against the grain' and engaging in an endless process of demystification. What is of relevance here, once again in critical difference from other traditions that also claim to be critical, is that Deleuze's process of demystification is defined as a differential and relative concept: as an ongoing process of differentiation from any system of representation, including those that claim critical attitudes. It is this ongoing differentiation – of resistance to *la bêtise* – that allows the movement towards the new, to what is yet to come, confirming the ultimate act both of resistance and of art.

It is in this constructive, demystifying gesture that one can appreciate the second dimension in Deleuze's understanding of the role of philosophy, a role that provides equally powerful insights for psychology. Deleuze refined his ideas through time with an increasing focus on the productive and affirmative role of philosophy. Writing more than twenty years after *Difference and Repetition*, in *What is Philosophy?* Deleuze unambiguously stated that 'philosophy is the art of forming, inventing, and fabricating concepts' (Deleuze and Guattari, 1991, p. 2). With this assertion, he relegated the critical activity in philosophy to a secondary role.

In order to fully understand this extra dimension to his work, it is important to note that, in line with his insights on locating difference at the core of metaphysics and of philosophical thinking, Deleuze separated the act of recognition from the act of thinking. Consistent with his critique of identity – of which understanding of thinking as a representational activity (thinking through ideas) is a companion – Deleuze conceptualised thinking as a 'different activity ... [one] that takes place when the mind is provoked by an encounter with the unknown or the unfamiliar' (Patton, 2010, p. 66). Thought is not about representing – not even about representing critiques of dominant knowledge, an activity that is reactive in nature – but about engaging affirmatively and creatively with actual problems so as to find novel and noble solutions. In such activity, what is ultimately affirmed is Life. Thought, then, as we indicated at the beginning of this chapter, becomes a key component in the endless immanent process through which life articulates itself, for thought is the process by which solutions to the problems of living are posed in the form of new and unexpected possibilities. These possibilities, these new concepts, cut across the paradoxes of life affording new types of organisations or forms of life. Thought, then, completes what is present by moving it to the new – to what is to come: a gesture that for Deleuze affirms the eternal return of Nietzsche.

Through Nietzsche, Deleuze challenges us further by raising the idea that there are noble ways of affirming difference as well as base ones. For Deleuze, differentiation as a human activity is not a laissez-faire activity. Nor is it the plurality so celebrated by social constructionism and by late capitalism alike, the plurality of the supermarket shelves. The differentiation that Deleuze calls for is a plurality *within the pack*. It is in this context that Deleuze's words quoted at the beginning of this second part of the book acquire their full sense: 'There is indeed catastrophe, but it consists in the society of brothers or friends having undergone such an ordeal that brothers and friends can no longer look at each other, or each at himself, without a "weariness," perhaps a "mistrust" ' (Deleuze and Guattari, 1991, p. 106). Noble responses are then responses where solidarity and connectedness are a horizon for which one can strive, a world where the tensions and violence imposed upon our lives may be constructively addressed. In the words of Deleuze we strive for 'the people to come'.

A good depiction of the challenges that are integral to an engagement with a noble response to the human condition is presented by the nineteenth-century American lawyer Adam Ewing, one of the characters in Mitchell's novel *Cloud Atlas* (2004). A complex novel presenting a number of interweaving narrations, *Cloud Atlas* commences and ends with Adam's experience. Adam is introduced as a genteel man visiting missionaries in New Zealand. Returning to the USA, Adam is close to having his life terminated by a seedy physician who he had counted as his only friend on the boat. Adam is rescued by a runaway slave, Jackson. Adam had seen Jackson being flogged earlier on and Jackson had then caught Adam's gaze of pity, a humane connection amidst his pain. Such a connection leads Jackson to risk coming out of his hideout to protect Adam in his vulnerability. Adam is deeply touched by this and resolves to commit himself to the Abolitionist cause once back home. His resolution is received with scorn by his father-in-law and the last paragraphs of the book encapsulate well the type of tribulations that a noble life brings forth. For Adam's gesture is not a charitable gesture of sorts but a gesture of a deep connection with those who are different, a gesture that conveys a sense of a different world to the one we know: a different world that – although not actual – is possible.

A further example of a noble life is described by García Márquez in one of his novellas, a novella he claims is better described as journalism (1970). The novella recounts the shipwreck of Luis Alejandro Velasco. It is not the shipwreck that is of importance but the circumstances in which it takes place. The navy is being used to illegally transport imported merchandise. Luis Alejandro had been welcomed as a national hero after the shipwreck so it is unexpected by the powers that be when he decides to tell the story as it really happened and, in doing so, to defy the government rather than maintaining a rather dubious 'heroic' standing. Through his noble gesture, Luis Alejandro's life becomes invisible to fame and power. His name is lost in oblivion until he is accidentally recognised by the narrator years later. The description of Luis Alejandro at this point is perhaps the best image of health we have found: a man who had aged, put on some weight and had 'intimately' lived. But, perhaps of more importance, García Márquez clarifies that through this journey Luis Alejandro was left with a serene halo that belongs to the heroes who have the bravery to destroy statues of themselves. Adam and Luis Alejandro are thought-provoking examples of a literature – good literature as Deleuze would clarify – that is central to the search for a noble way of living a life and, as we discuss in the last chapter, to the application of psychology to an understanding of the clinic and the search for health.

A discipline that aims to focus on the human condition as a minor Deleuzian science will need to embrace this diversity and organise itself as a productive response to dominant royal trends in psychology, so as to affirm alternatives.[5] Such a science needs to go 'against the grain' not to be oppositional for its own sake but to demonstrate that there are indeed exceptions and that these exceptions are perhaps of more importance than the rule. Such a science will ultimately orient itself to facilitate the becoming of endless minoritarian ways of living – the people, like Jackson and Luis Alejandro, to come.

A direct practical example of what such a science of psychology would look like can be seen in relation to psychology's conceptualisations of its unit of analysis: the individual. In Chapter 2 we emphasised the importance

of looking at assemblages and, ultimately, at life and the process of individ-
ualisation as the unit of analysis. How would this look for the individual?
What Deleuze invites us to do is to shake the image of thought, the yardstick of measure, to decentre the individual as it is construed through nor-
malising practices of the dominant culture. Instead of confirming such a
yardstick, Deleuze invites us to affirm the presence of and the ongoing
diversification within minoritarian groups, each in turn with its own
internal organisation. To do so, such a discipline will require that normalcy
and self are questioned in favour of larger processes of differentiation. In
this sense, methodology needs to reorient itself not to confirm what is there
but to survey and highlight what is different, so as to facilitate the emergence of new capacities and new modes of living. Deleuze and Guattari
employ a comic image of this type of knowledge in the person of 'Professor
Challenger', the professor (borrowed from Conan Doyle's *The Lost World*)
who presents a lecture on the geology of morals in the third plateau of *A
Thousand Plateaus*. As the lecture progressed, and as he approached the
domains we define as human, Professor Challenger 'seemed to be deterri-
torializing on the spot' (Deleuze and Guattari, 1987, p. 64).

This minor, minoritarian-making discipline is, by definition, rhizomic in
nature, which is to say that it is decentralised and non-hierarchical. It will
raise its 'head' – developing offshoots – in unpredictable places and times. It
will have no clear shape or form, forming itself instead in the contingencies
present at any one time *as a resistance to the present*, perhaps even a betrayal.
Betrayal is an important concept for Deleuze. As he writes,

> There is always betrayal in a line of flight. Not trickery like that of an
> orderly man ordering his future, but betrayal like that of a simple
> man who no longer has any past or future. We betray the fixed
> powers which try to hold us back, the established powers of the
> earth.
>
> *Deleuze and Parnet, 2006, p. 30*

This betrayal could be best understood 'as an attempt to transform the
world, to think a new world or new man insofar as they *create themselves*....
It is first of all the affirmation of a world in *process*' (Deleuze, 1997, p. 86).
In this sense, psychology as a minoritarian discipline will rescue psychology's history not as transcendental but as attempts to provide solutions –
noble solutions – to specific questions inherent to our human condition so
as to better position ourselves when it comes to our task: to live a life.
Deleuze makes the point that there is no good or bad philosophy but there

most certainly is good and bad history of philosophy. The latter – bad history of philosophy – looks at philosophical problems as if 'they appeared to go without saying, as if they weren't created' (Boutang, 2012, H for History), whereas the former attempts to understand not only the relevant concepts but also the problems and the conditions that such concepts attempted to solve. In this sense, a minor psychology would be interested in understanding the conditions of emergence of the discipline, and the conditions under which it continually re-emerges. It would attempt to address these problems not as transcendental but as making sense within a specific set of circumstances and at a specific moment. Such a gesture helps us to remember that such knowledge also needs to look at the variations between that specific moment in time and the set of dilemmas now at hand. It must also keep in view the continuing effects of prior solutions, especially those solutions that have been captured in the State apparatus of normalcy. Such a reading is crucial because, ultimately, such a minor psychology is not interested in 'what is' but in 'what is to come': 'what needs to come' to facilitate the becoming of the people to come.

We are now in a position to address the complex and promising Deleuzian notion of *becoming*. We will do so in the next, final chapter, where we will be discussing the clinical role so favoured by Deleuze not as a diagnosis of societies but as an individual engagement with the human condition and the challenges inherent to living a life.

Notes

1 There is a resurgence of interest in von Uexküll's work through the emerging science of biosemiotics (Brentari, 2015), where von Uexküll is seen as a predecessor of cybernetics (Rueting, 2004).
2 We make the distinction between Hegel's own writing and what has sedimented as a 'popular Hegel'. Smith (2000) provides a nuanced explanation of the difference.
3 This idea resonates with an equivalent idea in solution-focused therapy: 'there is not a necessary connection between problem and solution' (De Jong and Berg, 2013, p. 11).
4 They explain further: the brain is

> 'an uncertain system', with probabilistic, semi-aleatory, quantum mechanisms. Not that our thinking starts from what we know about the brain but that any new thought races uncharted channels directly through its matter, twisting, folding, fissuring it.... New connections, new pathways, new synapses, that's what philosophy calls into play as it creates concepts.

5 Cognate projects include Duff developing a 'Minor Science of Health' (2014, p. 52) and Castillo-Sepulveda and Tirado working in cancer as an assemblage (2012).

References

Bains, P. 2006. *The primacy of semiosis: an ontology of relations.* Toronto: University of Toronto Press.

Bateson, G. 1964. The logical categories of learning and communication. *In:* Bateson, G. (ed.), *Steps to an ecology of mind: collected essays in anthropology, psychiatry, evolution and epistemology.* Frogmore: Paladin.

Bogue, R. 2004. *Deleuze's wake: tributes and tributaries.* Albany, NY: State University of New York Press.

Bonta, M. and Protevi, J. 2004. *Deleuze and geophilosophy: a guide and glossary.* Edinburgh: Edinburgh University Press.

Borges, J.L. 1942. John Wilkins' analytical language. *In:* Weinberger, E. (ed.), *Jorge Luis Borges: selected non-fictions.* New York: Penguin Books.

Boundas, C.V. 1996. Transgressive theorizing: a report to Deleuze. *Man and World,* 29, 327–41.

Boundas, C.V. 2006. What difference does Deleuze's difference make? *In:* Boundas, C.V. (ed.), *Deleuze and philosophy.* Edinburgh: Edinburgh University Press.

Boutang, P.-A. 2012. *Gilles Deleuze from A to Z.* Directed by Boutang, P.-A. MIT Press.

Brentari, C. 2015. *Jakob von Uexkull: the discovery of the Umwelt between biosemiotics and theoretical biology.* New York: Springer.

Brown, S.D. and Reavey, P. 2015. *Vital memory and affect: living with a difficult past.* London: Routledge.

Buchanan, B. 2008. *Onto-ethologies: the animal environments of Uexkull, Heidegger, Merleau-Ponty and Deleuze.* Albany, NY: State University of New York Press.

Burman, E. 2015. Developmental psychology: the turn to deconstruction. *In:* Parker, I. (ed.), *Handbook of critical psychology.* London: Routledge.

Castillo-Sepulveda, J. and Tirado, F. 2012. Complexity, heterogeneity and medicine. *In:* Nelson, S. (ed.), *Anarchy in the organism: cancer as a complex system.* London: Black Dog Publishing.

Colombat, A.P. 2000. Deleuze and signs. *In:* Buchanan, I. and Marks, J. (eds), *Deleuze and literature.* Edinburgh: Edinburgh University Press.

Conley, T. 2005. Space. *In:* Parr, A. (ed.), *The Deleuzian dictionary.* Edinburgh: Edinburgh University Press.

De Jong, P. and Berg, I.K. 2013. *Interviewing for solutions.* Belmont, CA: Brooks/Cole.

Deely, J. 1986. Semiotic as framework and direction. *In:* Deely, J., Williams, B. and Kruse, F.E. (eds), *Frontiers in semiotics.* Bloomimgton, IN: Indiana University Press.

Deleuze, G. 1950s. Desert islands. *In:* Lapoujade, D. (ed.), *Desert islands and other texts: 1953–1974.* New York: Semiotext(e).

Deleuze, G. 1973a. Letter to a harsh critic. *In:* Deleuze, G. (ed.), *Negotiations, 1972–1990.* New York: Columbia University Press.

Deleuze, G. 1973b. Nomadic thought. *In:* Deleuze, G. (ed.), *Desert islands and other texts 1953–1974.* New York: Semiotext(e).

Deleuze, G. 1976. Three questions on six times two. *In:* Deleuze, G. (ed.), *Negotiations, 1972–1990.* New York: Columbia University Press.

Deleuze, G. 1988a. *Bergsonism.* New York: Zone Books.

Deleuze, G. 1988b. *Spinoza: practical philosophy.* San Francisco, CA: City Lights Publishers.

Deleuze, G. 1988c. What is a dispositif? *In:* Lapoujade, D. (ed.), *Two regimes of madness.* New York: Semiotext(e).

Deleuze, G. 1990a. Letter-preface to Jean-Clet Martin. *In:* Lapoujade, D. (ed.), *Two regimes of madness: texts and interviews 1975–1995.* New York: Semiotext(e).

Deleuze, G. 1990b. Postscript on control societies. *In:* Deleuze, G. (ed.), *Negotiations, 1972–1990.* New York: Columbia University Press.

Deleuze, G. 1994. *Difference and repetition.* New York: Columbia University Press.

Deleuze, G. 1997. *Essays critical and clinical.* Minneapolis, MN: University of Minnesota Press.

Deleuze, G. and Eribon, D. 1991. We invented the ritornello. *In:* Lapoujade, D. (ed.), *Two regimes of madness: texts and interviews 1975–1995.* New York: Semiotext(e).

Deleuze, G. and Guattari, F. 1984. May '68 did not take place. *In:* Lapoujade, D. (ed.), *Two regimes of madness: texts and interviews 1975–1995.* New York: Semiotext(e).

Deleuze, G. and Guattari, F. 1987. *A thousand plateaus: capitalism and schizophrenia.* Minneapolis, MN: University of Minnesota Press.

Deleuze, G. and Guattari, F. 1991. *What is philosophy?* London: Verso.

Deleuze, G. and Maggiori, R. 1986. Breaking things open, breaking words open. *In:* Deleuze, G. (ed.), *Negotiations, 1972–1990.* New York: Columbia University Press.

Deleuze, G. and Negri, T. 1990. Control and becoming. *In:* Deleuze, G. (ed.), *Negotiations, 1972–1990.* New York: Columbia University Press.

Deleuze, G. and Parnet, C. 2006. *Dialogues II.* London: Continuum.

Deleuze, G., Descamps, C., Eribon, D. and Maggiori, R. 1980. On a thousand plateaus. *In:* Deleuze, G. (ed.), *Negotiations, 1972–1990.* New York: Columbia University Press.

Deleuze, G., Bellour, R. and Ewald, F. 1988. On philosophy. *In:* Deleuze, G. (ed.), *Negotiations, 1972–1990.* New York: Columbia University Press.

Derrida, J. 2007. The transcendental 'stupidity' ('bêtise') of man and the becoming-animal according to Deleuze. *In:* Schwab, G. (ed.), *Derrida, Deleuze, psychoanalysis.* New York: Columbia University Press.

Derrida, J. 2009. *The beast & the sovereign.* Chicago, IL: University of Chicago Press.

Duff, C. 2014. *Assemblages of health: Deleuze's empiricism and the ethology of life.* Dordrecht: Springer.

Foucault, M. 1974. Psychiatric power. *In:* Rabinow, P. (ed.), *Michel Foucault: ethics, subjectivity and truth.* London: Penguin Books.

Foucault, M. 1979. The birth of biopolitics. *In:* Rabinow, P. (ed.), *Michel Foucault: ethics, subjectivity and truth.* London: Penguin Books.

Foucault, M. 1991. *Discipline and punish.* London: Penguin Books.

Foucault, M. 2004a. *Madness and civilization: a history of insanity in the age of reason.* London: Routledge.

Foucault, M. 2004b. *The order of things: an archaeology of the human sciences.* London: Routledge.

García Márquez, G. 1970. *Relato de un naufrago que estuvo diez dias a la deriva en una balsa sin comer ni beber, que fue proclamado heroe de la patria, besado por las reinas de la belleza y hecho rico por la publicidad, y luego aborrecido por el gobierno y olvidado para siempre.* Barcelona: Tusquets editores.

Gatens, M. 1996. Through a Spinozist lens: ethology, difference, power. In: Patton, P. (ed.), *Deleuze: a critical reader.* Oxford: Blackwell Publishers.

Gergen, K. 1985. The social constructionist movement in modern psychology. *American Psychologist*, 40, 266–75.

Goujon, P. 2006. From logic to self-organization: learning about complexity. In: Feltz, B., Crommelinck, M. and Goujon, P. (eds), *Self-organization and emergence in life sciences.* Dordrecht: Springer.

Haaken, J. 2015. Alienists and alienation: critical psychiatry in search of itself. In: Parker, I. (ed.), *Handbook of critical psychology.* London: Routledge.

Hoffman, L. 2008. *Lynn Hoffman and the rhizome century* [Online]. Available: http://christopherkinman.blogspot.com/2008/01/lynn-hoffman-and-rhizome-century.html [accessed 14 April 2010].

Holland, E.W. 2013. *Deleuze and Guattari: a thousand plateaus.* London: Bloomsbury Publishing.

Kesey, K. 1973. *One flew over the cuckoo's nest.* London: Penguin Books.

Kinman, C.J. 2012a. *About the Rhizome Network* [Online]. Available: www.rhizomenetwork.com [accessed 20 September 2012].

Kinman, C.J. 2012b. *Gregory Bateson and the rhizome century: building sustainable webs* [Online]. Available: www.therhizomecentury.com [accessed 20 September 2012].

Law, I. 2013. *Self research: the intersection of therapy and research.* London: Routledge.

Lorraine, T. 2005. Lines of flight. In: Parr, A. (ed.), *The Deleuzian dictionary.* Edinburgh: Edinburgh University Press.

Maturana, H. and Varela, F. 1998. *The tree of knowledge: the biological roots of human understanding.* Boston, MA: Shambhala Publications.

May, T. 2005. *Gilles Deleuze: an introduction.* Cambridge: Cambridge University Press.

Mitchell, D. 2004. *Cloud atlas.* London: Sceptre.

Morss, J.R. and Nichterlein, M. 1999. Spaces in the surface: the reading and writing of the rhizome. *Millennium Conference in Critical Psychology*, Sydney.

Parker, I. 1999. Critical psychology: critical links. *Annual Review of Critical Psychology*, 1, 3–18.

Parker, I. 2015. Introduction: principles and positions. In: Parker, I. (ed.), *Handbook of critical psychology.* Hove: Routledge.

Parr, A. 2005. Lines of flight + art + politics. In: Parr, A. (ed.), *The Deleuze dictionary.* Edinburgh: Edinburgh University Press.

Patton, P. 2010. *Deleuzian concepts.* Stanford, CA: Stanford University Press.

Postle, D. 2007. *Regulating the psychological therapies: from taxonomy to taxidermy.* Ross-on-Wye: PCCS Books.

Prigogine, I. and Stengers, I. 1984. *Order out of chaos: man's new dialogue with nature.* New York: Bantam Books.

Pulido-Martinez, H.C. 2014. Psy-complex. *In:* Teo, T. (ed.), *Encyclopedia of critical psychology.* New York: Springer.

Rajchman, J. 2000. *The Deleuze connections.* Cambridge, MA: MIT Press.

Rueting, T. 2004. History and significance of Jakob von Uexkull and of his institute in Hamburg. *Sign Systems Studies,* 32, 35–72.

Skott-Myhre, H.A. 2015. Deleuzian perspectives: schizoanalysis and the politics of desire. *In:* Parker, I. (ed.), *Handbook of critical psychology.* London: Routledge.

Smith, D. 2000. Deleuze, Hegel, and the post-Kantian tradition. *Philosophy Today,* 44, 119–31.

Stengers, I. 1997. *Power and invention: situating science.* Minneapolis, MN: University of Minnesota.

Stengers, I. 2000. *The invention of modern science.* Minneapolis, MN: University of Minnesota.

Stenner, P. 2009. On the actualities and possibilities of constructionism. *Human Affairs,* 19, 194–210.

von Uexküll, J. 1934. A stroll through the worlds of animals and men: a picture book of invisible worlds. *In:* Schiller, C.H. (ed.), *Instinctive behaviour: the development of a modern concept.* New York: International Universities Press.

Watters, E. 2010. *Crazy like us: the globalization of the American psyche.* New York: Free Press.

Watzlawick, P., Beavin, J. and Jackson, D.D. 1967. *Pragmatics of human communication.* New York: Norton.

Watzlawick, P., Weakland, J. and Fisch, R. 1974. *Change: principles of problem formation and problem resolution.* New York: Norton.

Zourabichvili, F. 1996. Six notes on the percept (on the relation between the critical and the clinical). *In:* Patton, P. (ed.), *Deleuze: a critical reader.* Cambridge, MA: Blackwell.

Zourabichvili, F. 2012. *Deleuze: a philosophy of the event together with the vocabulary of the event.* Edinburgh: Edinburgh University Press.

5
A PRACTICAL APPROACH
Deleuze and the clinic

It is hard to think of a more positive and productive application of psychology than its application in the clinic. This is so at two levels. On the one hand, clinical work is a direct and noble application of psychology's insights in order to improve human wellbeing. On the other, and due to this direct application, clinical psychology has an important function in terms of its contribution to the credibility and the standing of the profession in the larger community. Images that the lay public has of the work of psychologists – 'performing individual or group therapy, asking questions about psychiatric symptoms, measuring intelligence, or assessing personality' (Cook, 2011) – often fall in the realm of what psychology can do in the clinic rather than in its specific insights. In predictable ways, psychology's insights are valued for their potency in an area that is of direct interest to the wider community. 'Clinical psychology' as such is of course the specialty within the profession that claims mastery in this type of work. As a specialty within the discipline, it requires completion of highly competitive courses and is subject to increasing regulation.

There is, however, something missing in this description, something that relates to the complexities and tribulations that are central to what it is to work as a psychologist in this realm of the clinic. These 'hidden' dynamics seem distant from the images portraying the profession as a locus for rationality, mastery and progress, but once discerned they provide a good opening into the possibilities that Deleuze brings to the clinic. This invisibility highlights many of the points that we have been addressing through the book. In some ways, the clinic is the place not only where 'treatment' is 'provided' but also where one may observe most acutely the tensions between the two approaches to psychology: a psychology informed by royal science versus a psychology informed by minor or nomad science. For the purposes of this chapter, we will introduce some of these dynamics as a way of focusing on the core elements of clinical work: its territorial space and the characters inhabiting such space, the territorialisations taking place and the lines of flight emerging out of its assemblage. We will then discuss some ways in which Deleuze's project can offer powerful insights into the work of the clinic as ways forward to more humane conceptualisations both of the clinic and of our human condition.

What's in a name? Clinical psychology as a professional entity

If the lay person in the community knows of the promises of clinical psychology, they often are not aware how poorly the territory is delineated. An average citizen would not be aware that there are a variety of contesting approaches, wider than psychology as such, claiming knowledge in relation to the care of our suffering. This contestation quickly becomes apparent when a member of the community experiences distress. Should they search for a service to address that distress, they will encounter myriad, for a lack of a better word, 'trades' claiming to provide services that will 'effectively' address their concerns. Among these, there is a hierarchy that has, at its summit, psychiatry as the specialty in medicine that addresses mental pathology. Although psychiatry and its methods have been subject to extensive critique over the decades, critique is muted when issues of significant risk become evident. In these circumstances, a hidden alliance becomes evident that confirms psychiatry as the royal practice. Like the king in Foucault's reflections on Velasquez' painting *Las Meninas* (2004, ch. 1), while the psychiatrist is often physically absent his presence is central in the understanding of the clinic. This central presence is clear when two particular clinical dilemmas take place: the relation with the law and the relation with death. When the community has to make decisions regarding safety – when someone may be a danger to him- or herself or to others – it is the psychiatrist who is central in the negotiating practices. It is the psychiatrist who signs the sectioning papers whereby someone's liberty can be temporarily removed. Close behind the psychiatrist stands the psychologist. Yet at the same time clinical psychology claims scientific superiority over other specialties within the discipline of psychology. Other specialties within psychology include counselling psychology, neuropsychology, applied psychology and others that are more removed from the clinic. But the demarcation does not exhaust itself within psychology: there are also psychotherapists, counsellors, coaches, alternative therapists and even applied philosophers competing for trade. When clinical psychology positions itself as the psychological specialty with the most scientifically credible approach to the clinic, there are significant issues at stake that go beyond a marketing strategy. There are careers and identities, both individual and collective, at stake. These dynamics – the dynamics of the clinic – concern not so much a series of clients considered in isolation as if 'patients in quarantine', but a set of relational definitions that constitute the clinic itself.

In this context, it is important to consider the role of mastery in the clinician. This mastery conceals the mechanisms by which the relational aspects of the clinic are reduced to one specific type of relation: the clinical gaze of the clinician observing and treating the pathos of the client. By the time the student of clinical psychology comes out of training, he or she has the social sanction to occupy a position in the pack whereby the role of mastery may be performed. This is possible because clinical training introduces the apprentice to a nomenclature – *The Diagnostic and Statistical Manual of Mental Disorders* (DSM-5, 2013) – where a complex abecedary of symptoms is organised. The student is further introduced to a complex and highly disciplined set of information regarding what works and what doesn't work in terms of treatment for each specific disorder. Good and 'ethical' practice will require the clinician to uphold 'best practice' defined in those terms. To be familiar with this regime of signs is central to the credibility of the psychologist's practice. The funding of research is also organised around compliance with this language. It is not surprising, then, that the clinic insidiously becomes captured by that language. Clients – persons seeking help – are interrogated according to this professional nomenclature; their profile cleansed of its differences and singularities to comply with a specific profile, a specific standard. Such differences are only called upon when they are required for further clarification within the same system: *differential diagnosis* being perhaps the only time when difference has a significant status in the DSM, enabling the newly defined clinical subject to emerge as an entity for treatment. The mastery of the clinician relates to this ability to see and understand the condition of the person being treated better, more comprehensively, than the person in question her- or himself. Indeed, if we accept Deleuze and Guattari's notion of faciality as a type of subjectivity established within regimes of signs, and if we take note of the mechanisms by which royal clinical knowledge ignores differences, what a 'royal clinician' ends up with is a very particular presentation of the client. We return to this point later in the chapter.

The mastery of the clinical psychologist is intimately connected with medicine, a connection that has been extensively discussed (e.g. Routh, 2012). As Routh notes, 'to speak of "clinical" psychology is to invoke the medical metaphor of care at the bedside of the individual (the Greek word *klinein* refers to a couch or bed)' (2012, p. 23). In this sense, this mastery not only reflects a certain nomenclature but also brings to the fore a different set of relations. It highlights the way in which clinical psychology positions itself – finds its niche, defines its territory – in the clinic. Psychology jumps on the bandwagon of medicine which, in turn, affirms itself as the ultimate master over human suffering. Clinical psychology, at least as taught in mainstream training centres in the Anglo-Saxon countries, claims its privileged position by positioning itself in a kind of camaraderie – brothers in arms – with medical practice. Clinical psychology would claim that their relationship is not one of subservience but, as we said before, one of 'camaraderie' in front of their joined commitment to a scientific approach to the clinical work. Research in clinical psychology, with very few exceptions (Wampold, 2001; Wampold and Imel, 2015), is strongly biased in favour of research that uses psychiatric diagnostic categories. The clinical psychologist subtly accepts a respectable, subordinate role to that of the physician, in particular although not exclusively, to that of the psychiatrist. In this sense, the clinical psychologist aspires to be the most senior and most respected non-medical professional among the allied health workers supporting the work at the clinic, and might be thought of as a superior servant, perhaps the butler in an aristocratic mansion. The butler is a person in whom confidence is placed, someone the master can trust in terms of knowledge, experience and the skill to keep the affairs of a house in order. In order to gain this trust, the butler needs to strongly uphold the values held by the family, often showing more allegiance to those values than some of the family members themselves.

That psychology might be serving a role of a butler in an aristocratic household is a provocative claim to make. But it brings to the fore two elements of importance: it problematises the camaraderie with medicine and at the same time it confirms the image of psychology as a profession of 'service'. To whom is the service offered? From the perspective of a philosophy of difference, there are significant concerns when psychology as a royal science puts in practice its findings in an unreflective manner, and provides a service to the State in the management of those who are different. Psychology as minor science or as nomad science would be a challenging practice. Perhaps the best way to summarise this challenge is by asking whether the work in the clinic should serve the functions of only one (aristocratic if not royal) family or whether the profession could deploy its skills to the service of a universal fraternity.

In considering the differences between a royal and a minor psychological practice, it is important to recall that many of psychology's pioneers came from medicine. This is interesting because, in taking this position, these pioneers made a conscious choice *not* to practise as physicians; they were 'medicine men' who were in search of a different type of understanding. They chose to move away from the orthodox medical approach of their times. This movement reminds us of another series of differences around the clinic and psychology that often is set to the side: the distinctions between clinical psychology, counselling psychology and psychotherapy. Freud, for one, actively advocated that the work in the clinic was not limited to the contribution of the physician and that responding to the problems of the psyche also benefits from other types of knowledge. Bateson did something similar when teaching psychiatry registrars in San Francisco. As Bateson explains:

> In the 1950s, I had two teaching tasks. I was teaching psychiatric residents at the Veterans Administration mental hospital in Palo Alto and young beatniks.... To the psychiatrists, I presented a challenge in the shape of a small exam paper, telling them that by the end of the course they should understand the questions in it. Question 1 asked for brief definitions of (a) 'sacrament' and (b) 'entropy'.... I was offering my class the core notions of 2,500 years of thought about religion and science. I felt that if they were going to be doctors (medical doctors) of the human soul, they should at least have a foot on each side of the ancient arguments.
>
> *2002, pp. 5–6*

Certainly, medicine itself has suffered significant transformations as Foucault has described (1973), transformations that seem to have been ironed out, to have been erased, in the current image of a monolithic and natural-scientific medical discipline. This reduction of the profession of medicine to a monolithic idealisation seems to be mirrored by the often clichéd critiques of the medical model, critiques that unfortunately seem to dismiss the complexities of the clinic (Barney, 1994) as a space that offers ongoing resistance to systems that have tried to capture it.

What's in a name? The clinic as an assemblage

The problematic nature of the camaraderie between psychology and medicine highlights the importance of the second association between the disciplines, that by which medicine provides a scientific model for psychology. In line with the concerns we discussed in Chapter 3 in relation to science, when looking at these concerns in the clinic, we are left with a clear reduction of pathology to something that belongs to an individual person. Much of the effort of psychology to find ways to help those experiencing distress has been translated into formulaic consideration both of the psyche and of the suffering. It is ironic that clinical psychology might come to see the shortcomings of such an orientation not because of its own reflections but as a consequence of the struggles that psychiatry itself has had. In particular, clinical psychology has found itself reacting to and accommodating the vicissitudes of psychiatric classification schemes, for example in relation to the most recent (2013) version of the DSM. It is in this context that, using Deleuzian ideas, it now becomes important to consider whether psychiatry, the science called upon by psychology as a foundation for its practice in the clinic, is itself a royal or a minoritarian science. Foucault and those who expanded on his work have highlighted the ways by which psychiatry has oriented itself to the categorising and departmentalising of human experience and to establishing norms by which to judge the human condition. A Deleuzian framework makes us aware that the DSM needs to be considered as much more than a manual on 'how to approach pathology', a set of directions providing the criteria for establishing what is claimed to be 'sound diagnosis' of patients. A Deleuzian framework insists that such a manual is part of a larger State machine. At one level, the DSM can be understood as a useful repository of the ideas of the dominant regime of signs. Not only does it provide information as to what is said to constitute pathology, and what falls within the realms of 'normal' experience, but it also tells us who is being observed and who is doing the observing. Furthermore, the DSM needs to be understood in relation to the legal structure that defines the roles and responsibilities of citizens in the community. When is a crime mitigated by mental health considerations and to what extent? When is it appropriate for one citizen – namely, a psychiatrist – to curtail the liberties of another? The complexities of the clinic – of the clinical dimension – participates in a much larger set of regulations of life in the community. An understanding of the clinic from a Deleuzian perspective acknowledges the clinic as a particular place, a place that is constituted as an assemblage but also is a part of a larger assemblage. It is in this context that Foucault's considerations on the governmental functions of madness are vital.

Madness serves a number of functions that are not discussed in any version of the DSM: how we deal with difference in society, how we select and how we protect those who are healthy and those who are not.

The clinic is connected with the governmentality that defines norms and defines the processes of normalisation of the dilemmas that life presents. This brings us back to the psy-complex. The psy-complex is so pervasive these days because it constitutes a background not only for psychiatry, psychology and other psy-disciplines (McAvoy, 2014) but for society at large. It provides a stable opinion – instead of chaos – that provides a steady platform for the construction not only of a unified 'normal science' but of reality full-stop. This is why Deleuze warns us that opinion is more dangerous than the chaos from which it protects us. We need science in the same manner that we need other practices – art and philosophy – to engage constructively with chaos and to confront the tragic condition of our lives. At the same time, some degree of opinion and taken-for-granted reality helps us to keep some sanity through a sense of shared normality. As Deleuze says, we only need some subjectivity. Science is only one of the dimensions of the clinic and sanity is only one aspect of our complex lives. There are serious dangers in reducing the clinic to a science that makes an arbitrary claim to the status of paradigmatic, normal science (Bradley, 2005; Stenner, 2009). Falling in with this claim is an artificial wish that betrays our search for solace and, even worse, betrays both those who practise in the clinic and those who the clinic claims to serve. The search for support – for allies – while navigating through one's tribulations turns into a 'name' and becomings stagnate in predictable and oppressive roles.

More than the institutionalisation of what others have called the psy-complex, what interests Deleuze is the productive functionings of the assemblage, functionings that confirm the clinic as a genuine space in society. But this space, like everything else we encounter in Deleuze, needs to be reconceptualised and understood as variations present in all aspects of life. Consistent with his concerns with other major or royal activities, Deleuze does not see the task of the clinic as predominantly one of subjectification and domestication through the use of efficient royal science. There is of course an element of diagnosis involved in the clinic – a diagnosis of precisely these elements of subjectification – but, what is of more importance to Deleuze, the clinic involves processes of renewal and (re)engagement with life and with that which is healthy. Life presents a multitude of challenges – as Deleuze might say, we are confronted with the violence of a certain throw of the dice – and what is important is to find the noble solutions to the problems cast into our path. It is (Nietzsche's) eternal return that gives life its tragic and, at the same time, its joyful condition by affirming all the possible presentations that can manifest as life. Life is a dice-throw and to live requires people to affirm this multiplicity by engaging with the ordeals that present to ourselves – 'misfortune, sickness, madness, even the approach of death' (Deleuze, 1986, p. 125) – in ways that are transformative of the suffering. This tragic engagement is then transformed into a heroism of sorts by providing those enduring such circumstances – the specific throw of the dice embodied through their lives – with a certain nobility that escapes external evaluation (Nichterlein, 2013b, p. 241).

We have thus far discussed aspects of the clinic that centre on the conduct of the person occupying the professional role. We have done so to highlight how striated such space has become, when it is only understood and practised as an evidence-based practice. In such a practice the patient or client is often subordinated to the role of providing a clinical presentation, as a vehicle or a vector of symptoms. This description obscures complex processes present in the clinic. The clinic is fundamentally a space where change is sought, where the state of things that the person seeking help experiences has become intolerable and something needs to be done. The questions underlying the mechanisms of the clinic have a direct relationship with the clinicians' beliefs as to how to facilitate this change. But orthodox understanding of the clinic relegates change to the periphery, putting identity, the identity of pathos, at the centre. It is here that Deleuze's project provides such a powerful alternative to approach the clinic. With the move from identity to difference, change and transformation become central. It is thus essential for the clinic to come to terms with Deleuze's insistence that what best describes our human condition is not the concept of static beings but of fluid *becomings*.

People's becomings

Deleuze's 'becoming' is a very different concept from the orthodox, humanistic understanding of becoming. For Deleuze, 'becoming' does not pertain exclusively to humans, and it takes us in a very different direction from hermeneutics and general humanistic values. Indeed, Deleuze's ideas are often associated with machinic and post-human approaches (e.g. Clarke, 2008; Hayles, 1999; Wolfe, 1998, 2010).

The concept of becoming was present in Deleuze's work since his book on Nietzsche (May, 2003, p. 139). Becoming for Deleuze is not the romantic idea of a self that actualises its potential through a lineal mechanism of expression of a (transcendental) essence. Deleuze makes a clear distinction between becoming and history: 'Becoming begins in history and returns to it, but it is not of history. The opposite of history is not the eternal, but becoming' (Deleuze and Eribon, 1991, p. 377). Becoming is a Deleuzian version of the Nietzschean eternal return that articulates its own presence through the ongoing transformation of whatever is, including the self, into something else: into an-*other* to itself. As Deleuze explains, 'becoming itself as intrinsically transformative, creative, and marginal – and as intrinsically multiple. Becoming has "itself" no fixed identity or being, is always becoming-other' (1995, p. 186 n. 8).

Becoming is the concrete manifestation of the schizophrenic process described by Deleuze and Guattari in *Anti-Oedipus*: the process of the person being always open to the encounter with the outside and to the production of new combinations. This is possible because, as Gatens explains, 'the human body is radically open to its surroundings and can be composed, recomposed and decomposed by other bodies' (1996, p. 165). Becoming is also a relational term that affirms the profound ways in which the human body can be affected and can engage with its environment. In this sense, becoming is also 'always "between" or among' a (departing) self and an (attractive) other (Deleuze, 1997, p. 2).

Becomings are also always collective. There is no becoming of an individual that does not imply an equal process on the other side. The becoming of one's self is paired with the becoming of the other or of the context in such a way that any distinction between these processes is highly arbitrary. As we have already stated, both the self and the world are by-products of the same desiring machine and inherent parts of a unique assemblage. Deleuze and Guattari write:

> There is no such thing as either man or nature now, only a process that produces the one within the other and couples the machines together.... Not man as the king of creation, but rather as the being who is in intimate contact with the profound life of all forms or all types of being.
>
> *1983, pp. 2, 4*

It is in this sense that Deleuze identifies the becoming-imperceptible as the ultimate form of actualisation. That is to say, what is desirable is to establish a smooth connection with the assemblage to the extent that it – the assemblage – is highly unique but the person in itself is not central but facilitates the functioning of the assemblage. It is in this sense that Deleuze focuses his attention not on the self-sufficient figure of the 'master and commander' but on a more problematic and troubled figure of the human condition. Rather than a (sublime) hero, what defined for Deleuze the human condition is better expressed by the image of a stuttering anti-hero such as Melville's Bartleby (Deleuze, 1997, ch. 10; Ranciere, 2004) or of an artist struggling with ill-health.

Furthermore, for Deleuze it is a mistake to talk about human life as a 'privileged' – even perhaps 'superior' – entity that is neatly distinguishable from its geopolitical contingencies. As we have already discussed, for Deleuze the sense of self is a by-product of territorialisation. As a by-product, it always runs the risk of being a faciality; a part of a regime of signs serving a function within the State apparatus and positioning individuals in defined, definite and static spaces. As an alternative to State definitions – which Foucault called biopower – Deleuze and Guattari already clarify in *Anti-Oedipus* that subjectivity is *only* for consumption. The sense one has of one's self is a production; a product whose main functions are to express a certain state of affairs and, perhaps of even more importance, to provide elements for further experimentation. In such an analysis, it is the transgression of limits established by the definitions of the self – the moments when the self forgets its own definition – that are central to the constitution and the health of humane life. This forgetting is also important to understand the centrality of a key concept for Deleuze: becoming-imperceptible.

Deleuze's gesture should not be considered to be a nihilistic project. Humans have the capacity to fully engage in life when they no longer recognise an individuality that separates them from their larger ecology. In other words and in a manner that is paradoxical, humans are able to be more fully present when they are able to let go of their identities in favour of a vitalistic and affirmative connection with larger forces: when they 'cease to be subjects to become events, in assemblages that are inseparable from an hour, a season, an atmosphere, an air, a life' (Deleuze and Guattari, 1987, p. 263). In this sense, becomings are individuations that are not self-centred but event-centred. They constitute a 'logic of impersonal individuation rather than personal individualization' (Rajchman, 2001, p. 8). This impersonal individuation transcends the person and presents a singularity – a *haecceity*, a moment and a circumstance – that is unique and intimately associated with a time and place outside; 'a gust of wind' as Deleuze remarks. This moment of impersonal singularisation is an example of the articulation of immanence that Deleuze saw as central. As a process, it escapes all attempts of description, because descriptions return processes to familiar and predictable points of reference. Deleuze writes:

What is immanence? A life.... No one has described what *a* life is better than Charles Dickens.... Between [a disreputable man's] life and his death, there is a moment that is only that of *a* life playing with death. The life of the individual gives way to an impersonal and yet singular life ... a '*homo tantum*' with whom everyone empathizes and who attains a sort of beatitude. It is a haecceity no longer of individuation but of singularization: a life of pure immanence, neutral, beyond good and evil.... The life of such individuality fades away in favour of the singular life immanent to a man who no longer has a name, though he can be mistaken for no other. A singular essence, a life.

2001, pp. 28–9

In summary, 'Becoming is a verb with a consistency all its own; it does not reduce to, or lead back to, "appearing", "being", "equaling [*sic*]", or "producing"' (Deleuze and Guattari, 1987, p. 239). It is an untimely process, infinite and endless in nature. Like a Batesonian plateau that never reaches a culmination or a climax of some sort, the becomings that traverse our bodies never reach a 'final point', a destination and/or actualisation. It is instead an untimely becoming of the 'people to come'. 'The people to come' is a powerful image in terms of what we do in life and what is done in the clinic. Deleuze invites us to live a life that is decentred yet unique, affirmative and focused on the future.

Therapy as experimental becomings in the world: schizoanalysis and variations in the clinic

The concept of becoming helps to engage with the clinic in a very different way to current practices. Rather than a focus on what is – the identifying and categorising of signs – the focus shifts to the supporting of a process of change. Change is, however, not a 'controlled' exercise. It is instead an engagement with the constructive and experimental nature of both life and knowledge so as to free the becoming of the people seeking help. This transformative process is neither fully conscious nor interpretative. Nor is it a rational process of 'storytelling' because such a process is inevitably limited by the linguistic structures within which the story is organised. It is instead an attempt to *think otherwise*: an awkward self-awareness that arises from the insights that emerged out of structuralism (Dosse, 1997a, 1997b) into the ways in which linguistic structures shape one's experience, often unconsciously. In this sense, the (re)turn to health present in the clinic is conceived as a process of genuine experimentation that, rather than reflecting or interpreting pre-established definitions, creates a space and a 'sense' for the workings of a particular possibility of the people that seek help; a space that, recursively, facilitates further movement.

In *Anti-Oedipus*, Deleuze and Guattari introduced the idea of *schizoanalysis* as their alternative to psychoanalysis. Schizoanalysis honours the insights of psychoanalysis in terms of the production of desire. But in schizoanalysis, desire is no longer indexed to the family but to the historical, political and social world (Deleuze, 1984, pp. 238–9). This new way of engaging with desire makes it 'inseparable from its revolutionary component' (Holland, 1999, p. 99). The task of schizoanalysis is 'that of learning what a subject's desiring machines are, how they work, with what synthesis, what bursts of energy, what constituents misfires, with what flows, what chains and what becomings in each case' (Deleuze and Guattari, 1983, p. 338). Schizoanalysis does not aim to 'understand' but to engage more freely with life. This 'liberating' activity is not to be associated with any political or otherwise predefined movement: although social in nature, it is essentially experimental and anarchic. What is important to Deleuze and to Guattari is the ongoing process of differentiation and of experimentation that constitutes life. With this in mind, Deleuze and Guattari align themselves with Foucault (1978, 1984, 1986) who, in turn, had emphasised that rather than becoming preoccupied with 'the eternal' or with the attempt to 'reflect history', what is important is 'to diagnose our actual becomings'. Thus we discern a becoming-revolutionary distinct, as Kant himself in effect recognised, from the actuality not only of any historical revolution but of any future revolution (Deleuze and Guattari, 1991, pp. 112–13). The revolution that Deleuze and Guattari refer to in Kant has a direct connection with the Enlightenment and the idea of a fraternal society (Kant, 1784). Kant defined *Aufklärung* – the Enlightenment – as an exit from a heteronomous state of 'immaturity' of humankind and a move towards autonomy in one's thought. That is, a state where humankind no longer relies on an external source (the king or God) to decide what to do, but has the courage to think for itself. Deleuze's resistance to *la bêtise* resonates with Foucault's reading of Kant. For Foucault, *Aufklärung* needs to be considered both as a process in which people participate collectively (through their alignment into current regimes of truth) and as an act of courage to be accomplished personally. In this reading, *Aufklärung* is an attitude towards life that represents

> a difficult interplay between the truth of what is real and the exercise
> of freedom, an exercise in which extreme attention to what is real is

confronted with the practice of a liberty that simultaneously respects this reality and violates it.

Schmidt and Wartenberg, 1994, p. 301

The double gesture that Foucault reads in Kant's revolutionary spirit is the type of differentiation that Deleuze sees worth pursuing: a certain collective – a pack – within which the individual differentiates itself.

An important corollary of the model of psychic and social organisation called forth by schizoanalysis is that there is no 'necessary' tension between the individual and systems of social inscription – regimes of signs. The presence and degree of tensions between these two domains will depend on how able the social organisation is to respect the individual within the social (Holland, 1999, p. 31). In other words, the harmony of any social organisation will depend on its ability to respect the schizophrenic process proper to the individual psyche which, in its relationship with the outside, establishes and creates the social. It is in this sense that, for Deleuze, capitalism is such a powerful social organisation, since it affords the largest diversity of modes of being and also proves to be highly fluid in its operation. But capitalism returns production to the form of capital that can be alienated and appropriated, in the same way that psychoanalysis returns desires to the nuclear family. Like Marx, for whom the capitalist form of production unwittingly prepares the ground for socialist forms, Deleuze and Guattari see in capitalism a move in a necessary and perhaps a desirable direction: the consumer society cannot simply be shrugged off or narrated away. After all 'D and G' also refers to Dolce & Gabbana, and differentiation is inextricably connected with the forces that shape society.

Consistent with his commitment to ongoing transformation and to resistance to mechanisms of capture, the year after *Anti-Oedipus* was written Deleuze commented that 'we no longer want to talk about schizoanalysis, because that would amount to protecting a particular type of escape, schizophrenic escape' (1973, p. 280). Deleuze's statement is not a questioning of schizoanalysis per se but an affirmation of the multiplicity present in life, multiplicity that the clinic needs to take account of. Standing in stark contrast with the reductionist tendencies inherent to a royal science of evidence-based practice, Deleuze insists on the impossibility of controlling change and of predicting the flow immanent to life. There is no one method that will do the trick, and there is no one ending to the story. The presence of health is, in fact, measured by its gradient of differentiation, which is to say, by its creative and novel way to provide unique responses to the problems inherent to living a life. It is in this sense that, for Deleuze, the experimentation that takes place in the clinic is more like a stutter than a well-polished script, it is movement that takes place in '*regions far from equilibrium*' where '*a minor use* of the major language' is invented and is put to use (Deleuze, 1997, p. 109).

Despite the fluidity, Deleuze continued to discuss the clinic. His investigations into specific aspects of the clinic started in 1967, a year earlier than *Difference and Repetition*, when he published *Masochism: Coldness and Cruelty* (2006). *Masochism* was the beginning of a continuing investigation (Smith, 1997, p. xii) into the connections between literature and the clinic, more specifically a critique and an engagement with the clinic using literary tools. Deleuze's last collection – *Essays Critical and Clinical* (1997) – was also an investigation of the clinic in relation to this powerful ally, literature. Informed by these writings, for the remainder of the chapter we look at some of the most important structural elements that Deleuze identifies as characteristic of the clinic. In particular we address the points Deleuze makes in an interview in 1977 (Deleuze and Parnet, 2006). The three elements that Deleuze considered central to the clinic are: first, 'the function of the proper name'; second 'a regime of signs'; and third the movement away from such a regime through a line of flight.

The proper name in the clinic: a term of art

For Deleuze, the constructive nature of knowledge and the central role of the author or artist is of particular relevance for the modern condition where 'the order of the cosmos has collapsed, crumbled into associative chains and noncommunicating viewpoints' (2000, p. 113) and where 'the only wholeness and unity available is that which may be constructed in art' (Bogue, 2003, p. 58). In such chaos, the artist becomes a central image for the construction of chaosmos. The artist is the one that becomes, and he or she becomes through the creation of 'a life'. In Deleuzian terms this means a certain moment of singularisation: a unique individuality that populates the space in ways that are beyond good and bad (Deleuze, 2001, pp. 28–9). It is this individuality, more than the author of a clinical diagnosis or even the artist, to which Deleuze is referring with the 'function of the proper name'. The proper name that is being searched for in the clinic is that of a singular assemblage. As Deleuze explains, 'an assemblage may have been in existence for a long time before it receives its proper name which gives it a special consistence as if it were thus separated from a more general regime to assume a kind of autonomy' (Deleuze and Parnet, 2006, p. 89).

Clinicians have some awareness of this idea through the familiar process of diagnosis. Diagnostic categories provide a certain organisation for the constellation of symptoms. Such organisation acquires a certain autonomy that has its own effects. Something happens to the sense of self once a diagnosis, a proper name, is given. An example of these dynamics can be found in a story well-known among systemic thinkers. Told by Watzlawick but with reference to Gordon Allport, the story refers to a man gravely ill who is in a regional hospital where doctors are stymied by the absence of a diagnosis. They say to the man that, if they had a diagnosis, they could probably cure him. They also comment that 'a famous diagnostician' is soon to visit the hospital. When the diagnostician arrives he glances at the patient, murmurs 'moribundus' and passes on. To the surprise of the hospital and of the diagnostician, the patient recovers. He says, 'They told me that if you could diagnose me I'd get well, and so the minute you said "moribundus" I knew I'd recover' (Watzlawick, 1984, p. 109). Needless to say, a crucial part of the story is that the patient does not know the meaning of the word moribundus, affording him to engage with the diagnosis in a way other than as a death sentence. This is the power of voodoo and of placebos alike, a power that is often neglected in a society where pharmacology has so much invested in the use of medication as the path for cure.

With Foucault, Deleuze emphasised that symptoms are constellations of signs that point to the effects of the complex forces present in the life of individuals. For Deleuze these effects produce affects, pathos. Deleuze notes that these signs are ordered, 'named, renamed and regrouped in various ways' (Deleuze, 2006, p. 15) and that, through history, there have been significant changes to such ordering, as well as to the therapeutic practices they produce. As Deleuze states, 'Illnesses are sometimes named after typical patients [e.g. sado-masochism], but more often it is the doctor's name that is given to the disease.' This is so because 'The doctor does not invent the illness, he dissociates symptoms that were previously grouped together, and links up others that were dissociated. In short he builds up a profoundly original clinical picture.'

Like the scientist and the artist, the clinician establishes a certain order, an assemblage that defines not only the presentation of the patient suffering the condition but also the actions of the clinician treating it. In this sense there are many characters populating an assemblage. Families and significant others – including at times the justice system – also have their actions defined according to the presentation in question. The proper name of a diagnosis then can be considered as 'a collective that meets other collectives, that combines and interconnects with others, reactivating, inventing, bringing to the future, bringing about non-personal individuations' (Deleuze and Parnet, 2006, pp. 89–90). This is in fact the power of the diagnosis, of naming a condition in a certain manner. It is a direct reference to becomings. These constellations are orchestrated by the clinician, with the names of others often emerging as characters subordinate to the master voice of the clinician. In their standardisation, systems of diagnosis have a deeply conservative role, a role that restrains the movement of people's becomings: 'This is the diagnosis, this is the path to health and this is the way you enact this path.'

There is, however, a critical possibility, a possibility that Deleuze sees as supported by literature. Deleuze opens the first chapter of *Masochism* asking the question 'What are the uses of literature?' The question emerges as a way to question the aggregation of 'sadism' and 'masochism' into one diagnostic category. The gesture of Deleuze is double here: he not only critiques the amalgamation of these two clinical presentations into one presentation, 'sado-masochism', but he also critiques the appropriation of these names by different doctors through time. For Deleuze, there is more value in focusing on Sade and on Masoch as authors themselves of possibilities of life. This reorientation has significant effects for Deleuze. As he writes,

> Because the judgement of the clinician is prejudiced, we must take an entirely different approach, the *literary approach*.... The critical (in the literary sense) and the clinical (in the medical sense) may be destined to enter into a new relationship of mutual learning. Symptomatology is always a question of art.
>
> *Deleuze, 2006, p. 14*

Deleuze argues that the connection between literature and the clinical is possible due to the peculiar nature of the 'symptomatological' method, a method central to clinical practice. Symptomatology constitutes an essentially creative act of organising the symptoms in order to form a figure of either health or illness (Deleuze, 1990a, p. 237). Given that these symptoms are signs of possibilities of life, their interpretation is not limited to clinicians only. As Deleuze writes, 'symptomology is located almost outside medicine, at a neutral point, a zero point, where artists and philosophers and doctors and patients can come together' (Deleuze and Chapsal, 1967, p. 134). This movement of democratisation of the diagnosis, and allowing for authors other than the physician, is at the heart of the *open dialogue* (Seikkula and Olson, 2003) and the *recovery movement* in mental health (Duff, 2014, ch. 4; Kerman *et al.*, 2014): yet we think that its reach is even further.

A regime of signs in the clinic

The second element identified by Deleuze as pertaining to the clinic is that the clinic – like any other territorialised space – has a distinctive regime of signs. We have talked already of the DSM and we also point to the theoretical constellations that different clinical practices bring to the fore. Each clinical practice expresses a certain 'order of things' and, for Deleuze, it is central 'to ask, each time, what the flux of writing is connected with. . . . [T]he first task would be to study the regimes of signs employed by an author, and what mixtures he uses' (Deleuze and Parnet, 2006, p. 90).

Deleuze was also concerned with the practice of grouping symptoms into specific diagnoses, because of the implied danger of engendering totalitarian regimes of signs. He was particularly critical of the use that clinicians make of symptomatology. Following the example of masochism, Deleuze argued that Sade's and Masoch's projects were incommensurably and essentially different in their treatment both of sexuality and of violence, and thus of politics. That prevalent clinical traditions of the time were not able to notice this was a serious concern for Deleuze. He writes:

> there is an urgent need for clinical psychology to keep away from sweeping unities ... the idea of a sado-masochism is simply a prejudice [that] results from hasty symptomatology, such that we no longer attempt *to see* what is there, but seek instead to justify our prior idea.
>
> *Deleuze and Chapsal, 1967, p. 133*

This blindness is core to the vicissitudes of the clinic and is a key problem for ethical practice. Not only does the person experiencing distress have the challenge of learning to live with the anxieties inherent to finding a path to health, a path that often includes seeking help, but such a person also has to be guarded regarding the appropriations present in the place they seek refuge. This is a serious betrayal.

Clinicians have an ethical imperative to avoid the blindness of an uncritical engagement with the sets of conceptualisations that inform their very identity as clinicians. Iatrogenic damage – the damaged caused by the medicine – is perhaps more deeply felt in our discipline where clinicians are acutely aware that it is 'words' and what the clinician 'does with words' that is at the heart of their practice and that makes the difference in their practice. In the apparent simplicity of such 'tools' it is not surprising that clinicians find it hard at times to accept the impact of their inability to see the other – the person seeking help – both in their tribulations but also in their possibilities. We are not claiming that clinicians should have an omniscient gaze. The point we are making refers to the importance of maintaining deterritorialising spaces that position the clinician as more curious about what the person seeking help 'can do' rather than focusing on 'what they are' and, perhaps more worryingly, searching for the definition of a pathology (Nichterlein, 2013a).

There is a need for the clinician to establish a singularity within the regimes of signs in which he or she operates, a critical distance from its powers in the clinic, so as to be able to recognise its dangers. It is at this level that there is a need to study the regimes of signs employed not only by the people seeking help but also by those providing it. Such a study serves a number of purposes. As we have already indicated, it serves to identify the players and the territory demarcating the suffering that presents to the clinic. This process of naming the elements at play has not only a critical and diagnostic aspect but is in itself productive and therapeutic. In line with Deleuze's critique of representation, Deleuze and Guattari saw in 'cartography' an alternative to traditional clinical practices: no longer the search for assessment according to interpretive principles, but an active engagement with the act of creating maps of life. Understood this way, cartography is at the centre of the work in the clinic and, as an activity, it needs to be differentiated from the archaeology of psychodynamic pursuits. Consistent with the distinction between history and becoming, Deleuze critiques the traditional approach to the clinic because it is 'a memorial, commemorative, or monumental conception that pertains to persons or objects, the milieus being nothing more than terrains capable of conserving, identifying, or authenticating them' (1997, p. 63). Such an approach 'unearths' what is already there. In this process, there is an ongoing connection with static identity in a way that 'pegs down' change and difference. The clinic, then, is a box – a black box to be precise – where mysterious things are done by the master, operations that result in change. What takes place in the box is explained differently by different approaches. That is, it is to some extent irrelevant because the representational structure is the same. Cartography, Deleuze and Guattari claim, is something else. Cartography refers to making maps and 'a *map is not a tracing*' (Deleuze and Guattari, 1987, p. 12). Whereas 'The tracing has already translated the map into an image' (Deleuze and Guattari, 1987, p. 13), the map is 'entirely oriented toward an experimentation in contact with the real. . . . It fosters connections between fields, the removal of blockages' (Deleuze and Guattari, 1987, p. 12). For Deleuze and Guattari, cartography is a word for the rhizome and, as an activity, it is closer to pragmatics and empiricism than to pre-defined theoretical structures. 'We never know what the body can do' is a maxim used by Deleuze to summarise his admiration of Spinoza. The same phrase shows its potential in the clinic as Jenkins has discussed (2011a, 2011b). Jenkins approaches Deleuze through the use of 'resilience'. He asks how could this concept be approached 'in a world obsessed with the measurement and cataloguing of deficits and virtues alike; with predicting outcomes, producing certainty and the reification of stable identity?' (2011a, p. 33). The same considerations apply to each of the categories that we have learned as part of our disciplinarian approach to the clinic. The challenge, then, is to the regime of signs that constitute ourselves as masters in the clinic.

Deleuze's challenge, however, goes beyond this. He warns us also of the dangers of turning his ideas into a new set of predictable and stable mechanisms for the clinic. If there is anything to be learned from Deleuze, it is that life works by change and differentiation. Whatever the 'state of the art' in therapeutic intervention is at any one moment in time, it will move and change in the next. As with the untimely question of how one is to live one's life, there is also an untimely quest by the therapist to engage artistically with their trade so as to facilitate the clinical encounter in its untimely uniqueness. In such a context, perhaps the greatest dangers for clinicians are those identified long ago by Whitehead, the dangers of misplaced concreteness and of uncritically assuming that specific types of reifications of life (predefined subjectivities, diagnostic categories, etc.) are 'the real thing'. It is at this point that a regime of signs becomes a totalitarian mechanism of control. As we have tried to highlight in the course of this book, this is a practice that, as Foucault has warned us, turns our life into the life of 'docile bodies' and, as Deleuze equally warns, stops our schizophrenic wanderings. This danger is a continuous reminder of one's untimely need of owning our responsibility of becoming-imperceptible; of owning our engagement with life and with what is to come.

A line of flight in the clinic

Even more than the proper name and the awareness of the regimes of signs of the clinic, what is central for Deleuze is the search for opportunities of deterritorialisation available to the therapeutic encounter. For Deleuze the essential point is 'the way in which all these regimes of signs move along a line of gradient' (Deleuze and Parnet, 2006, p. 90). The lines of flight that are present in any therapeutic encounter is the third element to consider. These lines of flight are unpredictable. Here we disagree with authors who have tried to over-define this process and, through this gesture, turn the line of flight into a humanising activity (Winslade, 2009). The line of flight is closer to art than to technique. It refers to the opportunities that present themselves for the clinic to move towards smooth spaces, opportunities that escape the naming and the endless mechanisms of capture that transform our existence, both as a person who seeks help in the clinic and as clinicians, into a banality that is suffocating. What is most important for Deleuze is to chart the ways in which the clinic can move toward the formation of singularities, of what Deleuze calls *haecceities*, 'individuations which are precise and without a subject, which are definable solely by affects or powers (and it is not necessarily the strongest that wins; it is not the one who is the richest in affects)' (2006, p. 91).

In this gesture, Deleuze specifies the final connection between literature and the clinic in terms of the position of etiology in clinical practice. Whereas medicine sees a necessary connection between symptomatology and etiology, the creative literary writer is not bound to this connection and can explore other relationships. It is the openness found in the writer of great literature that Deleuze sees as most productive and relevant for the clinic. Literature – good literature Deleuze feels the need to clarify – engages not with pathology but with health and brings forth new possibilities of existence. What literature brings to the clinic is its appreciation of the affirmative and transformative powers inherent to 'the great books [that] give tomorrow's health' (Deleuze, 1985, p. 147). Deleuze discusses this productive aspect of literature in the second edition of *Proust and Signs* (2000), adding a chapter for this purpose. He writes: 'the modern work of art is a machine and functions as such' (2000, p. 145), producing signs and affects. Literature for Deleuze, rather than being an interpretation of what is 'out there', engages with the real in order to produce possibilities of life. The artist engages neither in the representation of an objective reality nor in a subjective interpretation, but in the articulation of a self-differentiating difference. Here, the clinician can take lessons from the great authors. This is possible because, for Deleuze, language is a 'heterogeneous assemblage in perpetual disequilibrium [that] cannot be broken down into its elements [but] can be broken down into *diverse languages ad infinitum*' (Deleuze, 1990b, p. 368, emphasis added). As Deleuze explains,

> The world is the set of symptoms whose illness merges with man. Literature then appears as an enterprise of health.... What health would be sufficient to liberate life wherever it is imprisoned by and within man, by and within organisms and genera? ... Health as literature, as writing, consists in inventing a people who are missing....

This is not exactly a people called upon to dominate the world. It is a minor people, eternally minor, taken up in a becoming-revolutionary ... a bastard people, inferior, dominated, always in becoming, always incomplete. *Bastard* no longer designates a familial state, but the process or drift of the races.

1997, pp. 3–4

Deleuze's understanding privileges stylistics and pragmatics over aetiology. Deleuze calls on Proust to explain this orientation: 'every great author speaks a kind of a foreign language.... When I say style is like a foreign language, it is none other than the language we speak – it is a foreign language *in* the language we speak' (1990b, p. 370). In this sense, 'Every language is a kind of Black or Chicano English ... there is always another language in every language ad infinitum. This is not a mixture, it is heterogenesis' (Deleuze, 1990b, p. 367). It is the creation of a new possibility of life. As Deleuze writes,

What counts for a great novelist – Melville, Dostoyevsky, Kafka, or Musil – is that things remain enigmatic yet nonarbitrary: in short, a new logic, definitively a logic, but one that grasps the innermost depths of life and death without leading us back to reason. The novelist has the eye of a prophet, not the gaze of a psychologist.

1997, p. 82

It is thus *in* language rather than *with* language that change is affirmed. It is not the articulation of specific storylines (for example following standardised treatment recommendations or even 'helping clients to tell their stories') whereby change takes place, but through the manipulation of the regimes of signs that not only shape the distress but also shape the characters who experience such distress. An author of great literature experiments with language and pushes it to its limits 'mak[ing] the language itself scream, stutter, stammer, or murmur' (Deleuze, 1997, p. 110). Bogue explains that 'The artist, the surrounding world and the work of art are all part of an apersonal unfolding of signs, and the finished artwork is a Joycean "chaosmos," a chaos-become-cosmos' (2003, pp. 3–4). This is becoming, this is 'a composed chaos, neither foreseen not preconceived' that is continually self-differentiating and, through this process, creating a multitude of plateaus. Similarly, a good clinician engages in a transformative process with the person seeking help so as to find new and often unexpected ways of dealing with the circumstances that lead the person seeking help to attend the clinic.

Literature, as a process productive of difference, enters in resonance with the clinic simultaneously at two levels. At one level, it addresses the individual life of its clients by understanding the individuality involved in their search for a humane life, a process that includes but is not limited to a personal construction of a storyline. This search for a humane life is a different process from the eradication of symptoms. It refers back to a joyful acceptance of one's throw of the dice, an engagement where suffering is to some extent inevitable yet is not destructive, is rather a mechanism to understand and engage with larger processes of life. Deleuze saw this process as one of becoming an 'original'. As he explains,

> Each original is a powerful, solitary Figure that exceeds any explicable form: it projects flamboyant traits of expression that mark the stubbornness of a thought without image, a question without response, an extreme and nonrational logic. Figures of life and knowledge, they know something inexpressible, live something unfathomable. They have nothing general about them, and are not particular – they escape knowledge, defy psychology.
>
> *Deleuze, 1997, pp. 82–3*

The challenge for the clinician, then is not to read the becomings of those accessing the clinic according to pre-established regimes of signs, but to engage in paradoxical ways with such regimes of signs so as to help those approaching the clinic to transcend those regimes, and become originals.

In line with this impossible task, and perhaps of even more importance, literature resonates with the clinic by fully integrating the social in its operation. Literature at this level reminds the clinic of its untimely political and ethical responsibility to focus its work on facilitating the emergence of minority becomings. In this, the clinic itself is conceived as a unique space that is in constant danger of being (over)defined, a process through which its ethos is transformed, from a space of healing into a stratified space serving other purposes, namely, the confirmation of a wider social order, an order with winners and losers. In the latter, the clinic is transformed into an institutional set of disciplinarian practices that position people's becomings within regimes of subjectification. Within such a regime, a literary approach to the clinic enters into a play of difference by creating lines of flight out of this present system of (re)presentation, articulating an untimely reminder that the clinic is, primarily, an art form rather than a technical exercise.

It is in this ongoing play of differentiation that the artist has a revolutionary potential and the clinic a therapeutic one. We have already talked about the notion of revolution for Deleuze, and there is value in looking at the notion of the revolutionary artist in its relationship with the *minor*. The minor is not a term that is part of a dualism – it is not the opposite of the major – but refers to a qualitatively different relation in the artistic engagement, one that is necessarily political. As Smith comments, 'If art was to find a political task, Deleuze argues, it would have to be on a new basis ... not that of addressing an already existing people, but of contributing to the invention of a people who are *missing*' (1997, pp. xli–xlii). Those who are missing, those who are not present in civil life, constitute a minority that is not quantitative in nature – for often there is a larger number of individuals in the minority groups – but refers to a unique and alternative way of existence: 'a minority by definition has no model; *it is itself a becoming or a process*' (p. xliii). Minorities can be seen as groups of people, as marginal neighbourhoods that resist mainstream definitions (Richardson and Skott-Myhre, 2012); a multitude of collectives actively engaged with their contingencies. In other words, they are nomad assemblages. Their literature is part of a Deleuzian war/nomad machine and articulates the endless variation of life by constantly imagining new possibilities of movement. It is in this light that we can understand the words of Milan Kundera: 'the writing of a novel takes up a whole era in a writer's life, and when the labor is done he is no longer the person he was at the start' (2007, p. 61). Minority writing is thus political because it is transformational. Like the author, the person seeking help in the clinic is also in search of a profound transformation, a transformation that for Deleuze has to do with accepting the dilemmas and circumstances that present in people's lives and finding new and noble ways of dealing with them. It is in the full acceptance of the originality of everybody's life, rather than in its normalisation, that health articulates itself. This is a profoundly different formula from that of the absence of suffering, a formula that escapes categorisation in the same way that life itself escapes standardisation.

Literature then has a fundamental therapeutic role for the clinic in that it facilitates its flight from the role of judge – an interpreter of what is sane and what is mad – into a continual ethical evaluation of possibilities of life in terms of their '"vitality", [their] "tenor of life"' (Smith, 1997, p. liii). The potential force of the clinic then lies in facilitating the emergence not of normality but of the minorities that Deleuze teaches us to value. It is minorities that populate this earth, transforming the desert, 'making it sacred' (Deleuze, 1950s, p. 10) through an infinite process of differentiation of 'a consciousness of the earth and ocean ... ready to begin the world anew' (p. 11).

References

Barney, K. 1994. Limitations of the critique of the medical model. *The Journal of Mind and Behaviour*, 15, 19–39.

Bateson, G. 2002. *Mind and nature: a necessary unity.* Cresskill, NJ: Hampton Press.

Bogue, R. 2003. *Deleuze on literature.* New York: Routledge.

Bradley, B. 2005. *Psychology and experience.* Cambridge: Cambridge University Press.

Clarke, B. 2008. *Posthuman metamorphosis: narrative and systems.* New York: Fordham University Press.

Cook, J. 2011. *Lesson 1: the evolution of clinical psychology* [Online]. University of Missouri. Available: https://services.online.missouri.edu/exec/data/courses/2382/public/lesson01/lesson01.aspx [accessed 5 January 2015].

Deleuze, G. 1950s. Desert islands. *In:* Lapoujade, D. (ed.), *Desert islands and other texts: 1953–1974.* New York: Semiotext(e).

Deleuze, G. 1973. Five propositions on psychoanalysis. *In:* Lapoujade, D. (ed.), *Desert islands and other texts 1953–1974.* New York: Semiotext(e).

Deleuze, G. 1984. Letter to Uno: how Felix and I worked together. *In:* Lapoujade, D. (ed.), *Two regimes of madness: texts and interviews 1975–1995.* New York: Semiotext(e).

Deleuze, G. 1985. Nomad thought. *In:* Allison, D.B. (ed.), *The new Nietzsche: contemporary styles of interpretation.* London: MIT Press.

Deleuze, G. 1986. *Nietzsche and philosophy.* London: Continuum.

Deleuze, G. 1990a. *The logic of sense.* London: Athlone Press.

Deleuze, G. 1990b. Preface: a new stylistics. *In:* Lapoujade, D. (ed.), *Two regimes of madness: texts and interviews 1975–1995.* New York: Semiotext(e).

Deleuze, G. 1995. *Negotiations, 1972–1990.* New York: Columbia University Press.

Deleuze, G. 1997. *Essays critical and clinical.* Minneapolis, MN: University of Minnesota Press.

Deleuze, G. 2000. *Proust and signs: the complete text.* Minneapolis, MN: University of Minnesota Press.

Deleuze, G. 2001. *Pure immanence: essays on a life.* New York: Urzone.

Deleuze, G. 2006. *Masochism: coldness and cruelty.* New York: Zone Books.

Deleuze, G. and Chapsal, M. 1967. Mysticism and masochism. *In:* Lapoujade, D. (ed.), *Desert islands and other texts: 1953–1974.* New York: Semiotext(e).

Deleuze, G. and Eribon, D. 1991. We invented the ritornello. *In:* Lapoujade, D. (ed.), *Two regimes of madness: texts and interviews 1975–1995.* New York: Semiotext(e).

Deleuze, G. and Guattari, F. 1983. *Anti-Oedipus: capitalism and schizophrenia.* Minneapolis, MN: University of Minnesota Press.

Deleuze, G. and Guattari, F. 1987. *A thousand plateaus: capitalism and schizophrenia.* Minneapolis, MN: University of Minnesota Press.

Deleuze, G. and Guattari, F. 1991. *What is philosophy?.* London: Verso.

Deleuze, G. and Parnet, C. 2006. *Dialogues II.* London: Continuum.

Dosse, F. 1997a. *History of structuralism. Volume 1: the rising sun, 1945–1966.* Minneapolis, MN: University of Minnesota Press.

Dosse, F. 1997b. *History of structuralism. Volume 2: the sign sets, 1967–present.* Minneapolis, MN: University of Minnesota Press.

Duff, C. 2014. *Assemblages of health: Deleuze's empiricism and the ethology of life.* Dordrecht: Springer.

Foucault, M. 1973. *The birth of the clinic: an archaeology of medical perception.* New York: Vintage Books.

Foucault, M. 1978. What is critique? *In:* Schmidt, J. (ed.), *What is enlightenment: eighteenth century answers and twentieth century questions.* Berkeley and Los Angeles: University of California Press.

Foucault, M. 1984. What is enlightenment? *In:* Rabinow, P. (ed.), *The Foucault reader.* London: Penguin Books.

Foucault, M. 1986. Kant on enlightenment and revolution. *Economy and Society*, 15, 88–96.

Foucault, M. 2004. *The order of things: an archaeology of the human sciences.* London: Routledge.

Gatens, M. 1996. Through a Spinozist lens: ethology, difference, power. *In:* Patton, P. (ed.), *Deleuze: a critical reader.* Oxford: Blackwell Publishers.

Hayles, K. 1999. *How we became posthuman: virtual bodies in cybernetics, literature, and informatics.* Chicago, IL: University of Chicago Press.

Holland, E.W. 1999. *Deleuze and Guattari's Anti-Oedipus: introduction to schizoanalysis.* London: Routledge.

Jenkins, A. 2011a. Becoming resilient: overturning common sense – part 1. *Australian and New Zealand Journal of Family Therapy*, 32, 33–42.

Jenkins, A. 2011b. Ethical practice and narratives of resistance to violence: becoming resilient part 2. *Australian and New Zealand Journal of Family Therapy*, 32, 271–82.

Kant, I. 1784. Was ist aufklärung? *In:* Lotringer, S. and Hochroth, L. (eds), *The politics of truth.* New York: Semiotext(e).

Kerman, N., Eckerle Curwood, S. and Sirohi, R. 2014. Recovery, overview. *In:* Teo, T. (ed.), *Encyclopedia of critical psychology.* New York: Springer.

Kundera, M. 2007. *The curtain: an essay in seven parts.* London: Faber & Faber.

May, T. 2003. When is a Deleuzian becoming? *Continental Philosophy Review*, 36, 139–53.

McAvoy, J. 2014. Psy disciplines. *In:* Teo, T. (ed.), *Encyclopaedia of critical psychology.* New York: Springer.

Nichterlein, M. 2013a. Losing the gaze: an unnecessary tragedy? *Context: The Magazine for Family Therapy and Systemic Practice in the UK*, 130, 30–4.

Nichterlein, M. 2013b. Recasting the theory of systemic family therapy: reading Bateson through Foucault and Deleuze. PhD, University of New South Wales.

Rajchman, J. 2001. Introduction. *In:* Deleuze, G. (ed.), *Pure immanence: essays on a life.* New York: Zone books.

Ranciere, J. 2004. *The flesh of words: the politics of writing.* Stanford, CA: Stanford University Press.

Richardson, C. and Skott-Myhre, H.A. (eds) 2012. *Habitus of the hood,* Chicago, IL: Intellect.

Routh, D.K. 2012. A history of clinical psychology. *In:* Barlow, D.H. (ed.), *The Oxford handbook of clinical psychology*. Oxford: Oxford University Press.

Schmidt, J. and Wartenberg, T.E. 1994. Foucault's enlightenment: critique, revolution, and the fashioning of the self. *In:* Kelly, M. (ed.), *Critique and power: recasting the Foucault/Habermas debate*. Cambridge, MA: MIT Press.

Seikkula, J. and Olson, M. 2003. The open dialogue approach to acute psychosis: its poetics and micropolitics. *Family Process*, 42, 403–18.

Smith, D. 1997. 'A life of pure immanence': Deleuze's 'critique et clinique' project. *In:* Deleuze, G. (ed.), *Essays critical and clinical*. Minneapolis, MN: University of Minnesota Press.

Stenner, P. 2009. On the actualities and possibilities of constructionism. *Human Affairs*, 19, 194–210.

Wampold, B.E. 2001. *The great psychotherapy debate: models, methods and findings*. Mahwah, NJ: Lawrence Erlbaum Associates.

Wampold, B.E. and Imel, Z.E. 2015. *The great psychotherapy debate: the evidence for what makes psychotherapy work*. New York: Routledge.

Watzlawick, P. (ed.) 1984. *The invented reality: how do we know what we believe we know? Contributions to constructivism*. New York: W.W. Norton & Company.

Winslade, J. 2009. Tracing lines of flight: implications of the work of Gilles Deleuze for narrative practice. *Family Process*, 48, 332–46.

Wolfe, C. 1998. *Critical environments: postmodern theory and the pragmatics of the outside*. Minneapolis, MN: University of Minnesota Press.

Wolfe, C. 2010. *What is posthumanism?*. Minneapolis, MN: University of Minnesota Press.

AFTERWORD

We have used some harsh words to describe the current state of psychology – *timid*, *stupid* – and we have some more adjectives to add. Harsh words come cheap, perhaps, at least from the one of us who walked away from the academic discipline of psychology some years ago and who never practised the profession. And harsh words serve no useful purpose except as a goad (in Latin, 'stimulus'), and a goad is not a goad if it does not elicit a response. In the spirit of Deleuze (both with and without Guattari), we believe, we are suggesting that psychology has so much more to offer than what we currently see and what we have seen in the past. Timidity is a deliberate self-restraint, a kind of false modesty or false deference, especially in dealings with other professions. Stupidity is also deliberate in the sense that what we mean by this term is a wilful narrowing of perspective, a collaboration with the low expectations held by other disciplines and other professions. These attitudes, or rather these functions, are like the 'mind-forg'd manacles' of William Blake, they are produced and maintained by the everyday decisions of human persons working as docile bodies in institutional arrangements, by psychologists among others.

To add to the catalogue, we suggest that psychology as we know it is *morbid*, *insipid*, *florid*. It is morbid in its focus on pathology, understood as such. It is insipid in its satisfaction with the bland and the ineffective, in the light of which allusions to the 'psy-complex' perhaps overstate the significance of the 'psy'. Florid in its self-promotion to the wider community despite its timidity with respect to medicine, the insurance industry and the incarceration industry. What is to be done? With Deleuze we find inspiration in the creativity of the artist for visions of an energised psychology. Here, we emphasise that art is the expression of minority, of a mobile kind of resistance, so that however canonical a 'great' writer may be (Proust, Melville, Woolf), their 'greatness' breaks out of their established niche. The place reserved for them by State processes, in the Pantheon or in the high school curriculum, proves unstable.

In its only similarity with 'great' literature, we hope that this book deserves re-reading. But before that, it is time for that walk in the park.

INDEX

actualisation 17, 129, 150, 152
Adkins, B. 6
Allport, G. 16
Anti-Oedipus 3, 5–6, 22, 41, 45, 48, 71–2, 101, 150–1, 153
apprenticeship 29, 32, 144
Aristotle 56, 58
art 23, 66, 74–7, 106–7, 127, 132, 148, 155, 157, 161, 164, 169
Artaud, A. 57, 74
artist 76–7, 151, 155–6, 157, 161, 162, 164, 169
assemblage 5, 22, 37, 40, 45–7, 56, 70, 73, 76, 103–7, 115, 125, 147, 150, 155–6, 164
autopoiesis 39

Bagehot, W. 66
Bains, P. 102
Baker, J. 43
Barbetta, P. 55
Barney, K. 79, 146
Bateson, G. 7, 28, 40–1, 48, 54, 70, 75, 82, 107, 146, 152
becoming 17, 23, 46, 77–8, 115, 116, 129, 137, 149–53, 157, 159–60, 163–4
Bell, J. 40, 68, 71–2
Benjamin, J. 37
Berg, I.K. 137n3

Bergson, H. 8, 10, 13–15, 18, 39, 104
Berkeley, G. 61, 68, 71
biology 40, 72
Blake, W. 168
body without organs 70
Bogue, R. 12, 110, 155, 162
Bonta, M. 128, 130
Borges, J.L. 102
Boundas, C. 61, 67–8, 120, 132
Boutang, P-A. 12, 107, 137
Bowden, S. 57
Bowen, M. 37
Bowlby, J. 41
Bradley, B. 33, 36, 48, 83, 148
Braidotti, R. 35
Brentari, C. 137n1
Brown, S. 37, 58, 94
Buchanan, B. 46, 100–1, 103
Burman, E. 41, 119

Candland, D. 43
capitalism 6, 116, 134, 154
Carroll, L. 15, 57
cartography 46, 82, 159
Castillo-Sepulveda, J. 137n5
Challenger, G. 136
chaosmos 22, 38–9, 44, 75, 104–5, 118, 162
Clarke, B. 149

Colebrook, C. 4, 21
Colombat, A. 109
common or good sense 16, 56, 63, 74,
    78, 81, 96–7, 116
communication 59, 91, 109–10, 122
concept 9–10, 77, 114, 133–4, 137n4
conceptual persona 114–15
Conley, T. 125
consciousness 5, 14, 19, 21, 35, 42, 61,
    68, 71, 74, 122, 124, 164
Cook, J. 142
Copernicus, N. 77
Crossman, R. 66

Darwin, C. 71–2
De Jong, P. 137n3
Deely, J. 101
Delpech-Ramey, J. 43
Derrida, J. 9, 46, 98–9
Descartes, R. 22, 40, 58–66, 68, 77, 123
desiring machine 6, 19, 21, 45, 72
deterritorialisation 56, 78, 127–9, 136,
    159
diagnosis 122, 124, 137, 144, 147, 148,
    155–7
*Diagnostic and Statistical Manual of Mental
    Disorders* 144, 147–8, 158
difference 8, 10–11, 12, 15–18, 20, 28,
    38, 40, 46, 54, 68, 75, 83, 97, 99,
    109, 112, 133, 144, 159, 161, 163
Difference and Repetition 9, 15–18, 67,
    74, 97, 104, 120, 133, 155
differentiation 12, 17, 21, 37, 39, 47,
    80, 94, 97, 107, 112, 118–19, 121,
    123, 127, 133, 153–4, 160–1, 163–4
Dodds, J. 43
Dosse, F. 7–8, 10, 17, 20–1, 74, 152
Duff, C. 94, 137n5, 157

ecology 39, 47–8, 70, 106–7, 109, 122
Einstein, A. 77
empiricism 8–10, 57–8, 60–2, 65–8,
    80–1, 83, 159
Empiricism and Subjectivity 9, 12, 67
Enlightenment (*Aufklärung*) 11, 67–8,
    153
environment 36
Epston, D. 65
Essays Critical and Clinical 155
eternal return 12, 15, 38, 134, 149–50

ethics 12–13, 16, 18, 23–4, 34, 49, 69,
    84, 93, 97, 100, 144, 158, 164
ethology 23, 46, 72, 100–2, 117, 131
experimentation 8, 22, 40, 58, 65, 129,
    151, 153, 155, 159

faciality 23, 108–9, 113–15, 144
familial 41, 46, 153, 156, 162
family 36, 41, 54, 118, 153, 154, 156
fascicular 123
Ferenczi, S. 104
Foucault, M. 13, 40, 55, 57, 74, 76,
    82–3, 92, 97, 102, 120, 123, 127,
    143, 146–7, 153–4, 156
Freud, S. 3, 5, 31, 41, 43–4, 55, 104, 133

Gao, Z. 83
Garcia Marquez, G. 135
Gatens, M. 150
Gergen, K. 55, 64, 109
Goujon, P. 127
Gould, S.J. 36
Guattari, F. 3, 5, 7, 20

Haaken, J. 119
Hacking, I. 62
Haley, J. 55
Hayles, K. 149
Hegel, G.W.F 20, 67, 123, 137n2
Heidegger, M. 18, 38
Heraclitus 29, 56
herd 45, 48, 83, 92, 97, 99–100, 108,
    121, 131
Hoffman, L. 130
Holland, E. 15, 22–3, 42, 44–5, 48, 94,
    97, 100, 104–8, 110–11, 131, 153–4
Hume, D. 42, 61, 65, 67–72, 74, 77,
    84, 102
Husserl, E. 18–19, 75

identity 15–16, 64, 66, 69–72, 77
image of thought 16, 28, 54, 57, 77,
    119, 131
Imel, Z. 145
immanence 10–11, 15, 18, 19, 22, 39,
    75, 99, 151–2
Intra-Species Social Organisation 44–5,
    94, 107

James, W. 31

Jenkins, A. 160
Jensen, C. 40
Joyce, J. 22, 38, 76, 162

Kafka: Toward a Minor Literature 45
Kant, I. 11, 15, 18, 22, 42, 55, 67, 72, 153–4
Kerman, N. 157
Kesey, K. 123
Kierkegaard, S. 124
Kinman, C. 130
Klein, M. 70
Kratochwil, F. 29
Krause, I-B. 55
Kuhn, T. 55, 77
Kundera, M. 164

Lacan, J. 22, 42
language 20, 23, 57, 102, 109, 155, 161–2
Latour, B. 94
Law, I. 94
Lawlor, L. 19
Lecercle, J-J. 7
Lehrer, J. 32
Leibniz, G. 55
line of flight 129–31, 136, 143, 160–4
literature 155, 157, 161, 163–4
Locke, J. 61, 68
Logic of Sense, The 41
Lorenz, K. 101
Lorraine, T. 129–30

McAvoy, J. 148
MacGregor Wise, J. 45
machine 3–4, 20–2, 39, 46, 101
McNamee, S. 64
Marx, K. 5, 20, 79, 120, 133
Masochism: Coldness and Cruelty 155, 157
Maturana, H. 39, 84, 94, 102
May 1968 4–5, 21, 93
May, T. 6, 8, 10–11, 15, 21, 46, 125, 128, 149
medicine 145–7, 157–8, 168
Melling, B. 61
Melville, H. 47, 151, 162, 169
Millican, P. 68, 72
minor science 78, 80, 82, 94, 135–6
misplaced concreteness 54, 160

Mitchell, D. 134
money 115–17
morality 13, 16, 72, 100
Morss, J.R. 40, 45, 57, 130
Motzkau, J. 31

Negri, A. 125
neuroscience 32, 35–6, 39, 59, 84
Newton, I. 68
Nichterlein, M.E. 41, 45, 53, 55, 130, 149, 159
Nietzsche, F. 5, 8, 10, 13–18, 38, 47–8, 57, 75, 81, 108, 121, 134, 148–50
Nietzsche and Philosophy 12, 97
nomad 16, 23, 46, 49, 128, 164
nomad science 79, 82, 111, 113

Olson, M. 157
Open Science Collaboration 81
original 76, 114–15, 163
Ouroboros 124

pack 44–5, 47, 49, 83, 92, 97, 99–100, 107–8, 124, 131, 134, 154
Pankejeff, S. 42–8, 98–9
Parker, I. 119–20, 123, 132
Parr, A. 129
Patton, P. 7, 15, 133
phenomenology 11, 18–20, 61, 75, 84, 109
Pickering, A. 40, 82
Pisters, P. 35
Plato 15, 17, 34, 38, 55–6, 59
politics 23, 46, 78, 92–5, 107, 116
positivism 14, 55, 84
Postle, D. 121
Prigogine, I. 127
prophet 76
Protevi, J. 19, 38, 55, 78, 128, 130
Proust, M. 30, 32, 111, 162, 169
Proust and Signs 97
Pulido-Martinez, H. 79, 120
psy-complex 79, 103, 117, 119–20, 148, 168
psychiatry 143, 145–8
psychoanalysis 5–6, 22, 31, 41, 43, 54, 70, 96, 99, 117, 122, 153–4

Rajchman, J. 19, 66, 125, 151
Ranciere, J. 151

Raphael 56
Reavey 94
refrain 104, 108, 114, 118
regime of signs 23, 46, 114, 144, 158–60, 163
representation 15, 17, 23, 56, 84, 133, 159
rhizome 81, 130–2
Richards, G. 29
Richardson, C. 164
Roazen, P. 44
Rodje, K. 40
Rose, N. 79
Routh, D. 145
royal science 65, 78–82, 94, 111, 120, 143
Rueting, T. 137n1

sacred 146, 164
Sade, Marquis de 157–8
Saussure, F. de 109–10
schizoanalysis 46, 152–5
schizophrenia, schizophrenic 5, 21, 57, 130, 154
Schmidt, J. 154
science 6, 15, 27–9, 33, 38, 40, 55, 57, 66, 68, 73–6, 78, 81, 92–4, 120, 132, 148
Seikkula, J. 157
Semetsky, I. 43
semiotics 103, 106, 108–9, 115, 137n1
Shotter, J. 64
Skott-Mhyre, H. 110, 164
Skott-Mhyre, K. 55
Slife, B. 61, 66, 118
Smith, D. 38, 42, 66, 78, 137n2, 155, 164
smooth and striated space 49, 105, 125–7, 132, 161
social constructionism 48, 55, 64–5, 108–9, 134
Spinoza, B. 8, 10–17, 46, 57, 65, 103, 124, 129, 160
state 21, 23, 46, 48–9, 73, 78–83, 105, 110, 115, 117–18, 125, 128–9, 131, 137, 145, 147, 151, 169
Stengers, I. 63–5, 94, 121, 127
Stenner, P. 37–8, 58, 61, 148
Stivale, C. 12
structuralism 18–20, 152

stupidity (la bêtise) 95–9, 107, 118, 121, 127, 131, 153, 168
style 47, 162
subjectivity 35–6, 47, 68, 78, 99, 106, 109, 113, 115, 123, 144, 148
symptom 13
systemic 40, 53–5, 106, 110, 114, 127, 156

territorialisation 47, 56, 104, 106, 115, 127, 143, 151
territory 22, 46, 73, 76, 104–5, 107–8, 124, 159
Thousand Plateaus, A 6–7, 22, 45, 72, 78, 104, 109, 113, 126, 128–30, 133, 136
timidity 29, 96–7, 119, 131, 168
Tirado, F. 137n5
Tolstoy, L. 54
transcendence 11, 19, 39, 69

Umwelt 101–3, 106
unconscious 41–2, 48, 71
Urdoxa 19, 75–6, 113

Varela, F. 39, 94, 102
Villani, A. 38
Vitalism 14, 37, 39, 72, 75, 164
Von Foerster, H. 127
Von Masoch, L. 157–8
Von Uexküll, J. 101–2, 137n1

Wampold, B. 145
war machine 22–3, 46, 78, 127–30
Wartenberg, T. 154
Watters, E. 95
Watzlawick, P. 110–11, 156
What is Philosophy? 74, 133
White, M. 64
Whitehead, A. 9, 31, 54, 59, 65, 84
Widder, N. 15
Wilkins, J. 102
Williams, B. 58, 63
Williams, J. 57
Winslade, J. 161
wolf 100
Wolf-Man 42–8, 98–9
Wolfe, C. 149
Woolf, V. 169

Zourabichvili, F. 46, 97, 127, 132

Taylor & Francis eBooks

Helping you to choose the right eBooks for your Library

Add Routledge titles to your library's digital collection today. Taylor and Francis ebooks contains over 50,000 titles in the Humanities, Social Sciences, Behavioural Sciences, Built Environment and Law.

Choose from a range of subject packages or create your own!

Benefits for you

» Free MARC records
» COUNTER-compliant usage statistics
» Flexible purchase and pricing options
» All titles DRM-free.

REQUEST YOUR FREE INSTITUTIONAL TRIAL TODAY

Free Trials Available
We offer free trials to qualifying academic, corporate and government customers.

Benefits for your user

» Off-site, anytime access via Athens or referring URL
» Print or copy pages or chapters
» Full content search
» Bookmark, highlight and annotate text
» Access to thousands of pages of quality research at the click of a button.

eCollections – Choose from over 30 subject eCollections, including:

Archaeology	Language Learning
Architecture	Law
Asian Studies	Literature
Business & Management	Media & Communication
Classical Studies	Middle East Studies
Construction	Music
Creative & Media Arts	Philosophy
Criminology & Criminal Justice	Planning
Economics	Politics
Education	Psychology & Mental Health
Energy	Religion
Engineering	Security
English Language & Linguistics	Social Work
Environment & Sustainability	Sociology
Geography	Sport
Health Studies	Theatre & Performance
History	Tourism, Hospitality & Events

For more information, pricing enquiries or to order a free trial, please contact your local sales team:
www.tandfebooks.com/page/sales